1993

ECONOMICS FOR THE WILDS

ECONOMICS FOR THE WILDS

Wildlife, Diversity, and Development

Edited by Timothy M. Swanson
and
Edward B. Barbier

ISLAND PRESS

Washington, D.C. ❑ Covelo, California

Library of Congress Cataloging-in-Publication Data

Economics for the wilds: wildlife, diversity, and development / edited by
   Timothy M. Swanson and Edward B. Barbier.
      p. cm.
   Includes bibliographical references and index.
      ISBN 1-55963-211-9 (cloth).—ISBN 1-55963-212-7 (paper)
      1. Wildlife conservation—Economic aspects.   2. Wilderness areas—
   Economic   aspects. 3. Economic development—Environmental aspects.
   I. Swanson, Timothy M.   II. Barbier, Edward B., 1957- .
   QL82.E26 1992
   333.95—dc20   92-15757
                                                                  CIP

Printed on recycled, acid-free paper

Manufactured in the United States of America
10 9 8 7 6 5 4 3 2 1

CONTENTS

NOTES ON THE CONTRIBUTORS

Bruce A. Aylward	Research Associate, London Environmental Economics Centre
Edward B. Barbier	Director, London Environmental Economics Centre
John I. Barnes	Senior Wildlife Resources Economist, Department of Wildlife and National Parks Botswana
Joanne C. Burgess	Research Associate, London Environmental Economics Centre
Nigel Leader-Williams	Department of National Parks and Wildlife, Tanzania and Large Animals Research Group, Department of Zoology, University of Cambridge
Richard Luxmoore	Director, Wildlife Trade Monitoring Unit, World Conservation Monitoring Centre, Cambridge
E.J. Milner-Gulland	New College, Oxford and Renewable Resources Assessment Group, Imperial College, London
David W. Pearce	Professor of Economics, University College London, Associate Director, London Environmental Economics Centre and Director, Centre for Social and Economic Research on the Global Environment, London
Timothy M. Swanson	Faculty of Economics, University of Cambridge, Associate Fellow, London Environmental Economics Centre and Director of Biodiversity Programme, Centre for Social and Economic Research on the Global Environment.

FOREWORD

While it is generally appreciated that conserving the world's wildlife and wildlands is an investment in the future of humankind, it is often suggested that such investment primarily serves aesthetic rather than economic or social values. Our dependence on these resources for our long-term economic well-being is not broadly recognized. Where it might be recognized, a deepening philosophical rift between resource managers and protectionists threatens to undermine the adaptive strategies that this recognition might entail.

In the "North", affluent industrial economies continue to rely on wild resources for production, yet its inhabitants are reluctant to argue for their conservation in utilitarian terms, particularly where use is consumptive rather than non-consumptive. In the "South", from which most of these wild resources derive, strategies for economic development are, inevitably, focused on utilization of these resources as, for many countries, they are the only ready asset. These resources will continue to be utilized until they are exhausted or replaced by other forms of economic activity. From such a context has sprung the very simple and compelling conservation counter-philosophy: use it or lose it. A growing sector of the conservation community, realistically but not cynically, is coming to recognize that wildlife and wildlands must pay their way if they are to compete with other forms of land use and general trends in economic development.

The protectionist, anti-use philosophy is rapidly gaining momentum but is short-lived because, dangerously, it is based on a lack of understanding of complex economic relationships. It also perpetuates the increasing tensions between "North-South" trading partners, as it overlooks the fundamental requirements of developing economies. This philosophy is also short-sighted in its failure to recognize the threats posed by non-consumptive resource use, on which there is a growing body of evidence.

The pro-use philosophy, however, has problems too. While often theoretically robust, practical and positive examples of sustainable use of wild resources as a conservation strategy in all but the most local of contexts are few and poorly documented, lending credence to arguments that such use is still in the conceptual or experimental phase and has yet to be proved a viable conservation strategy.

Fundamental to this conflict in conservation philosophies is the way we measure and value our renewable resources. Buildings and equipment, as traditional economic assets, are easily valued and accepted as productive capital, and are written off against the value of production as they depreciate. Renewable resource assets are not valued along the same lines. A result of negligence in both economic and conservation thinking, their loss entails no charge against current income to account for the decrease in potential future production, even though it is patently clear that, whether used sustainably or not, these resources make important contributions to long-term economic productivity (Repetto *et al.*, 1989). The real tragedy, however, lies in the lack of formalized connection between measured income and wild assets. Under existing economic accounting practices, a country could exhaust its renewable resources without affecting measured income in the process (Repetto *et al.*, 1989; IUCN/UNEP/WWF 1991). Unless these accounting practices are altered to reflect the full economic value of wild assets, there will be no incentive to preserve them for future generations. They will only be changed with wider acceptance of wildlife and wild lands as economic assets, to which the same principles as for other capital assets apply.

Economics for the Wilds provides a strong theoretical and practical basis for refining common thinking on the value of wild resources and the strategies for conserving them over the long term. It promises to bridge the gap between pro-use and anti-use constituencies.

Jorgen B. Thomsen
Director
TRAFFIC International
– a programme of WWF and IUCN

References

IUCN/UNEP/WWF, *Caring for the Earth. A Strategy for Sustainable Living* (Gland, Switzerland, 1991).

Repetto, R., W. Magrath, M. Wells, C. Beer and F. Rossini *Wasting Assets: Natural Resources in the National Income Account* (Washington DC, World Resources Institute, 1989.)

PREFACE

One of the important global challenges we currently face is determining the role of conservation in economic development. Too often, the debate over the world's remaining wild resources is polarized between *preservation* and *development* views. In this book we take a different perspective. Do the dwindling natural habitats contain a wealth and diversity of goods and services that indicate an important *asset* that can be tapped for greater economic development and welfare? If so, what are the best uses to which these goods and services can be put, and what are the implications for our choice of land use options? How best can developing countries "capture" some of the value of their remaining sources of natural wealth without excessively depleting their wild resources, and what public policies and reforms are required? In short, is it possible to reconcile the conservation of wild resources with economic development so as to ensure that developing societies with these resources have an incentive to ensure their long-term management and survival?

This book attempts to address these key questions at the heart of conservation and development. Moreover, we are unabashedly "economic" in our approach to these issues. An unfortunate misconception is that economics has little to say about wild resource conservation, and that what it does say usually works against conservation of natural areas. As with most misconceptions, there is an element of half-truth: in the past economists have not paid sufficient attention to the economic role of wild resources in development, and as a consequence the economic value of these resources has been frequently overlooked in analysis of land use options, public policies and investment strategies. In the past economics may have paid insufficient attention to the role of wild resource conservation in development, but rejecting economic analysis altogether will only serve to further the gap between conservation and development views. Instead, what is needed more than ever is an *economics for the wilds* that attempts to place wildlife, wildlands and their diversity in the proper economic development context.

Throughout this book we have emphasized the important role of economic analysis in redressing the balance between conservation and development. Economics has several contributions to make:

- Proper economic analysis of the market and policy failures affecting resource use and degradation is required in order to understand better the distortions that work against efficient and sustainable resource management. A recurrent theme in many chapters of this book is how these distortions work against wildlife and wildland resource conservation as viable economic development options.

- Better economic analysis is also required of the full economic values that wild resources afford developing societies. The direct subsistence use of these resources by local communities, the support and protection of economic activity by ecological services and the existence and cultural values of natural habitats are just some of the many benefits provided by the remaining natural areas in developing regions. Only by better valuation of these and other economic benefits of wild resources can developing societies make appropriate decisions as how best to allocate these resources.

- Further economic analysis is also needed of the distributional implications of resource loss. Who gains and who loses when natural areas are appropriated or depleted? To what extent are poorer households and communities dependent on sustainable and seasonal exploitation of wild resources, and to what extent are these entitlements disappearing as natural areas become depleted or degraded? Too often, the assumption is that conversion or appropriation of natural areas leads to greater economic benefits for all, yet many of the case studies explored in this book would suggest otherwise.

- Finally, only by improving economic analysis of the allocative distortions affecting wild resource use, the proper valuation of these resources and their distributional consequences can we begin to understand the important range of economic incentives governing wildlife and natural habitat exploitation. Eliciting this incentive structure through better analysis is the first step, and indeed a prerequisite, for designing more appropriate policies for integrating wildlife and wildland utilization in economic development.

One of the legacies of this book, we hope, will be to inspire others to take up this challenge of applying economic analysis to the pressing problem of wild resource conservation in development.

EB, TS
London Environmental Economics Centre

ACKNOWLEDGEMENTS

We gratefully acknowledge the support of the core donors to the London Environmental Economics Centre (LEEC), the Swedish International Development Authority (SIDA), the Norwegian Ministry of Foreign Affairs and the Dutch Ministry of Foreign Affairs. Much of the case study material presented by the various authors in this book resulted from research supported by and conducted for the World Conservation Union (IUCN) and the World Wide Fund for Nature (WWF). We are grateful to these two organizations for their support as well as their pioneering interest in the economics of wildlife and wildlands. Special thanks must also go to all our colleagues at the International Institute for Environment and Development (IIED) and the Economics Department, University College, London (UCL). We would also like to recognize the important role played by the worldwide TRAFFIC network in the formulation and careful consideration wildlife conservation issues.

Neil Middleton of Earthscan is responsible for originally commissioning this book. We are grateful to him for his interest in LEEC books over the years, and especially for his appreciation of the value and potential contribution of this volume. We are indebted to Kate Griffin for following through on this commitment, and to Jonathan Sinclair-Wilson and Sian Mills for seeing the book through the various publication stages.

Numerous other individuals are responsible for influencing our work. We thank them all and hope we have not misinterpreted them. Of course, any errors or omissions remain our responsibility alone.

1

WILDLIFE AND WILDLANDS, DIVERSITY AND DEVELOPMENT

Timothy M. Swanson

Few would question the value of wildlife and wildlands, yet these most irreplacable of all resources are dwindling rapidly. What remains is largely in the still-developing countries, and a clear threat currently hangs over that. This apparent contradiction between values and realities raises several fundamental questions. Why has the development process been so destructive of our natural resources? Must it continue to be so in the future? Are we destined to share the world with just a few dozens of species? Or can development be compatible with the maintenance of the natural environment? These are the issues that we address first in this chapter, and then in more detail throughout this volume.

We believe diversity and development need not be mutually exclusive. In fact, to a large extent, maintaining the diversity of wild resources is one of the necessary conditions for sustainable development. As such wild resources should be treated more often as an input into the development process; they cannot be left entirely out of the equation.

However important these diverse resources are intrinsically, they are also important because we – the human species – use them. And, whether we welcome or deplore the fact, it is the latter value that will be the key to their continuing survival in the near term. As soaring human populations cause the pressures for development to build, there will be a need to stress wildlife utilization in order to preserve wildlands throughout the next century. For all those who appreciate and enjoy the wilds, this is a very important lesson to learn.

Diversity and development

At the broadest level this is a book about the conservation of biological diversity, which is one of the most fundamentally important international environmental problems facing the world community today. The conservation of biological diversity, or "biodiversity", was one of the chief concerns of the World Conservation Strategy, developed by UNEP, IUCN and WWF in 1980, and it will be one of the topics for the 1992 United Nations Conference on Environment and Development.

Biological diversity is closely related to the number of species that exist within the earth's ecosystems – the loss of a species represents a loss of genetic diversity, and an examination of the problem of endangered species, therefore, is an important part of any attempt at understanding the reasons for diversity losses.

Biodiversity conservation is, at base, concerned with the world's continuing losses of genetic capital, i.e. the amount and extent of genetic variety within the earth's ecosystems. Genes determine the particular characteristics of a given organism and encode the information that determines the specific capabilities of that organism. The greater the variety of genetic material in existence, the greater the variety of organisms that exist or that will exist in the near future.

The motivation to conserve biological diversity is not an altruistic one. There are clear and positive links between biological diversity and human development. At the global level, the loss of biodiversity means the loss of options for all of us and for future generations (Reid, W. and Miller, K., 1989). These are irreversible losses. They can also be very substantial losses. The variety of microbes, plants and animals that have only recently been discovered to be of human usefulness illustrate the potential value of the undiscovered.

In addition to any yet-to-be-discovered economic values, there is also the very real dependence of our ecosystems, and hence our economies, on the diversity that exists. The crops and animals that we currently rely upon are continually under threat from outbreaks of pests and disease, and it is the diverse strains that exist in the wild that we must ultimately rely upon in these circumstances to provide more resistant strains.

Biodiversity also provides insurance against such situations. Recently introduced wild relatives of domestic wheat and barley have been estimated to provide annual disease protection worth between $50 million and $160 million for US crops alone (Briefbook: *Biotechnology and Genetic Diversity*, 1985). But the reliance of our livelihoods on diverse lifeforms is still much broader than these few categories indicate. Humans live within and are part of ecosystems, and we depend in every way upon the web of services that they provide. The intrinsic value of such dependence is impossible to quantify (although in many senses *all* value may ultimately derive from these systems); however, the risks involved in altering these systems must be recognized and the costs of such risks internalized. We will expand on this theme further in Chapter 3.

Box 1.1: Market values of recently utilized varieties

Most of the world's biodiversity remains untapped by humans, and for this reason often remains undervalued. However, the fact that a species has no apparent value at present is no reason to suppose that it will have no value in the future; many recently utilized varieties have proved to be highly valuable.

Year of first marketing	Species	Origin	Estimated market value
1963	Rosy Periwinkle	Madagascar	$ 88m. p.a. (1985)
1976	Lycopers. chmielewskii	Peru	$ 8m. p.a. (1986)
1981	Wild Hops	- - - -	$ 15m. p.a. (1981)
1990s	Zea diploperennis (Perennial maize)	Mexico	Potentially $ billions

Sources: Wilson, E., 1986; Hoyt, 1988.

Finally, there is also the very tangible value obtained by those persons who rely upon the diverse products of our earth for their subsistence and development. Most of these people belong to groups who have traditionally used and consumed the products of natural habitats, and to them "biodiversity" represents real and concrete resources. For example, in many parts of the developing world, the majority of the daily intake of protein continues to come from wildlife (Prescott-Allan, R. and Prescott-Allan, C., 1982).

It is very clearly in the interest of global human development to attempt to conserve biodiversity for all of the various values that it represents. There has been quite a substantial literature developing recently that makes this point. (Wilson, E., 1986; McNeely, J. et al., 1990; Reed, W. and Miller, K., 1989; Office of Technology Assessment, 1988; Orians, Brown, Kunin, and Swierzbinski, 1990). Biological diversity conservation and human development are closely linked. It should be not only our appreciation and enjoyment of the world's natural diversity that should motivate our actions in this regard; but also our "self-interest". This is true not only at the local level of communities that are dependent largely upon the diverse products of natural habitat for subsistence purposes, but it is also true at the global level for the insurance and options that biodiversity preserves for us all.

Wildlife and wildlands

The conservation of biological diversity is closely linked to the conservation of "wildlife" and "wildlands". This is known as *in situ* conservation, or the conservation of diversity "in its natural place". There are various *ex situ* alternatives, seed banks, botanical and zoological gardens, etc., however these are not practical options for the conservation of more than a small fraction of threatened species. The world's biodiversity is too great and too poorly known to be catalogued and stored in a "genetic library". Long-term storage facilities even for that stock that has already been well-catalogued is difficult to acquire, and this represents only the tiniest fraction of all species known and unknown. Even considering the "higher" species alone, *ex situ* conservation is a difficult and expensive task (Wilcox, B., 1990).[1]

In addition to the expense of *ex situ* conservation methods, the two methods have very different effects. The conservation of biodiversity implies the need to conserve not only a given stock of genetic capital but also the evolutionary process itself, i.e. the capacity for species to mix, mutate and evolve in an ongoing interactive process. *Ex situ* conservation maintains a one-time "snapshot" of existing diversity; it does not provide the background against which diversity thrives and develops.

For these reasons, *in situ* methods are generally both more effective and more cost-efficient in conserving biodiversity. Following this reasoning, many conservationists have come to equate the conservation of biological diversity with a strategy of "preservation of natural habitats". The obvious fallacy of this equation lies in the observation that, by definition, all species contribute to biological diversity; they do not have to derive from wilderness. Even the most common breed of domestic livestock represents an individual and unique set of genes, and many of these species are the most highly valued (by markets) in existence.

However, it is equally obvious that a policy of biodiversity conservation need not be focused primarily on such species. None of the heavily utilized species, e.g. none of the 80 to 100 species listed in the Food and Agriculture Organization tables on world food production, are in any danger of immediate extinction. Therefore, despite the importance of these species it is clear that proponents of genetic conservation need not be most concerned with their preservation.

What distinguishes these from the many other species that are endangered are the incentives that exist to assure their conservation.[2] The genetic traits of heavily utilized species are conserved for their known economic value alone. In addition, the closest relatives of these species are also being conserved through active international programmes.[3] Thus financial incentives have produced diversity conservation programmes for these heavily utilized species, and their very closest of kin. Yet, millions of other species remain threatened, on account of the absence of any similar programmes for their protection.[4] There are, quite simply, no incentives for the protection of the vast majority of the world's species.

An understanding of the nature of the process that has resulted in many species being "threatened", and a few others not so, is essential to the understanding of the terms "wildlife" and "wildlands".[5] That is, the conservation of wildlife is not concerned simply with the preservation of that small number of species well known from visits to the zoo and media campaigns. Rather, it concerns the management of a process by which a small and select group of domesticated species are being maintained at the expense of all other species.

For thousands of years people have been splitting the products of the natural world into two groups: one, a set of closely managed "domesticated" species and another, a group of virtually unmanaged ones. This is no accident of nature; it is the work of human choice and economic forces. The group of "threatened species" are inevitably those that are often undervalued and under-utilized and almost always unmanaged.[6] For this group, economic forces dictate that there is negligible investment in their conservation, and hence these species come under threat when humans begin to compete for their habitats. The prospect of mass extinctions is raised when human population growth threatens the habitats of large numbers of unmanaged species.[7]

Although this explains the differential characteristics shared by the group of "threatened species" and why they are in danger of extinction, it does not explain the relative sizes of the two groups. Why are so many more species currently threatened than not? What economic pressures support a relatively tiny number of maintained species, rather than a much larger number?

Economic "specialization" has contributed most to the homogeneity in species seen first throughout the developed world, and increasingly now in the developing world. The law of specialization is one of the principles of economics. In simple terms it states that uniformity can contribute significantly to productivity. This is so because repetition allows for the application of capital to the production process. As a single undifferentiated task is repeated more and more times, it becomes economically feasible to introduce more and more powerful tools to assist in the production process. Of course, this implies a clear-cut trade-off between lack of diversity and productivity in the production process. This is why "mass-produced" goods are nearly always less expensive than "hand crafted" items (Swanson, T., 1990).

Specialization came to the countryside long ago. Settled agriculture has usually involved the clearing of diverse habitats and their replacement by one or a few species. Such monocultural production creates the possibility for huge productivity gains. Converting a piece of land to a single crop allows the use of machinery for planting and harvesting, and it also allows the use of chemicals that are capable of targeting all competitors (or "pests") of the crop.

In addition, as more and more producers turn to capital intensive methods of production, the costs of such capital goods fall as the producers of such goods are then allowed to specialize further. In this manner cost differentials become so great that there is pressure for all producers to adopt the same methods. As these methods spread with the global economy, the economic pressures for uniform production techniques are applied throughout the world (Norgaard, 1986).

Finally, not only does this process narrow down the thousands of possibilities to a small number of species of plants and animals that are then the subject of worldwide production, but it also reduces the amount of diversity to be found within the gene pools of each of the heavily utilized species (Office of Technology Assessment, 1988). This is because the species become segregated from their wild kin and have a narrower base from which to evolve. Specialization has not only narrowed the range of species utilized, but it has also reduced the scope for interaction within those that remain.

Therefore, although the conservation of biological diversity concerns the conservation of all genetic resources *per se*, the primary focus is the conservation of "wildlife", *defined as those species that have been left out of this closely managed process*. These species are important for their existing uses, their yet-to-be-discovered individual usefulness (either for themselves or in interaction with another species) and as support for the ecosystem or otherwise; however, because they have never entered into the human management system, they are currently in danger of "falling through the cracks" as more and more of the world's resources are invested into a small number of closely managed species.

To the extent that this process of global specialization underlies the problem of biodiversity losses, the nature and importance of "wildlife" and "wildlands" in conservation efforts becomes concrete. "Wildlife" species are the focus of these efforts because, as refugees from the international economic system, they are under threat of being excluded from all other global systems as well.

"Wildlands", or natural habitat, can then be defined with respect to these economic concepts. In this framework, wildlands are those which have not been substantially modified by the force of specialization.[8] And "wildlife" is then defined as all of the existing and potential goods and services flowing from such wildlands.[9]

Therefore, biodiversity conservation must indeed be focused on the conservation of wildlife and wildlands, but not only for the purposes of preservation. It is important to integrate these sources of value into the economic process rather than simply shield them from it. This is the means by which wide- ranging incentives for the conservation of these wildlands, and the wildlife they contain, can be implemented. This is the basis for the policy of wildlife utilization as a means of biodiversity conservation.

The development and use by local communities of wildlife and wildlands as a method of conserving threatened species, and biological diversity, is what this book is about. It may seem paradoxical to propose use as a means of retaining the very special characteristics of all that which has been "natural" historically, but this is one of the clear messages that economics can provide in this context.[10] This is the economics of wildland conservation through wildlife utilization, or the "economics for the wilds".

The global nature of the problem

The crux of the current crisis in biodiversity is the projected rate of extinctions relative to the historical rate of extinctions. Extinction is itself a natural process; the fossil record indicates that the natural longevity of many species lies in the range of one to ten million years. Indeed, even periods of "mass extinctions" have been located within the fossil record. There are at least five distinct occasions in which over half of the then-existing mammal species were rendered extinct. However, even taking into account these periods of mass extinctions, the historical rate of extinctions has averaged only about 9 per cent of the existing species per million years (Raup, 1986).

At present, however, the rate of extinctions in the tropical regions of the world appears to be about 1000 to 10,000 times the historical rate (Wilson, 1986). And a range of projections by eminent scientists indicate that the earth is facing a major mass extinction crisis over the next 50 to 100 years. These projections are debatable as they rely upon estimates of the numbers of unknown species of insects and plants, many of which are being extinguished without ever being identified, far less analysed. However, as was discussed previously, it is the loss of unknown values (and the options they represent) that makes up much of the potential costliness of biodiversity losses. It is not possible, given our present state of understanding, to discount the costliness of many of these losses, even though the majority may represent barely noticed or understood lifeforms.

Box 1.2: Projections of possible extinctions

Several leading scientists have estimated the possible extinction losses that may result if the present trend of wildland losses continues. These estimates range from 20 to 50 per cent over the next 50 to 100 years.

Estimated extinctions (as a percentage of existing species)	Basis	Source
33-55	Forest area losses	Lovejoy (1980)
50	Forest area losses	Ehrlich and Ehrlich(1981)
25-30	Unspecified	Myers (1983)
33	Forest area losses	Simberloff (1986)
20-25	Present trends	Norton (1986)

Why are mass extinctions occurring now? There are many important factors contributing to these species losses: the over-exploitation of unprotected species; the introduction of exotic species into unprotected habitats; the general degradation of habitats from pollutants released into air and water supplies, and the conversion of natural habitats to other uses.

The first point to note is that all these contributing factors can be traced to human beings: the earth's genetic stock is being severely depleted by human activities. Moreover, with the technology now available, the amount of genetic capital to be retained is one of the many environmental variables which we can in principle determine. The conclusion is clear, whether through action or inaction, the future stock of genetic capital will henceforth be determined by human decision making.

There is one factor that currently dominates the others. Note that in Box 1.2 most of the estimates of species losses were based on projections regarding forest area losses. Such projections are made possible by reason of an empirically demonstrated link between the loss of habitat and the loss of species. Although it is an inexact science, studies of "islands" of natural habitat (whether in oceans or in human civilization) indicate that the loss of natural habitat area leads directly to species extinctions.[11]

Most of the estimates listed in Box 1.2 were derived by applying such formulas to the current rates of deforestation occurring throughout the world's tropical zones. The rate of deforestation is currently estimated to be in the region of 10 to 20 million hectares per year, over the past decade and a half (Office of Technology Assessment, 1988). It is estimated that about 2 per cent of the world's forests have been cleared in the past decade (World Resources Institute, 1991).

The tropical forested regions are of special importance because they are believed to retain the vast majority of the world's remaining species. In fact, a very small number of countries, Brazil, Colombia, Indonesia, and Mexico, are known to be especially species rich. A list of about a dozen countries, most of them within the world's tropical forested zones are believed to account for at least 60-70 per cent of all the world's biodiversity (Mittermeier, 1988).

In general, a quick look at the distribution of "species wealth" throughout the world reveals this clear correspondence between diversity and location and geographical features of the country.

Box 1.3: Countries with greatest "species richness"

A listing of the countries with the greatest number of species reveals several patterns. Many of these countries share common characteristics: they are typically tropical, forested, developing countries.

Mammals	Birds	Reptiles
Indonesia (515)	Colombia (1721)	Mexico (717)
Mexico (449)	Peru (1701)	Australia (686)
Brazil (428)	Brazil (1622)	Indonesia (600)
Zaire (409)	Indonesia (1519)	India (383)
China (394)	Ecuador (1447)	Colombia (383)
Peru (361)	Venezuela (1275)	Ecuador (345)
Colombia (359)	Bolivia (1250)	Peru (297)
India (350)	India (1200)	Malaysia (294)
Uganda (311)	Malaysia (1200)	Thailand (282)
Tanzania (310)	China (1195)	Papua N.G. (282)

Source: McNeely et. al. (1990).

Perhaps the single most striking characteristic of the distribution of species wealth throughout the world is the extent to which it is located in developing countries. Virtually all of the most significant sites for diversity conservation are situated in countries with some of the lowest per capita incomes in the world.

The core of the threat to the remaining biological diversity derives from the scale of the changes now occurring throughout the developing world. First and foremost is the current rate of population growth throughout the developing world. Between 1950 and 1990, the population in the developing world grew by 150 per cent (from 1.6 to 4.0 billion people) while that in the developed world grew by 50 per cent (from 0.8 to 1.2 billion people) (World Resources Institute, 1991). This rate of growth places a tremendous strain upon the resources of a given country, and creates demands for the most intensive use of all resources at a populations' disposal.

In addition, this pressure on the developing world's resources is not likely to ease off in the near future. The past population gains have a natural momentum which, even with a slowing of the pace of growth, will inevitably lead to much greater population sizes in the developing world in the next 50 years. Even assuming a very rapid decline in the rate of population growth, the world's human population is likely to reach about 10 billion by the year 2100, with about 85 per cent of these people situated in the developing world (Repetto, 1986; Western, 1989).

Therefore, against the forces for conservation in the developing world must be placed the demand for food, land and opportunities in a world that will double in population over the next 100 years (from 4.0 to 8.7 billion people). The next century's pressures must be dealt with now, there is very little prospect that future governments will not come to re-examine their commitments to the "preservation" of substantial areas of their territories (of which about 4 per cent of natural habitat is now protected) in light of changing circumstances.

It is the irony, and the core, of the problem of biological diversity conservation that in this one respect the "poorest" of the world's nations hold most of the world's "wealth". However, a stock of wealth does not always generate an obvious return to its holders, and sometimes return from an investment flows to persons other than those in possession of it. This is the case for much of the value of biological diversity; although it is chiefly held in the developing world, most of its value flows to the developed.[12]

The problem of biodiversity conservation can then be reconstructed as follows: How is it possible to develop a flow of the full value of this stock of wealth to its holders in a manner that creates incentives to maintain it? One possible solution is to utilize this wealth, thereby generating a flow of goods and services for both local benefit and for trade with the developed regions. The role of wildlife utilization is to provide compensation for the developing countries for conserving wildlands and wildlife .

Economics for the wilds: an overview

The economic approach to wildlife and wildlands is distinguished by the emphasis that it places upon the link between the two. The economic link between wildlife and wildlands is found in the concept of *utilization*. The use of wildlife can provide the funds necessary to sustain and conserve wildlands; equally, many of the non-use or indirect use values of natural environment are also important to human welfare. This is the message provided by Chapter 2 on Economics for the Wilds. This chapter provides a "toolkit" for the understanding of how the economics of wild resource utilization and natural habitat conservation can be made compatible with human development goals.

Chapter 3 raises a theme that will recur again and again throughout the book; this concerns the limitations of wildlife utilization policy. The most important limitation is its inapplicability to the facets of wildlands that are not appropriable: ecosystem services, genetic information, even the existence rights of other species. The design of an effective wildlife utilization policy requires a clear understanding of its limits, and Chapter 3 on Appropriating the Value of Wildlands begins the process of analysing where these constraints exist.

The implications of wildlife and wildland utilization are wide-ranging and involve some of the most important issues of our times. The scale at which these issues operate ranges across the entire realm of human interaction. Wildlife utilization involves issues of sustainable development in some of the smallest and most remote communities on earth, and it also involves the issue of the conservation of an important global resource, biological diversity, requiring collective action by the whole of the international community. Chapters 4 and 5 are juxtaposed in order to present this contrast between the local and the global roles of biodiversity policy.

Chapter 4 examines the international policy element to wildlife utilization; it analyses its role in biodiversity conservation. The fundamental international environmental problem with regard to biodiversity is the transference of funds from North to South in a way that creates incentives for conservation. Not only wildlife utilization, but also natural habitat funding mechanisms, property right transfers (such as debt-for-nature exchanges), intellectual property right systems, and trade regulation are surveyed. Chapter 4 identifies the provision of an ongoing system of compensation as the necessary condition for natural habitat maintenance, and it assesses all of these various policy options against this requirement.

At the national level, it is equally important that the correct policies be undertaken in order to conserve diversity, both human and natural. Chapter 5 analyses the capacity of community utilization schemes to bring wildlife into the local economy. Two case studies are examined, the CAMPFIRE programme in Zimbabwe and the LIRDP Project in Zambia. The main theme of the chapter is to stress the importance of community participation and sharing in the returns from wildlife utilization.

The following two chapters are case studies designed to illustrate some of the concepts developed earlier in the book. Chapter 6 surveys the role of wildlife tourism in the maintenance of natural habitat. The economic studies of wildlife tourism in Chapter 6 illustrate the need to have careful analysis of wildlife management and utilization schemes before appropriate strategies are chosen. The assumption that wildlife tourism is always a "peripheral" development activity is laid convincingly to rest in this chapter. Chapter 7 addresses the range of uses that are afforded by rainforest utilization. Case studies are also used in this chapter to illustrate the market and policy failures that are currently leading to excessive deforestation. Because of the linkages between economic policies and large-scale land use changes, careful analysis of the factors contributing to deforestation is necessary. These chapters then provide some of the illustrative detail necessary to make clear the role of natural habitat utilization in development programs.

The penultimate two chapters are included in order to illustrate some of the important differences and problems implied by production in the context of wildlands and wildlife. Chapter 8 on the conservation impact of wildlife utilization demonstrates that, to the present time, very little effective conservation has resulted from wildlife utilization in the past. This record clearly contributes to the public perception that wildlife exploitation is a threat to wildlife. The analysis of the range of utilization options makes clear that different approaches to utilization have very different conservation impacts. Clearly, these problems must be tackled if utilization is ever to be applied as a constructive force for wildlife and wildland conservation.

Chapter 9 addresses the problems of illegal exploitation of wildlife, an issue that is always in the news. Ironically, much that is now "illegal" was "traditional" in the not-too-distant past. Part of the solution to these crimes is to return the resources to the local people, as discussed in more detail in Chapter 5. However, with any allocation of rights, there is always lawbreaking, and then it is important that the resources are protected. This chapter provides an interesting case study of how enforcement can be "economically adjusted" to fit the crime.

The economic approach to wildlife and wildland conservation, therefore, emphasizes the role of utilization, as one prong of a much broader strategy for the conservation of the world's species and diversity. Against the background of substantial and continuing losses of natural habitats, we believe that this is a fundamentally important message to convey. However, with the proposal of any policy, its limitations must be carefully scrutinized. These are the dual roles of this volume: to make the case for the policy of wildlife utilization while analysing its capabilities and shortcomings. The point that we wish to make is that diversity conservation efforts must be focused on the solution to these shortcomings, not on the jettisoning of wildlife utilization as a policy altogether.

Notes

1. *Ex situ* conservation is an important mechanism for the conservation of a very small number of very highly valued species, such as a few domesticated crops and animals. Genetic libraries for these species do exist, although they remain incomplete, difficult to maintain and expensive to operate.
2. One of the important points to make clear at the outset is that the threat of possible extinction in the near term is one that currently faces the vast majority of the world's species, not a selected few that are always in the press. The reasons for this are detailed in this and the immediately following section.
3. Since early this century, with respect to plants, substantial germ plasm collections have been developed with an eye to conserving the closest kin of heavily used species. Over the past few decades a network of international storage banks has been created for the *ex situ* conservation of the nearest relatives; these are the "seed banks" established at International Agricultural Research Centres (IARC) under the auspices of the International Board for Plant Genetic Research (IBPGR).
4. In addition, as noted earlier, such *ex situ* methods are not realistic options for the vast majority of species, but only for these exceptional few.
5. It is apparent from the historical record that nearly every species can pass from one group to the other, *i.e.* nearly every "wild" species has the capacity to be domesticated, nearly every domesticated species can become feral. Therefore, it is not a specific genotype that determines on which side of the roster a particular species lies.
6. By "under-valued", it is intended to include those wild breeds of domestic stocks that would be highly valued if discovered and utilized. Much of the cost of undervaluation of unused resources lies with those that could most easily be brought into existing production processes, but these are often lost with others whose usefulness would be much more difficult to discover.

7. This is precisely the situation in which we find ourselves at present, with human population pressures projected to impact severely on previously unmanaged habitats over the next century.

8. It is important to note that natural habitat cannot be defined by reference to human intervention, simply because there is no land mass on earth (possibly excepting Antarctica) where humans have not intervened over the last 10,000 years. The human species appears to have originated in Africa and spread to Europe and Asia about one million years ago, reaching Australia about 50,000 years ago and the Americas 20,000 years ago (Daimond, 1989). Therefore, it makes little sense to speak of habitat without humans; it is the nature of the process affecting the habitat, not the presence of humans, that determines its produce.

9. Under this valuation "wildlife" represents a broad spectrum of under-valued and under-managed species. The two most significant wildlife products are, by far and away, trees and fish, representing about two-thirds of the world trade in wildlife together (Hemley, 1985). The remainder of the wildlife trade represents a wide variety of products, including (in order of annual US import values) furs, reptiles, ivory, ornamental fish, coral and shells (Fitzgerald, 1989). The annual value of the international trade probably approaches $20 billion (Prescott-Allan, R. and Prescott-Allan, C., 1989).

10. This book primarily concerns itself with the development of "traditional" uses that have long existed within particular systems as a means of keeping them in their "natural" state.

11. It has been shown in certain studies that a reduction in area of 90 per cent leads to a loss of half of the habitat's species. For example, in one study of terrain lost during flooding that occurred with the construction of the Panama Canal, there was a loss of about 12 per cent (of a projected 15 per cent) of the initial stock of species within 50 years of the habitat alteration (Terborgh, 1974).

12. This is evident from the proportion of biotechnology patents lodged in the developed and developed world. In the EC, for example, the US holds 36 per cent of such patents, EC states hold 32 per cent of them, and Japan 23 pr cent (leaving 9 per cent for the remainder of the world). In Latin America, once again, only 11 per cent of biotechnology patents are held by residents; the remainder are held by developed countries. Therefore, the value of genetically engineered products are being captured, both in the developed and the developing world, by developed countries, even though most of the genetic value originates from the former.

2

ECONOMICS FOR THE WILDS

Edward B. Barbier

The following chapter introduces some basic principles of economics that are relevant to wildlife and natural habitat preservation and management. As the main theme of this book is to illustrate that conservation of wildlife and natural habitat has economic value and a role to play in development, a brief review of this economic argument serves as an important introduction to subsequent chapters.

Conservation and development: the role of economics

Chapter 1 has outlined the global nature of the current biodiversity "crisis". The loss of the woeld's remaining natural areas and habitats for wild species is usually portrayed as a conflict between *development* and *preservation* options. Equally, the over-exploitation and extinction of key wildlife species is seen as the failure to preserve these species by controlling or limiting harvesting, hunting and extractive activities. Thus development is perceived as the principal threat to the continued survival of wildlife and wildlands, and "stopping" development – at least for key species and select natural areas – is advocated as the best means for ensuring their preservation.

Portraying the alternative options as a "polarized" choice between, at the one extreme, development, with the complete conversion or loss of natural areas and wildlife and, on the other, preservation, with no or extremely limited human use, is not always helpful. As the previous section noted, the vast majority of the world's remaining natural habitats are in the developing world, and only a modest fraction of this area is officially protected. For many developing countries, the option of "preserving" all or most of their remaining areas of natural habitat as "nature reserves" is unfeasible, given the social and economic pressures for increased economic development and poverty alleviation.

On the other hand, all societies must be made aware of the full costs of natural habitat conversion and loss. Too often, wildlands are treated as "wastelands" and wildlife as "free goods" to be exploited at little or no cost. Individuals undertaking the decision to exploit these resources face only the direct costs of converting natural habitats, extracting and harvesting natural products or hunting wildlife – and often these costs may be inadvertently or even deliberately subsidized through public policies. The wider social and environmental costs of habitat and wildlife loss – the "external" costs imposed on others who benefited from the use of these resources, the disruptions to important ecological functions, the sacrifice of future income from depleting these assets today and the loss of unique species and natural areas that some may value merely for their existence – all these costs are rarely borne by the individual exploiters of wildlife and wildlands.

In sum, both the extreme development and preservation options for the remaining wildlife and natural areas of the world may have important and increasing social costs. Nevertheless, under certain conditions, the preservation option will be viewed as economically worthwhile – even in poorer developing countries – provided that the net benefits of creating a "reserve' out of the natural area are perceived to be greater than any that development of the area could yield. Complete conversion of the natural area may also be justified if all the social and environmental costs of irreversible loss of this resource are properly accounted for and considered less than the gains from conversion.

Economics of sustainable management

In the majority of circumstances land and wildlife use options other than the conventional development and preservation extremes may be more attractive. There are a variety of conservation or sustainable management options that serve to maintain natural areas broadly in their original state and conserve wildlife species while at the same time allowing important human uses of these resources. Sustainable management regimes for these resources are extremely diverse, ranging from commercial wildlife ranching and harvesting to non-timber forest product extraction to community-based wildlife and wildlands development to tourism and recreation, and so on. Many examples of these conservation options and their implications for the economics of wildlife and wildland utilization are given in subsequent chapters of this book.

Because they appear to reconcile development and conservation objectives, sustainable management options for wildlife and natural areas are extremely attractive. However, just like any other option, a sustainable management regime will have a range of economic costs and benefits associated with it. These costs and benefits will, of course, vary considerably for different sustainable management options and for different locations and at different times. Thus it may be presumptuous to assume that a given sustainable management regime may always be economically worthwhile in all times and places. Box 2.1 illustrates this with the example of wildlife culling in Africa.

Careful economic assessment of the costs and benefits of a sustainable management option is required, both from the financial perspective of the individual or individuals undertaking the activity and from the economic perspective of society as a whole. The net benefits of sustainable management must also be compared to the net benefits of any other land and wildlife use options – perhaps a conventional development or preservation alternative – in order to determine which option is indeed the most economically worthwhile to pursue. Such an approach offers the best chance of encouraging efficient and sustainable use of our remaining, and rapidly dwindling, natural areas and wildlife resources.

Box 2.2 illustrates the usefulness of assessing the comparative returns to wildlife management options with an example from Botswana. The financial and economic returns indicate that, with the exception of game ranching, most wildlife management schemes are more profitable than cattle ranching for beef production, which is the main alternative use of rangelands in Botswana.

Total economic value

Unfortunately, it is rare that such an assessment as the one illustrated in Box 2.2 takes place. Moreover, even this example was only a partial analysis of comparative economic returns. To reflect accurately the costs and benefits of different land and wildlife use options, it is necessary to assess the total economic value (TEV), both marketed and non-marketed, that each option entails. TEV comprises direct and indirect use values, option values and existence values (see Box 2.3). Direct use values include wildlife and other harvested products (e.g., skins, hides, tusks/horns, plants, resins) and direct use of natural areas for tourism and recreation. Indirect use values are essentially the ecological functions of species and natural areas (e.g., protection, microclimatic and material cycling functions). All these values may have an "option value" component if we are interested in preserving them for future use.

Box 2.1: Commercial wildlife cropping in Africa: successes and failures

Wildlife cropping or *culling* essentially implies the harvesting of wild animals to provide continuous, sustainable supplies of animal products – meat, hides, trophies, etc. As distinct from traditional hunting practices for food and other subsistence needs and safari hunting for recreational sport, commercial cropping involves organized hunting operations to supply wildlife products to markets for financial gain. In some cases, control of wildlife populations is also an objective. More recently, cropping has been promoted as a viable sustainable management option for wildlife utilization and natural habitat conservation, and as a means to generate employment and revenues for local communities (see Chapter 5).

Since 1960, many commercial cropping schemes of elephants, hippos and smaller animals have been implemented with varying degrees of success in East, Central and Southern Africa. Although many projects have failed because they were unable to produce a safe, hygenic source of meat or had misjudged population densities, the vast majority were unsuccessful because the projects were simply financially unviable due to misjudgement of market demand, the costs of production and the constraints of rural subsistence economies. Very few commercial cropping schemes are ever subject to economic and financial analysis even to give a rough indication of their relative costs and benefits.

One exception is the analysis of the cropping scheme run by the Tanzanian Wildlife Corportation (TAWICO), which was appraised after four months of operation. The scheme essentially produced both skins (lion and zebra) and meat (zebra and wildebeest). The financial analysis indicated that after four months of operation the scheme returned a modest profit of about US $6650 (1988 prices). Other observed points were:

- neither the skins nor the meat alone led to a profit; profitability depended on both being taken;

- although the average costs of shooting and marketing products were high (around US $73 per animal), these costs were standard for commercial cropping schemes of this kind and do not indicate any inefficiencies;

- the type of operation would not benefit from economies of scale; on the contrary, any increase in yield must be achieved either by changing cropping methods or by increasing the number of shooting parties in the field.

A further analysis was conducted to see whether a larger operation could increase foreign exchange earnings through selling wildebeest meat to external markets in Gulf states (zebra meat is not acceptable in these countries). The results are shown opposite.

Box 2.1 (continued)

Returns to exporting 1 kg of culled wildebeest meat from Tanzania to Gulf markets (in US$)

Gross revenue	**3.12**
Major costs	**2.72**
of which:	
Freight and handling	2.10
Shooting	0.62
Net revenue	**0.40**

Additional (unquantified) costs
e.g.:

> Transportation within Tanzania
> Chilling
> Butchering
> Packing
> Administrative overheads
> Contingencies

Project net revenues   **<0.0**

The analysis shows that estimated net revenues of US$0.40 per kg are unlikely to meet the unquantified additional costs associated with this kind of operation. The conclusion reached was that the existing medium-scale cropping schemes run by TAWICO are close to optimal for the special conditions of Tanzania. Any attempt to expand the operations to export meat would probably undermine their profitability.

Source: I.S.C. Parker, "Perspectives on Wildlife Cropping or Culling", Chapter 16 in R.H.V. Bell and E. McShane Caluzi (eds), *Conservation and Wildlife Management in Africa*, US Peace Corps, Washington DC, 1984. Ministry of Lands, Natural Resources and Tourism, Tanzania, in collaboration with the International Trade Centre and IUCN, *Wildlife Utilisation in Tanzania*, IUCN, Gland , Switzerland, 1988.

Finally, existence value includes the values that people place on wildlife and natural areas "in themselves" and is unrelated to any use. (See Chapter 3, for more on the indirect use and non-use values provided by natural areas.)

Box 2.2: Botswana — comparative returns to wildlife management options

The following table shows financial and economic rates of return in Botswana to different wildlife management options, in comparison to cattle ranching for beef production. With a cut-off rate of 10-12 per cent (i.e., options exhibiting rates of return at this level or higher are acceptable), most wildlife management options should proceed. In comparison, beef production appears to be unprofitable. Moreover, the returns to cattle ranching do not take into account the subsidies for beef production in Botswana. Thus the subsidy is very uneconomic as it supports an industry that would not otherwise break even, displaces other more profitable wildlife management options and over the long term gives rise to land degradation. Surprisingly, game ranching also shows an unacceptable rate of return, which underlies the need to assess carefully the costs and benefits of different wildlife management options before selecting the appropriate one to pursue.

| Project | Internal rate of return (%) | | Comment |
	Financial	Economic	
Group small scale game harvesting	21	28	Biltong, skins, trophies, hunting
Ostrich farming	19	14	Skins, feathers, meat
Crocodile farming	18	14	Skins, tailmeat
Tourist lodge	18	35	See chapter 6
Safari hunting	16	45	<3% animal offtake, 12 bed lodge
Game ranching	6	7	Meat, hunting, live animals, 9000 ha
Cattle ranching	5	na	Beef, 6500 ha

Source: J. Barnes and D.W. Pearce, "The Mixed Use of Habitat", *mimeo.*, Centre for Social and Economic Research on the Global Environment, London, 1991.

Calculation of the above components of total economic value is important for assessing the costs and benefits of different

Box 2.3: Total economic value of wildlife and wildlands

The table indicates the many *use* and *non-use* values of wildlife and wildlands that may comprise their *total economic value* (TEV):

Classification of total economic value for wildlife and wildlands

Use values			Non-use values
(1) Direct value	(2) Indirect value	(3) Option value	Existence value
Sustainably harvested products (meat/fish, timber, plants etc)	Ecological functions/ roles Protection functions	Future uses as per (1), (2)	Biodiversity Culture, heritage
Recreation Tourism	Waste assimilation		
Genetic material	Microclimatic functions		
Education	Carbon store		
Human habitat			
Other services (water transport/supply)			

Direct use values are the resources and "services" provided directly by natural areas, or by directly harvesting and exploiting wildlife. *Indirect use values* comprise mainly the environmental functions of natural areas – ecological functions, such as nutrient cycling, protection functions, such as ground cover for key watersheds, waste assimilation functions, such as the retention or detoxification of pollution and wider functions such as microclimatic stabilization and carbon storage. These environmental functions all indirectly support economic activity and human welfare. However, wildlife species may also have important indirect use value through key ecological roles; for example, elephants are known to have an essential ecological role in African savannahs and forests through diversifying ecosystems, dispersing seeds, reducing

Box 2.3 (continued)

bushlands, expanding grasslands and reducing tsetse fly, which is of value to livestock grazing (Western 1989).

Option value relates to the amount that individuals would be willing to pay to conserve wildlife and wildlands, or at least some of their direct and indirect applications, for future use. Individuals are essentially valuing the guaranteed "option" of future supply of these uses, the availability of which might otherwise be uncertain. *Existence value* relates to valuation of these resources as unique assets in themselves, with no connection to their use values. This would include the worth of wildlife species, natural areas and overall biodiversity as objects of intrinsic and "stewardship" value and as unique cultural and heritage assets. As essentially an *attribute* of natural areas rather than a resource or function, biodiversity has a special value relationship (Aylward and Barbier, 1991). In addition to having existence value, the diversity of biological resources may contribute to the direct use value of a natural area for scientific research, education and as a source of genetic material. Biodiversity may also have additional indirect use value in protecting ecological stability and functions.

wildlife and wildland use options. For example, if conversion of a natural area to agriculture entails the loss of natural habitat and environmental functions, we need to know exactly what economic values are being sacrificed by taking up this development option. However, care should be taken in adding up the various components of TEV, as there are inevitable trade-offs among them. Furthermore, a measure of TEV in itself does not tell us anything about the opportunity costs – the next best wildlife or wildland use option forgone – of a given development option. Only by carefully comparing the full costs and benefits of different options is it possible to determine which ones should take place. As noted above, even complete conversion of natural areas may be warranted if the benefits of this development option exceed the full economic and social costs of conservation.[1]

A major problem is that many of the components in total economic value have no market – especially subsistence use of wildlife and wildland products and the indirect use, option and existence values of natural areas. These values are often difficult to assess in developing countries, yet the few studies that have been made suggest that the various values of wildlife products and natural areas are considerable (see Table 2.1).

Table 2.1: Some recent wildlife and wildlands valuation estimates for developing countries (US$)

Direct use values

Pre-ban ivory exports, Africa (Barbier et al. 1990)	$35–45 million/year
Fruit and latex forest harvesting, Peru	$6330/ha
Sustainable timber harvesting, Peru (Peters, Gentry and Mendelsohn 1989)	$ 490/ha
Buffalo range ranching, Zimbabwe (Child, 1990)	$3.5–4.5/ha
Wetlands fish and fuelwood, Nigeria (Barbier, Adams and Kimmage, 1991)	$38–59/ha
Viewing value of elephants, Kenya (Brown and Henry, 1989)	$25 million/year
Ecotourism, Costa Rica (Tobias and Mendelsohn, 1991)	$1250/ha
Tourism, Thailand	$385–860,000/year
Research/education, Thailand (Dixon and Sherman, 1990)	$38–77,000/year
Tourism, Cameroon	$19/ha
Genetic value, Cameroon (Ruitenbeek, 1989)	$7/ha

Indirect use values

Watershed protection of fisheries, Cameroon	$54/ha
Control of flooding, Cameroon	$23/ha
Soil fertility maintenance, Cameroon (Ruitenbeek, 1989)	$8/ha
Carbon storage, tropical forests (Pearce, 1990)	$1300/ha/year

Option/Existence values

Elephants and other species, Thailand (Dixon and Sherman, 1990)	$4.7 million/year
Amazonian forests (Pearce, 1990)	$3.2 billion

Source: See references.

Unless valuation of these resources in developing countries is made specific, actual choice of natural land and habitat use is usually biased in favour of development and conversion options that do have marketed outputs, e.g. ranching, timber exploitation, agriculture, mining, hydroelectricity. Alternatively, only marketed wildlife and wildland products, e.g. game meat, hides/skins, horns/tusks, fruits/nuts, rattan/bamboos, are seen to have "value', and these products are harvested or exploited exclusively for this purpose. The result is often too much conversion and over-exploitation, and too little sustainable management, of natural lands and products.[2]

Many of the studies indicated in Table 2.1 have shown that, when proper account is taken of the values of natural areas and products, sustainable management of these areas makes sound economic sense. Peters, Gentry and Mendelsohn (1989) have shown that the discounted financial returns from non-timber harvesting of fruit and latex plus selective cutting of timber from a rainforest in Peru easily exceed the returns from alternative options, such as clear-cutting timber, plantation harvesting and cattle ranching. Barbier, Adams and Kimmage (1991) demonstrated that the direct uses of the natural Hadejia-Jama'are floodplain in Northern Nigeria for fishing, fuelwood and recession agriculture appear to offer much higher economic returns than upstream irrigation developments that are diverting water away from the floodplain. The study by Ruitenbeek (1989) for the Korup Project, Cameroon, concluded that the economic benefits from preserving Korup National Park and from sustainable management of buffer zones were much greater than the direct costs of the project plus any forgone timber earnings and the lost production from resettling six villages. Similarly, Dixon and Sherman (1990) maintain that the various direct and indirect benefits of Khao Yai National Park place it in the socially beneficial category (i.e., the net benefits to society at large are positive), thus deserving continued public support as a protected area.

Economic decision-making over resource use

The failure to appreciate and assess the total economic value of wildlife and wildlands often results in a distortion in economic incentives. That is, excessive loss of natural areas and habitats is the outcome of their values not being fully recognized and integrated into decision-making processes by individuals in the market place and by government. If markets fail fully to reflect these values, then market failure is said to exist. Where government decisions or policies do not fully reflect the "socially beneficial" values of natural areas, there is government or policy failure.

Throughout the developing world, the presence of environmental "externalities", poorly defined property rights for resources, incomplete markets for labour and capital, endemic poverty and income constraints, imperfect competition, and high levels of uncertainty have limited the effectiveness of markets in reflecting the full social benefits of wildlife and wildlands. The existence of poorly formulated economic and regulatory policies has further exacerbated problems of natural resource management. By failing to make markets and private decision-makers accountable for for-gone values of natural areas, habitats and species, these policies may contribute to market failure. At worst, the direct private costs of resource-using and conversion activities are subsidized and/or distorted, thus encouraging the excessive loss of wildlife and wildlands.[3]

Appropriate incentive structures must be set against the context of management regimes – access and rights to land and other resources. Throughout the developing world, four types of resource management regimes exist – private ownership, common property ownership, state ownership and open access. In private ownership, resource rights and ownership are conferred on a private individual or group of individuals. For example, much farmland in developing countries is privately owned. In state or public ownership, resource ownership is vested in the government, which also tries to determine and control resource rights and ownership. Officially protected areas and many other natural resources – forests, mines, coastal seas, even wild animals – are often subject to state ownership in developing countries. However, the ability of these governments to control or regulate access to these resources is frequently undermined by high costs and lack of funds. Common property is the ownership and management of resources by a reasonably defined community. Often, communities will jointly own grazing land, forest, woodlots and even farmland.

A frequent misperception is that common property leads to over-exploitation by individuals – the "tragedy of the commons" – and should be replaced by state or private ownership of resources. However, many common property regimes traditionally have involved the sustainable use of resources, but may break down due to overpopulation, policy failures and the expropriation of resource ownership and rights. This often occurs in the case of wildlife and wildlands, where community management of these wild resources consists mainly of important social rules and rituals governing traditional "rights of access" and harvesting. Such management systems are easily undermined by external forces of change.[4]

Open access exploitation increases the risks of rapid resource degradation of wildlife and wildlands. As exclusion (or control of access) of users is problematic, each individual has the incentive to exploit the resource as quickly as possible. Each individual will therefore ignore any user costs of exploitation; that is, the concern will be with maximizing returns today – before they are lost to somebody else – rather than with the loss of future income owing to resource depletion. Perversely, the presence of surplus profit, or economic rent, will also encourage over-exploitation.[5] If large profits are available from resource exploitation but they accrue exclusively, say, to a single individual or to the government, then the single resource owner can sustain the income earned indefinitely by limiting over-exploitation. However, if it is impossible to exclude others from exploiting the resource as well, then the existence of excess rents will be an incentive for many individuals to undertake this activity, or alternatively for the individuals already exploiting the resource to expand their activities. The result is that any profits will be quickly dissipated, as returns become rapidly dispersed over a growing number of individuals, none of whom will have any incentive to conserve the resource. In many developing countries, government policies – fiscal incentives, pricing policies, regulations and land titling – often exacerbate these tendencies by reducing or distorting the direct costs of rapid resource exploitation and conversion.[6]

Comparative returns and discounting

Another major problem affecting the incentives for managing natural areas and wildlife in developing economies is whether the returns realized in "conserving" or "holding on" to these resources is greater than the income earned from alternative sources. If wildlife and wildlands are considered a valuable asset, i.e. a source of wealth that increases in value over time, then it may be worthwhile to maintain these resources into the future to take advantage of this increasing value. We have already seen how open access exploitation can undermine this incentive. In addition, there are other forms of wealth, or assets, that yield income. The comparable returns from these assets will determine the general rate of interest in the economy. Individuals therefore have the choice of harvesting or converting wild resources today and investing the returns in alternative economic assets, or "holding on" to these resources to reap future income from them. Thus, the opportunity cost of conserving wildlife and other natural resources is the forgone earnings from alternative assets, as represented by the interest rate. Or another way of looking at it, in order to be economically worthwhile, the future income earned from maintaining wildlife and wildlands must be discounted at the rate of interest earned on other assets.

In addition, the rate at which we discount the future value of wildlife and natural areas is affected by individuals' time preference. That is, people may be reluctant to wait for future returns from maintaining wild resources because they are simply impatient for money now, because of uncertainty over the future (including a high risk of death) and because improving incomes mean that additional wealth in the future is less valuable today. In rural areas in developing countries, uncertainty of the future is compounded by threats of drought and other natural disasters, political instability and warfare, economic disruptions and policy changes and the cumulative impacts of widespread natural resource degradation. Finally, poverty itself may force individuals to have a high rate of time preference: under conditions of extreme poverty, a household's major concern is securing sufficient means for survival today.

Public policies also can affect the comparative returns to conserving wild resources by distorting capital markets and affecting individuals' perceptions of the future. For example, in many developing countries, scarce financial credit is often allocated through subsidies and tax inducements to certain economic activities, such as investments in large-scale commercial agriculture and industry, while the vast majority of rural households must rely on informal sources of credit with effective interest rates of 50 to 200 per cent or even higher. Thus, on the one hand, subsidized formal credit assists large-scale conversion of wildlands and natural habitat to "income-earning" activities such as commercial ranching, agriculture and forestry. On the other, the lack of formal credit in many rural areas means that small farmers and pastoralists are discouraged from "conserving" wild resources for future gain. They are also discouraged from borrowing to invest in land improvements and intensification that will contribute to future productivity. Instead, extending production into the remaining "frontier" areas of natural habitat is the only means of guaranteeing subsistence and income.[7]

Sustainable development and resource management

So far we have argued that by affecting the relationships between

prices, costs and the return on comparable investments – as
reflected in the interest or discount rate – market and policy
failures in developing countries distort the incentives for conservation of wild resources. Yet, paradoxically, excessive exploitation
of wildlife and wildlands leads to the loss of important economic
values. As these values are "socially beneficial', appropriate public
policies must be designed to ensure the protection and sustainable
management of wild resources.

Wildlands and wildlife also have an important role to play in
the sustainable development of developing countries. Sustainable
development has been defined by the World Commission on Environment and Development (1987) as "development that meets the
needs of the present without compromising the ability of future
generations to meet their own needs". Underlying this concept is
the notion of *intergenerational equity*; that is, future generations
should enjoy at least the same, if not greater, economic opportunities as present generations. Since our economic opportunities
are determined by our wealth, i.e. by the value of the capital stock
that we hold, then we can meet our obligations to the future by
leaving them an inheritance of wealth no less than we inherited.

Now, if we are confident that our stock of man-made capital,
skilled labour and environmental assets are totally interchangeable
– i.e. they can all perform the same functions and yield similar
goods – then any irreversible loss of environmental assets would not
matter as the environmental values foregone could be compensated
for by greater man-made assets or labour. However, if future and
current environmental values are unknown, particularly if there
is uncertainty concerning cumulative environmental impacts, and
if some of the ecological functions and goods provided by our
"natural" capital cannot easily be substituted for by man-made
capital or labour, then irreversible loss of natural resources should
be avoided.[8]

As argued in this chapter, and in the rest of this book, much
of the world's remaining wildlands and wildlife have substantial
economic values that are not fully accounted for when decisions
concerning their utilization are taken. Moreover, many of the
environmental goods and services lost when natural resources
such as wild species, wetlands, coral reefs, primary forest and
so on are irreversibly degraded or depleted cannot be simply
replaced by accumulation of more man-made capital or increasingly skilled labour. As the stock of natural capital declines, even
in developing countries the increasing "relative" scarcity of the
economic values it provides will be felt in terms of diminishing
economic welfare. Widespread environmental degradation and species loss can also push "ecologically vulnerable" economic activities

– fishing, pastoralism, fuelwood extraction, dryland farming – into the thresholds of carrying capacity, and ultimately environmental collapse.[9]

However, the emphasis of much of the sustainable development literature on the role of natural resources in securing the needs of future generations often obscures the important function of environmental assets in current development efforts. As argued by Barbier (1991b), there are several reasons why efficient and sustainable management of natural resources should be an important development goal, particularly for low income countries.

First, many of the low and lower-middle income economies of the world are currently dependent, and will continue to be dependent, on natural-resource based commodities for the largest share of their export-led development efforts – in terms of both economic growth and meeting debt repayments. Many of these economies rely on only one or two commodities for the majority of their export earnings. If these economies are to diversify their export base, their comparative advantage will most likely lie in the development of other natural resource-based products. Sustainable management of wildlife and wildlands will figure prominently in providing these products (Swanson, 1991).

Second, even if natural resource systems do not directly provide additional products for developing economies, they have important indirect use value in supporting and maintaining economic activity. As will be discussed in the following chapter, the role of natural systems and resources in protecting watersheds, maintaining soil fertility, controlling flooding, preventing storm damage and mitigating pollution is often vital to human welfare and economic production in developing regions.

Finally, wildlands and wildlife are also important resources to the livelihood security of the poorest groups in developing countries. The vast majority of the rural "core" poor live in ecologically fragile areas, cultivating marginal lands of low agricultural potential and directly dependent on natural resources for their livelihoods, i.e. dependent on woody biomass and vegetation for livestock fodder, fuelwood and raw materials; wildlife meat and fish for protein; water supplies for domestic use; and so forth. Dependence on wild foods and resources by the rural poor increases when cultivated food and market supplies are scarce and during times of emergency brought on by drought, war and famine. Thus, more often than not, sustainability of the livelihoods of the poor is linked to the sustainability of natural resource systems and wildlife resources. Sustainable management of these assets may therefore be just as important for *intragenerational equity* – the need for the poor to gain better livelihoods – as it is for *intergenerational equity* – meeting the needs of future generations, or alternatively, the future needs of the present generation.

Conclusion

This brief chapter has introduced some of the important economic principles underlying management of the wilds in developing countries. The main message has been to emphasize that wildlife and wildland management decisions are essentially "economic" choices that have important implications for the allocation of resources, and as a consequence, economics has an important role to play in determining appropriate management decisions for the wilds. Moreover, if wild resources are important to the economic development and welfare of developing countries, then more effort is required to ensure that proper economic analysis of this role is taking place. Further economic issues, as well as illustrations of the main points raised in the overview provided by this chapter, will be discussed in subsequent chapters.

References

Aylward, B.A. and Barbier, E.B., "Valuing Environmental Functions in Developing Countries", paper prepared for the Economics and Ecology Workshop, CATIE, Turrialba, Costa Rica, 29- 30 January, forthcoming in *Biodiversity and Conservation*, Vol. 1, 1991.

Barbier, E.B., *The Economic Value of Ecosystems: 1 – Tropical Wetlands*, LEEC Gatekeeper Series GK 89-02, [London: London Environmental Economics Centre, 1989a.]

Barbier, E.B., *Economics, Natural Resource Scarcity and Development: Conventional and Alternative Views* [London: Earthscan, 1989b.]

Barbier, E.B., "Environmental Degradation in the Third World", in D.W. Pearce et al., *Blueprint 2: Greening the World Economy* [London: Earthscan, 1991a.]

Barbier, E.B., "Environmental Management and Development in the South: Prerequisites for Sustainable Development", Paper prepared for the UNCED Symposium Sustainable Development: From Concept to Action, The Hague 1991b.

Barbier, E.B., *The Economic Value of Ecosystems: 2 – Tropical Forests*, LEEC Gatekeeper Series 91-01 [London: London Environmental Economics Centre, 1991].

Barbier, E.B., Adams, W.M. and Kimmage, K., *Economic Valuation of Wetland Benefits: The Hadejia-Jama'are Floodplain, Nigeria*,

LEEC Discussion Paper 91-02 [London: London Environmental Economics Centre, 1991].

Barbier, E.B., Burgess, J.C., Swanson, T.M and Pearce, D.W., *Elephants, Economics and Ivory* [London: Earthscan, 1990].

Bojo, J., Maler, K-G. and Unemo, L., *Environment and Development: An Economic Approach* [London: Kluwer, 1990].

Brown, G. Jr. and Henry, W., *The Economic Value of Elephants*, LEEC Discussion Paper 89-12 [London: London Environmental Economics Centre 1989.]

Child, B., "Assessment of Wildlife Utilization as a Land Use Option in the Semi-Arid Rangeland of Southern Africa", in A. Kiss (ed.), *Living with Wildlife: Wildlife Resource Management with Local Participation in Africa*, Technical Paper No. 130 [Washington DC, World Bank, 1990].

Dixon, J.A. and Sherman, P., *Economics of Protected Areas: A New Look at Benefits and Costs* [London: Earthscan 1990].

Hodgson, G. and Dixon, J.A., *Logging Versus Fisheries and Tourism in Palawan*, East-West Environment and Policy Institute Occasional Paper No. 7 [Honolulu: East-West Center, 1990].

Marks, S.A., *The Imperial Lion: Human Dimensions of Wildlife Management in Central Africa*, [Boulder, Colorado: Westview Press, 1983].

Moorehead, R., "Changes Taking Place in Common-Property Resource Management in the Inland Niger Delta of Mali", in F. Birkes (ed.), *Common Property Resources: Ecology and Community-Based Sustainable Development*, [London: Belhaven Press, 1989].

Pearce, D.W., *An Economic Approach to Saving the Tropical Forests*, LEEC Discussion Paper 90-05 [London: London Environmental Economics Centre, 1990].

Pearce, D.W., Barbier, E.B. and Markandya, A., *Sustainable Development: Economics and Environment in the Third World*, [London: Earthscan and Edward Elgar, 1990].

Peters, C., Gentry, A. and Mendelsohn, R., "Valuation of an Amazonian Rainforest", *Nature* 339:655-6, 1989.

Repetto, R., *Economic Policy Reform for Natural Resource Conservation*, Environment Department Working Paper No. 4 [Washington, DC, World Bank, 1988].

Richards, P. (1985). *Indigenous Agricultural Revolution*, [London: Hutchinson, 1985].

Ruitenbeek, H.J., *Social Cost-Benefit Analysis of the Korup Project, Cameroon*, Report prepared for the World Wide Fund for Nature and the Republic of Cameroon, London, 1989.

Swanson, T.M., "Conserving Biological Diversity", in D.W. Pearce et al., *Blueprint 2: Greening the World Economy*, [London: Earthscan, 1991].

Tobias, D. and Mendelsohn, R. (1990), "Valuing Ecotourism in a Tropical Rain-Forest Reserve", AMBIO 20(2):91-93, 1990.

Turner, R.K., "Economics and Wetland Management", AMBIO 20(2):59-63, 1991.

Western, D., "The Ecological Value of Elephants: A Keystone Role in African Ecosystems", in the ITRG Report, *The Ivory Trade and the Future of the African Elephant*, Prepared for the Second Meeting of the CITES African Elephant Working Group, Gabarone, Botswana, July, 1989.

Notes

1. For further discussion of the methodology for economic appraisal of different land use options for natural areas, e.g. tropical forests and wetlands, and of environmental functions see Aylward and Barbier (1991), Barbier (1989a and 1991c) and Pearce (1990). See also Chapters 3 and 7 in this volume.

2. For a recent overview of the conversion versus conservation dilemma facing natural lands and wildlife, see Swanson (1991). There are also specific studies relevant to developing countries on the economic appraisal of land use options for protected areas (Dixon and Sherman, 1990); tropical wetlands (Barbier, 1989a; Barbier, Adams and Kimmage, 1991; Turner, 1991); tropical forests (Pearce, 1990; Ruitenbeek, 1989); and coastal systems (Hodgson and Dixon, 1988). Further studies are cited throughout this volume.

3. For an overview of market and policy failures and their impact on environmental degradation in developing countries, see Barbier (1991a and 1991b); Pearce, Barbier and Markandya (1990) and Repetto (1988).

4. For example, Moorhead (1989) details the process of rapid breakdown in the common-property management systems that have developed over hundreds of years in the inland Niger delta of Mali. Richards (1985) describes a similar process for traditional harvesting and access rights to forest and forage resources in Sierra Leone. Marks (1983) argues how the displacement and abrogation of traditional hunting rights in the Luangwa Valley of Zambia encourages "illegal hunting" of wildlife and the alienation of local communities from conservation efforts. For further discussion, see also Chapter 5.

5. In economics, *rent* is the difference between the total value of selling a commodity and the costs of supplying it. Thus, rent can in principle be determined by deducting from the gross income earned the costs of labour, material and capital imputs (including the costs of paying a normal return, or profit, to capital). The existence of rent therefore implies more remuneration than is required to keep an activity in operation – hence the term *surplus profit*.

6. Barbier et al. (1990) analyse how inappropriate international and domestic management of the ivory trade has contributed to rent dispersion and dissipation, thus leading to over-harvesting of the African elephant and undermining conservation efforts. Chapter

6 emphasizes the major role of policy failures in tropical deforestation, especially in encouraging open access conversion of forest land for frontier agriculture expansion.

7. For further discussion of environmental problems in developing countries and discounting see Pearce, Barbier and Markandya (1990, ch. 2).

8. For further discussion of this particular economic interpretation of sustainable development and its implications for developing countries see Bojo, Maler and Unemo (1990) and Pearce, Barbier and Markandya (1990).

9. On the role of pervasive environmental degradation in natural resource scarcity and development, see Barbier (1989b).

3

APPROPRIATING THE VALUE OF WILDLIFE AND WILDLANDS

Bruce Aylward

Much of this book is concerned with the economic value of wildlife and wildlands in developing countries. The following chapters demonstrate that many values of wildlife and wildlands – including their direct use for subsistence, tourism, game ranching, culling, tradeable products and so forth – are important benefits that can be captured by individuals, firms and communal groups. However, as discussed in Chapter 2, the presence of market failures in the management of many wild resources prevents markets from fully reflecting the economic value of these resources. As a result, many of these wild resources are managed unsustainably and in a fashion that precludes the full realization of their value to society.

One common source of market imperfection in the case of a number of wild resources is their characteristic as "public goods", by which it is meant goods with *diffuse and uncapturable benefits*. This chapter examines three wild resources that are considered to be public goods and are increasingly recognized for their economic importance to developing countries: species and habitat existence, ecosystem services and genetic resources.[1] It is important to recognize that although these benefits of wildlands are not exchanged in markets (as are many of the other resources covered in this book) the value they provide is an integral, and often crucial, component of the total economic value of wildlands.

This chapter briefly summarizes what is known about the economic value of these wildland resources and points to the significant role this information can play in developing an economic argument for wildlife and wildland conservation. However, it is not enough merely to indicate the current and potential benefits to society of species and habitat existence, ecosystem services and genetic resources. If these values cannot be appropriated by wildland managers a sub-optimal and unsustainable level of wildland management may be the end result. By investigating the "public good" nature of each of these wild resources this chapter clarifies the constraints that impede the appropriation of the benefits they provide. Chapter 4 then goes on to examine existing efforts and prospective methods for confronting the public goods problem.

Appropriability and public goods

The preceding chapter argued that the ability of resource users to secure the multitude of economic values attributable to wild resources appears to be a precursor for sustainable management. When the value accruing to wildlife managers falls short of the total economic value produced by the wildland, perverse incentives exist that cause wildlands to be overused and degraded. For example, logging companies only garner the timber value of rainforests, they do not garner the value of non-timber forest products and are not held responsible for the negative effects of logging on economic activities downstream. As a result loggers have little incentive to manage the forest in such a way as to maximize the total benefits that a rainforest is capable of providing. Sustainable management will only occur if the full range of benefits and costs of resource use feed into the decision-making process of the *de facto* managers of wild resources. The failure to appropriate the total economic benefits of a wild resource leads to an under-supply of wild resources because the individual does not take these "other" values into account in consumption and investment decisions.[2]

The strategies for wildlife utilization described in later chapters involve products and services of wildlands that can be owned, controlled and marketed by individuals or groups within society. However, there are other wild resources such as existence values, genetic resources and ecosystem services that are not so amenable to exchange in markets and whose value is not so easily captured by resource managers. Box 3.1 discusses how the benefits of these other wild resources may be spread across different groups in society. If wildlife managers are capable of securing only a portion of the value from such a resource they are unlikely to undertake comprehensive conservation efforts. As a result, such wild resources will be maintained at a level short of that which would maximize the welfare of society as a whole.[3]

The inability of individuals or groups to appropriate the value of wild resources may be due to the public good characteristics of the resource. As explained in Box 3.2, few "pure" public goods exist, but many wild resources exhibit differing degrees of the public good characteristics of non-rivalness and non-exclusiveness. The

Box 3.1: Appropriating the value of wildlands

A given wildland may produce a range of valued products and services. Each product or service may in turn provide benefits to a number of individuals or groups within societies and across the globe. Given the multitude of benefits and users it may be very difficult for wildlife managers to actually appropriate the full value of wildlands. The following hypothetical example briefly examines this problem in the case of a wildland producing four types of benefits: (1) direct use benefits; (2) genetic resource values; (3) ecosystem services and (4) existence values. Benefits from the wildland are assumed to go to three broadly representative groups: "management", "local", and "global", groups.

The "management" group exerts direct control over the resource. They harvest wild species for a variety of uses and may derive psychological satisfaction from the mere existence of local species and habitat. In addition they may crossbreed varieties and species thereby obtaining value from genetic resources. On-site ecosystem services may provide support and protection to the daily activities of the management group. All four of these benefits produced by the wildland are captured by the managers. In this example it is assumed that these are the only benefits that the management group receives from the resource, and they are not compensated for benefits that other groups receive from the resource.

The second, "local" group, has no legal access or control over the wildland. Nevertheless, ecosystem services that originate within the wildland may provide off-site benefits to the locals such as watershed protection or groundwater recharge. Similar to the managers, the locals may enjoy existence values originating from the species or habitats of the wildland. It is also possible that the local group may derive benefits from encroachment on the wildland for the purpose of collecting wild species for direct consumption or use in breeding activities. Clearly, the locals may capture some of the economic benefits of this wildland, however the benefits that accrue to the locals are not captured by the management group.

The final group in this example, the "global" group, consists of those living at a distance from the wildlands concerned. Although these people have little direct interaction with the wildland's resources they may receive

Box 3.1 (continued)

indirect use benefits from ecosystem services that have global impacts and existence benefits from exotic or endangered species with a global appeal. The benefits of genetic resources freely collected from the wildlands may also provide marketable benefits to multinational companies or farmers benefiting from public breeding programmes. Again, these are benefits captured by the global group with no compensation paid to the management group in return.

The table below summarizes the economic values of the hypothetical wildland and indicates which values are captured by the management group. If the values experienced by the local and global groups are large, but are not captured by the management group, then the management group may chose to provide less of the wildland than is socially optimal. That is, they fail to take account of the preferences of society as a whole. The table demonstrates the complexity of the problem – for any one wildland there may be a number of wild resources that have economic values that go appropriated. In practice, it is likely that intervention to correct such market failures will have to take into account the distribution of these unappropriated values across a much larger range of societal groups than is represented by this simplified example.

Capturing the economic values of wildland resources: an example

Groups	Direct uses	Genetic resources	Ecosystem services	Existence values
Managers	■	■	■	■
Local	□	□	□	□
Global		□	□	□

Key: captured = ■

uncaptured = □

practical implications of these characteristics is the classic public
goods problem – that of *free riders*. Free-riding occurs when
the cost of initiating the supply of a public good outweighs the
benefits that any one individual or group will gain in return. As
a result there is no clear motive for a single group to supply the
good – if one group supplies it they do so at a loss while all
the others receive the benefits for free, i.e. they free-ride. Thus
a waiting game develops as each group sits tight in the hope
that another group will take action first – the outcome being
a stalemate of inaction. In sum, wild resources that display the
characteristics of public goods have values that are difficult to
appropriate, thereby causing the market to underprovide conservation activities.

Public goods are often juxtaposed with private goods. The general
idea is that private goods *are* allocated efficiently by a market
system based on private ownership. Public goods, on the other
hand, are not supplied by the market in quantities sufficient
to maximize the welfare of society and a case for intervention
by central authority to correct the market failure is justified. In
many developing countries government intervention consists of
nationalizing large areas of wildland – by making wild resources
public property. However, there is growing recognition that alternative schemes such as communal management may be more appropriate in managing resources that are neither "pure" public goods
nor private goods. As Chapter 5 reveals, communal management
schemes in developing countries often prove a more effective means
of appropriating the value of wild resources than either public or
private management and encourage sustainable management of
such resources.

Communal management may provide a reasonable solution to
the problem of appropriating the local values of mobile wildlife
resources such as game and fish. However, the resources discussed
in this chapter suffer from the problem of appropriating values
that may be dispersed not just locally, but globally. Providing
incentives to manage such resources in a sustainable fashion
may require the development of additional management schemes
and compensation mechanisms. An assessment of a wild resource's
public good characteristics yields important clues to the manner
in which the benefits of the resource are, or are not appropriated.
Such analysis forms the basis for economics input to the design of
policy measures. The remainder of this chapter gathers evidence
on the magnitude of the benefits generated by species and habitat
existence, ecosystem services and genetic resources and then provides an analysis of the public good and appropriation problems
characterizing these important wild resources.

Box 3.2: Public goods

Public goods are commodities or services that once produced can be supplied to additional users without affecting their availability to the original consumer – i.e. at no extra cost. "Pure" public goods must be both non-rival and non-exclusive. *Non-rivalness* implies that consumption by one individual does not reduce the quality or quantity of the good available to other consumers. *Non-exclusiveness* means that there is no way to prevent others from making use of the good. Security from external threat – i.e. the provision of national defence – provides an excellent example of a "pure" public good. All members of a nation state have access to the security afforded by effective national defence forces and the security enjoyed by one citizen does not detract from that felt by his compatriot.[4]

However, such pure public goods are few and far between. The matrix displayed below shows that there are goods that fall between the extremes of pure public goods and private goods. For example, some goods are non-exclusive but are not fully non-rival – the classic example being the fishery. In a market setting, fishermen cannot exclude one another from the resource, but the fishery is only non-rival up to a point. The larger the number of fishermen trying to make a living off the same fishery, the more chance that their consumption of fish will become rival. Randall (1983) classifies goods that are neither rival nor non-rival as *congestible* goods. As demonstrated in the matrix below, *common pool resources* are defined as non-exclusive goods that are either rival or congestible.

The matrix also points to the potential existence of goods that are exclusive but not rival. As discussed in detail later on in this chapter, genetic resources are an example of a wild resource that is potentially exclusive and non-rival. The use of genetic material by one researcher does not impede the use of the original material by another so germplasm is non-rival. While genetic material is currently exchanged freely and on request, nations may in the future choose to exert their sovereignty over natural resources by controlling and marketing their national stock of genetic material. There is no traditional nomenclature for non-rival and

---

Box 3.2 (continued)

exclusive goods, but this discussion suggests *sovereign resources* as an appropriate label. Finally, resources that are exclusive and congestible are likely to be rare as the ability to exclude consumers may provide a mechanism to keep the congestibility of the good down to a minimum. For this reason such resources are also classified as sovereign resources.

A classification of wild resourses

	Non-exclusive	Exclusive
Non-rival	'Pure' public goods	Sovereign resources
Congestible	Common pool resources	
Rival		Private goods

Species and habitat existence

Non-use values are those benefits that are completely divorced from the use of a resource. Such benefits occur when people are willing to pay simply for the pleasure they derive from knowing that particular species or habitats continue to exist – irrespective of any plans they may have to hunt, observe or otherwise use these wild resources. Box 3.3 shows that such non-use values are best characterized as *existence values* – with the two terms being used interchangeably throughout this chapter.

The satisfaction that comes from knowing that a particular animal, habitat, micro-organism, etc., continues to prevail on earth is felt by all who wish to know and care in this manner. Once existence is provided there is no way to exclude people from appropriating existence values. The emotional, spiritual or ethical satisfaction derived from existence value is in no way diminished or affected by the degree of pleasure that others may also derive from a particular source of existence value. Therefore, "consumption" of existence values is both *non-excludable and non-rival* and existence value is an example of a "pure" public good.

People in both the developed and the developing world may experience

Box 3.3: Non-use values

The literature on non-use values is full of different typologies and taxonomies that seek to illustrate and define different non-use elements. Along with *existence value* – value associated with the knowledge that a resource exists – Krutilla (1967) suggested that *vicarious use values* represent the enjoyment received by people from the picture, print and broadcast media. The satisfaction people attach to setting aside wildlife resources for future generations is considered as a *bequest value*. *Stewardship values* have a similar connotation: the value found by guarding or preserving wildlands. Cultural or religious influences determining non-use values are often labelled *cultural values*. Finally, *intrinsic value* is often used as if it were synonymous with existence value

The plethora of types of non-use values can lead to confusion over what is and what is not a pure non-use value. If the motivation behind these expressions of value are to preserve the resource for future use broadly-defined (vicarious) or for the future use of others (bequest and stewardship) then the criteria of non-use is not met and these values are better considered as use values. If bequest or stewardship values are indeed non-use values they probably reflect the satisfaction derived from the knowledge that species or habitats will be around for a long time to come. Thus these values do not really differ substantially from existence values *per se.*

Culturally defined values – whether use or non-use values – are not distinct from economic values since people's preferences depend on their cultural backgrounds. Existence values may have a pronounced cultural or religious edge such as the Hindu belief in the sacred nature of cows. On the other hand they may have nothing to do with societal or institutional norms such as purely emotional responses to the pending extinction of a particularly charismatic or "intelligent" species. For this reason, cultural *non-use* values may simply be regarded as a subset of existence values.

Interpreting intrinsic value to mean value in and of itself, or in other words the satisfaction other species derive from their own existence, puts this value outside the scope of economic analysis. Economics is anthropocentric; it is based solely on the expression of human preferences. For this reason intrinsic value is neither a use nor a non-use value. Of course, if a human observes an animal "enjoying life" this may affect the value that person puts on the animal or species, but this is in no way a measure of the "satisfaction" the animal itself is feeling. In sum, "existence value" is the term that most effectively conveys the psychological nature of non-use benefits, while covering the full range of potential non-use values.

an existence value for the wildlands of developing countries. The suggestion that such values are much larger in developed countries is usually based on the assumption that existence values are a luxury of the rich. This, however, does not necessarily square with the reverent attitude toward nature exhibited by many indigenous forest dwellers and other aboriginal rural peoples in developing countries. When the habitats of tribal peoples are degraded and they are deprived of their normal environmental setting the resulting anomie should suggest that they have lost more than just the material use values gained from their habitat. As with many other aspects of existence values, further empirical work is necessary to determine the extent of existence values in both developed and developing countries. Unfortunately, the "psychological" nature of existence values means that economic theory provides little in the way of *a priori* expectations to guide such research.

Existence valuation studies

Empirical evidence of the magnitude of existence values is limited and is based mainly on research in the developed world, in particular in the United States (see Box 3.4). However, despite the preliminary nature of these studies they have produced some interesting results. Three illustrative studies are discussed below. They are selected as much for the questions they raise as for the light they shed on the extent of people's willingness to pay for non-use benefits in developed countries. All three studies are based on the use of the *contingent valuation method* (CVM). In order to elicit the use and non-use values individuals place on species and habitats, CVM typically involves the use of survey interviews or questionnaires. Since there are no markets for existence values the creation of a hypothetical or "contingent" market in which to survey peoples willingness to pay is generally regarded as the only reliable way to obtain an economic measure of such values.

A critical ingredient of CVM studies is the extent to which respondents are informed about the object of the studies and correspondingly, how much information is disclosed during the survey process. Samples et al. (1986) investigated the effects of information disclosure on preservation bids for endangered species. Although preservation bids may be interpreted to have both use and non-use components, the authors assumed that the endangered status of the species would cause responses to reflect mainly on the value of "saving" the species as there was little real prospect for "using" species close to extinction.[5]

In an experimental setting, questionnaires were used to record bids for humpback whales in the presence of differing amounts of information on the whale's characteristics and its endangered status. Preservation bids were recorded in the $30-$65 range per year. The effect of an informational video on the behaviour and plight of the humpback whale caused a relatively higher increase in bids by the experimental group as versus the control group, but the results did not indicate a clear impact from information disclosure.

Box 3.4 Empirical measures of non-use values

Value per adult respondent
in mid1980s US dollars

Animal species

Bald eagle	11
Emerald shiner	4
Grizzly bear	15
Bighorn sheep	7
Whooping crane	1
Blue whale	8
Bottlenose dolphin	6
California sea otter	7
Northern elephant seal	7

Natural amenities

Water quality (S. Platte River Basin)	4
Visibility (Grand Canyon)	22
Additional park facilities (Australia)	6

Source: Pearce 1990; Majid et al., 1983;

In the next stage, the respondents were given a hypothetical lump-sum cash payment and varying degrees of information about three species. They were then asked to divide the money as they wished amongst preservation funds for the three species. The results indicated that physical appearance and endangered status are significant determinants of allocation of preservation monies. More interestingly, when information on endangered status and physical appearance were revealed at the same time, respondents chose to dedicate a significantly larger share of their money to the unattractive and endangered, but savable species. The mean bid to preserve a rat-like creature out of a $30 endowment came to $21.60. Given that the other two species in the study were monkey-like and rabbit-like species this result flouts the common perception that people care only about preserving "friendly", fuzzy or human-like species.

The easiest way to avoid the problem of information disclosure is to survey a group that is well acquainted with the subject at hand. Brookshire et al. (1983) conducted a CVM study of preservation bids for bighorn sheep and grizzly bears in Wyoming. At the time of the study the grizzly bear was considered an endangered species and hunting had been outlawed for almost a decade. Hunting permits for the bighorn sheep, also under pressure from human encroachment upon its habitat, were limited to 350 per year. Questionnaires were distributed to three thousand Wyoming residents with a past history of hunting elk, antelope and deer. This group was expected to be well informed about the characteristics and status of these two species.

In addition to measuring the respondents' willingness to pay for hypothetical future permits to hunt bighorn sheep and grizzly bears, the questionnaire also identified existence values and observer preservation bids. The bids of respondents indicating that they would neither hunt nor directly observe the animals were taken to reflect existence values. The results of the study revealed a range of hunting bids from just under $10 to almost $30. Observer option bids for the two species were in the vicinity of $20. Existence bids for the bighorn sheep were in the $7 range with those for grizzly bears averaged $15. This study reveals that non-use values for species may be of the same order of magnitude as use values such as hunting and game-watching.

Another survey – this time of the value of habitat – provides even stronger evidence that existence values are of a significant size when compared to recreational use values. Majid et al. (1983) surveyed the willingness to pay for additional park facilities in a region of New South Wales, Australia. The first set of questions asked how much individuals would pay for recreational use benefits and total benefits originating from each of a number of existing and proposed parks. The difference between respondents willingness to pay for recreational visits and total willingness to pay indicated that existence values actually exceeded the recreational use values in all cases. For example, respondents indicated they would pay an average of A$5.50 (US$4.60) for recreational use of one of the proposed parks and A$12.90 (US$10.75) in total. By implication, the willingness to pay for existence values came to A$7.40 (US$6.20).

The study then went on to see how the willingness to pay (WTP) for the proposed park facilities would change when the responses were phrased in terms of the incremental value of the parks.

Thus the value of the eighth park was derived by subtracting the respondent's WTP for a system of eight parks from his WTP for seven parks. When the questions measured total WTP as preferences for explicitly adding new parks to the existing facilities the total WTP for the sites fell quite dramatically. In the case of the park cited above the total WTP dropped from A$12.90 (US$10.75) to just over A$5.00 (US$4.20).

The studies by Majid et al. (1983) and Brookshire et al. (1983) raise interesting questions regarding the degree of confidence and ultimate practicality of CVM results for policy purposes. In the case of the Australian park facilities it is difficult to determine the exact meaning of the lower willingness to pay that results when it is measured in an incremental fashion instead of in isolation. For example, when explicitly confronting other demands on their funds did the respondents reduce the value they placed on the non-use or the recreational values? Would bids have declined again if the interviewer had set the incremental value of the park facilities off against donations to other worthy causes? The Majid et al. study clearly illustrates the difficulty of accounting for the role of competing philanthropic causes in CVM studies.

The Brookshire et al. study raises the question of aggregation. Is it possible to extend the fairly narrow range of results for the existence value of grizzly bears and bighorn sheep beyond the sample of well-informed Wyoming residents to all individuals in Wyoming – or for that matter New York? The uncertainty involved in trying to apply such information to wider policy issues and populations is compounded if the results are extended from the preservation of domestic species to the protection of habitats of international importance.

Pearce (1990) made a bold attempt to "guesstimate" the value of the Amazon rainforest. Making the assumption that all the adults in the richest countries would contribute $8 per year to save the Amazon rainforest, Pearce calculated that the proceeds would pay as much as 55 per cent of the compensation needed to halt unsustainable activities in Amazonia. While the studies above may allow us to quibble with the size of Pearce's guesstimates they tell us very little about the economic rationale or practical likelihood of such donations. Pearce's suggestion is that a resource transfer from existence valuers in developed countries to the Amazon would be an ideal way to save the Amazonian rainforest. Is such action very likely? In order to answer this question the implications of the public good characteristics of existence values must be investigated.

Existence values and free riders

As stated earlier, public goods such as existence values are often subject to free-riding. In the case of existence values, there is little incentive for individuals or groups to act unilaterally to conserve the species or habitat if all other existence valuers would obtain the benefits for free. However, the extent to which free-riding is a problem in terms of the provision of the wild resource may vary considerably.

In culturally uniform societies free-riding may be restrained as an entire society may be appropriating the benefits of existence – the management group extends beyond individuals and groups to the entire society. Societies that traditionally place a great cultural significance on particular species may benefit disproportionately from its provision – and therefore be willing to incur the costs of conservation. Such groups are called "privileged groups".[5] For example, the preservation of sacred cows is of such importance to Hindus that they are willing to pay the costs of protection – which include the loss of potential use values as well as the direct costs of preservation.

In the case of "global" existence values, free-riding may be much more of a problem. The disparity between the number of global recipients of non-use benefits and those managing the resource may mean that significant existence values for wild resources will go unappropriated. This discourages the provision of an optimal level of conservation activities by undervaluing the survival of species and habitats. In order to overcome the dilemma of free-riding and provide socially beneficial levels of conservation, either direct policy intervention by central authority or co-operative action between societal groups is necessary. Financial resources for conservation may be generated either through public or non-governmental initiatives. Efforts to initiate action may be unilateral or reflect a broad consensus between groups within a nation or between nations themselves. Outside of public relations gestures, actions by private firms are unlikely because existence values accrue to individuals rather than to corporate entities.

Intervention by national authorities or co-operation at the international level are common mechanisms for providing the collective benefits of species protection. Examples of this include the 1973 Endangered Species Act in the United States and the Convention on Trade in Endangered Species (CITES) at the international level. The aim of such policy actions are to limit activities that threaten endangered species with extinction. Public funds for conservation in developing countries may be mobilized through international development assistance programmes. In recent years, increasing concern over the environmental impacts of past lending policies of the major aid donors has led to a greater emphasis on the promotion of environmentally sustainable development. The World Bank-led Global Environmental Facility is designed to funnel development aid to projects that provide global environmental benefits – which include existence values.[7]

Non-governmental organizations (NGOs) may also seek to provide public goods. National and international conservation organizations such as the World-Wide Fund for Nature, Friends of the Earth, Conservation International, etc., are funded by charitable donations from the private and public sector. Data from the United States on donations to philanthropic causes and resulting implications for existence values are examined in Box 3.5. The mixture of motivations behind donations to conservation organizations indicate that they represent an amalgam of existence and use values. For example, people may contribute simply because they feel better thinking that they have helped the golden tamarin survive, or because they anticipate a future journey to Brazil to actually observe the tamarin in its native habitat. Wealthy environmentalists who can afford to travel to exotic natural sites in developing countries constitute another example of a privileged group – they contribute to saving endangered species and habitats secure in the knowledge that they are likely to be the only ones able to pay for visits to such sites.

Despite the financial resources dedicated by developed countries to NGO and public sector conservation activities in developing countries such efforts are unlikely to reflect the full value of non-use benefits attributable to wild resources. NGO programmes will tend to be underfunded as some individuals may decline to make financial contributions in the expectation that the species they care about will be preserved through the actions and donations of other individuals and groups. Free-riding is likely to remain a problem.

Action at the international level is also likely to fall victim to similar difficulties. The next chapter describes current mechanisms and future prospects for transferring financial resources to developing countries in attempts to compensate for "global" values accruing to developed countries. Should international regimes be established, free-riding would likely be minimized due to the negative public attention non-payment might attract. However, there is no guarantee that the total level of funding chosen at the outset, or the amount subscribed by any one country would be sufficient to the task.

Further empirical research is necessary to ascertain the magnitude

Box 3.5 Charitable contributions in the United States

Total funds in 1990: $122.6 billion

Destination of funds	%	Sources of funds	%
Churches and synagogues	53.7	Individuals	83.0
Education	10.1	Bequests	6.4
Human services	9.6	Foundations	5.8
Health	8.1	Corporations	4.8
Arts and culture	6.4		
Public benefit	4.0		
Environment	1.9		
International	1.8		
Undesignated	4.4		

Source: Weber in The Economist (1991)

In a report for the US-based Trust for Philanthropy, Nathan Weber compiled information on the destination of charitable contribution by US individuals in the United States. Based on the figures shown above, it is possible to estimate that charitable giving for environmental and international causes came to an average of roughly $10 per person in the United States in 1990. Poorer families with incomes of $10,000 gave 5.5 per cent of their income to charity, while richer families with $100,000 gave only 2.9 per cent. Assuming that all families gave the same proportion to the environment, Americans with incomes between $10,000 and $100,000 donated between $10 and $55 dollars a year *per family* towards the environment in 1990.

A number of observations can be made from these rough figures. First, if the Brookshire et al. (1983) survey provides an accurate barometer of people's willingness to pay for local species then it would appear that actual giving in the United States falls well short of expressed existence values for domestic species, to say nothing of global values. None the less, the addition of an $8 donation per adult just for the Amazonian rainforest, as suggested by Pearce (1990), would represent a very substantial increase over current donations to environmental action. This is particularly true if other habitats and species the world over were to receive similar treatment. Finally, in light of the results obtained by Samples et al. (1986), it will be interesting to observe the extent to which increasing media attention and scientific research devoted to wildlands and wildlife in developing countries influences empirical measurement of WTP and actual donations in the years to come.

of existence values originating in developing countries and the extent of their appropriation. Without such information, estimating the needs for supplemental funding to cover these "global" values is very difficult. If reliable data on existence values were available, the chances of expediting negotiations over compensation issues between developed and developing countries would be improved. None the less, actually obtaining this information remains a major obstacle. Few countries in the developed world are likely to allocate substantial sums of money for applied research that would only add ammunition to the calls for increased North-South resource transfers.

Ecosystem services

The value of ecosystem services are difficult to appropriate and, like species and habitat existence, tend to be undersupplied as a result. Ecological processes support economic activity by recycling important elements such as carbon, oxygen and nitrogen; and protect economic property and activity by acting as a buffer against routine and excessive variations in weather, climate and other natural events outside the control of human beings. Most of these ecosystem services are examples of *indirect use values*. They offer support and protection to economic activity, but do not themselves directly enter into human preferences. Box 3.6 illustrates the complex interactions that often link ecology and economics.

The urgent need to conserve natural habitats because of their important regulatory role rests on growing empirical support for claims that:

> many of the less cuddly, less spectacular organisms that *Homo sapiens* are wiping out are more important to the human future than are most of the publicized endangered species . . . the most anthropocentric reason for preserving diversity is the role that micro-organisms, plants, and animals play in providing free ecosystem services, without which society in its present form could not persist. (Ehrlich, 1988)

The value of ecosystem services stem largely from intact wildland areas. In certain cases, "redundant" species may be extracted with little harm, while conservation of specific "keystone" species may warrant special consideration. However, the interlinkages between species involved in producing just one ecosystem service often defy a reductionist approach to providing ecosystem services. This is not to deny that certain functions of natural habitat may be replaced by managed habitat.

Box 3.6: Impacts of upper watershed degradation – Java

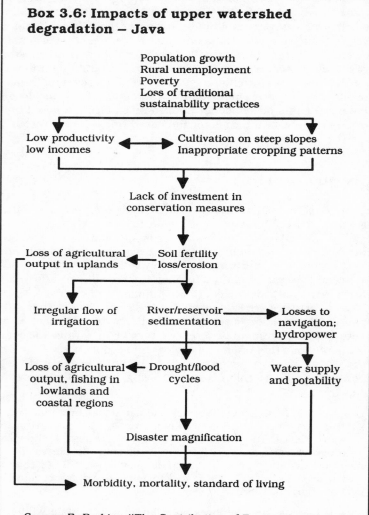

Population growth
Rural unemployment
Poverty
Loss of traditional
sustainability practices

Low productivity low incomes ↔ Cultivation on steep slopes Inappropriate cropping patterns

Lack of investment in conservation measures

Loss of agricultural output in uplands ← Soil fertility loss/erosion

Irregular flow of irrigation

River/reservoir sedimentation → Losses to navigation; hydropower

Loss of agricultural output, fishing in lowlands and coastal regions ← Drought/flood cycles

Water supply and potability

Disaster magnification

Morbidity, mortality, standard of living

Source: E. Barbier, "The Contribution of Environmental and Resource Economics to an Economics of Sustainable Development", *Development and Change*, vol. 20, no. 3, July 1989, pp. 429-59

Plantation forestry can be a good substitute for natural forests when it comes to maintaining the carbon storage function provided by trees or in providing ground cover for protecting critical watersheds. Of course, even relatively non-diverse tree plantations themselves depend on ecological processes. McNeely (1988) points to the role wild birds play in maintaining the productivity of Albizia plantations by feeding on caterpillars that would otherwise defoliate the trees. In general, managed monocultures are far less biologically and ecologically diverse than wildlands so that the provision of ecosystem services is likely to remain an area of comparative advantage for wildlands for the foreseeable future.

Box 3.7: Wetland characteristics: Petexbatun, Guatemala

Components	Direct	Indirect
1. Forest resources	xxx	
2. Wildlife resources	x	
3. Fisheries	xx	
4. Forage resources	xx	
5. Agricultural resources	xx	
6. Water Supply	xxx	

Functions		
1. Groundwater recharge/discharge		x
2. Flood and flow control		xxx
3. Shoreline/bank stabilization		xxx
4. Sediment retention		xxx
5. Nutrient retention		x/xx
6. External support		xxx
7. Recreation/tourism	x	
8. Water transport	xxx	

Key: x   = low
      xx = medium
      xxx = high

Source: Barbier (1989)

Ecological processes originating from specific wildland areas may support and protect economic activity on a local, regional or global scale, proving difficult to appropriate. Examples of local benefits from ecological processes include nutrient/waste cycling, nutrient retention, microclimatic regulation and ecological buffering against extreme weather conditions such as excessive rainfall, wind, etc. Box 3.7 provides some salient examples of the local environmental functions originating from a wetland in Guatemala.

Local and regional indirect use values are often measured by investigating the damage done to productive activities by the degradation of ecosystem services. If it is indeed possible to model the damage functions of the ecological interrelationships, the resulting damage costs give a reasonably accurate picture of the benefits of the service. For instance, contrasting a depletion scenario of increasing loss of groundwater storage versus a conservation scenario in which the recharging function is preserved may demonstrate the additional "externality costs" caused by degradation of a recharge function. Munasinghe (1990) used this approach to indicate a benchmark value of over $29 million for the damage costs of aquifer depletion in the Philippines.

Deforestation and the ensuing loss of the watershed protection function provided by the forest are also frequently cited as causing severe disruption of fisheries and ecotourism industries based on coral reef ecosystems. Ruitenbeek (1989) assessed the loss of a coastal fishery that would occur due to deforestation of the Korup rainforest in Cameroon and the ensuing deposition of eroded soils. Given the projected scenario for conserving the forest, Ruitenbeek found that the value of the watershed protection function came to just under £4 ($7) million. Additional on and off-site values from flood control and soil fertility maintenance brought the total contribution of ecosystem services to over £5 ($8) million. In this case these indirect use values outweighed the direct benefits from sustainable use of the forest which totalled just over £3 ($4) million.

Unfortunately, the strong assumption Ruitenbeek makes about the ecological consequences of deforesting the Korup area raises questions about the magnitude of the watershed protection value associated with the coastal fishery. It is evident that Ruitenbeek considers the fishery to be a total loss if the Korup forest is removed. The ecological substantiation of this implicit assumption is not presented by Ruitenbeek, nor is it likely to be justified. Valuable though the watershed protection function may be, it is unlikely to be so essential that the entire fishery will be eliminated by the loss of this function. In fact it is probable that the low rates of deforestation projected by the cost-benefit scenario may have a proportionately smaller impact on the fishery than that implied by a more rapid rate. This clarifies an essential point. The rate of deforestation will be an important factor in determining the extent of the damage done to the fishery when the watershed protection function is fully destroyed.

None the less, an important aspect of the Ruitenbeek study is its effort to communicate to the Cameroonian government how the cost of conserving the Korup forest would be balanced by benefits such as the survival of Cameroons onshore fishery. By differentiating between the damage done to the Cameroonian fishery and the Nigerian fishery the analysis also lays the groundwork for determining the scope for regional co-operation and the resolution of potential transboundary disputes. At both the local and regional level this type of economic and distributional analysis provides the basis for government intervention to solve the problem of appropriating the value of wildlands.

The carbon storage function of tropical forests is an excellent example of the global environmental benefits derived from ecosystem services in developing countries. Pearce (1990) estimated that on average one hectare of deforested land releases 100 tonnes of carbon. Nordhaus (1990) has suggested that the potential damage done by one tonne of carbon in terms of the costs of global warming equals $13. Pearce simply multiplies these two figures to arrive at a figure of $13,000 per hectare that could be credited to tropical forest areas left intact. Since the benefits attributable to intact tropical forests accrue to those who would suffer from the impact of climate change – such as small island nations – the values are not likely to be appropriated by those managing tropical forests. Again, the failure to appropriate the value of wildlands works against wildlife conservation.

Characterizing an ecosystem service solely by means of the end product consumed by people does injustice to the complex interdependencies that make up ecosystem services. As the review above indicates, benefits of ecosystem services that are not appropriated are characterized by the geographic distance between the site of their production and the location of their end-use. The distinction that emerges between the process itself and the product actually consumed is useful in analysing the public good nature of ecosystem services.

The value of these end products of ecosystem services are typically non-exclusive. For example, it is difficult to exclude humans, plants, animals, motorized vehicles, etc., from consuming oxygen and producing increased levels of carbon-dioxide. Similarly, the benefits of local or global climatic regulation, flood control, storm protection and other regulatory process are non-exclusive in nature. The more diffuse and mobile the output of the ecological process the more difficult or costly it is to exclude prospective consumers.

For example, organic waste recycling and nutrient retention are vital to the survival and successful rearing of fish fry in coastal mangroves. However, fishermen harvest adult fish and prawns not their fry. In addition, the harvest occurs offshore. Thus, the value of the catch (including the value added by the ecosystem services) is garnered by fishermen who may have no explicit link to the management of the mangroves. Not only that, but the local fishermen may be powerless to object to a government or privately-run scheme aimed at converting the mangrove swamps into prawn farms. Should the prawn farms become a reality both the fishermen and local inhabitants will suffer as the organic waste recycling and nutrient retention functions are degraded and the productivity of the fishery declines.

Ecological products produced by "wild" soil processes such as the regeneration of soil fertility by soil micro-organisms and natural inhibition of pests and diseases by natural agents represent the other end of the spectrum. The proximity of process and product is due to the relative immobility of soil. In the case of products like fertile soil the benefits are likely to be exclusive. Soil and its "wild" processes are often part and parcel of land tenure arrangements. Thus – barring ineffective arrangements – the benefits of soil fertility will be appropriated by farmers and other land managers.

Even non-exclusive ecological products will not qualify as "pure" public goods unless they satisfy the additional criterion of non-rivalness. However, the non-rivalness of ecological products is not assured. For example, at low levels of demand for a particular oxygen and carbon dioxide balance, such as that demanded by a single internal combustion engine, the regulatory function is clearly non-rival. However, as the density of users increases (as in any large city) the demand may swamp supply as the local capacity of the ecological process is overwhelmed. At this point the consumption of oxygen by any vehicle does negatively influence pedestrians' ability to breathe "clean" air as the ecological system can no longer balance the oxygen/carbon-dioxide budget. The nature of many other ecological products is much the same – the product becomes rival as the density of users and the effects of congestion increase. Thus, non-exclusive ecological products are likely to be congestible goods and common pool resources (as described in Box 3.2), not "pure" public goods.

It is difficult to make a blanket statement about the public good characteristics of ecosystem services as the ecological processes originate from every conceivable type of wildland. It is possible, however, to suggest that a large number of wildlands in developing countries tend to be non-exclusive and congestible. Technically speaking, governments in developing countries have nationalized forests, fisheries and rangelands. In reality, however, a combination of institutional and technological constraints such as a lack of funds, the cost of manpower and enforcement infrastructure, mean that wildlands are essentially non-exclusive resources. As development pressure and high value species encourage movement into this management vacuum the damage to ecosystem services grows and the congestible nature of the resource base is increasingly evident.

In sum, neither the end product nor the ecological process that make up ecosystem services consistently demonstrate the characteristics of pure public goods. Instead ecosystem services often appear to be common pool resources. In the absence of effective local community structures or national management of public property to forestall what is essentially an open access situation, wildlands are overexploited as encroachment occurs on an ever larger scale. As a result ecosystem processes are degraded and the quantity and quality of their end products are reduced considerably.

Public or private solutions aimed at ensuring that ecosystem services are provided in adequate quantities will need to account for the number of users and the degree to which technological or institutional options exist for excluding other consumers. As described in Chapter 5, common property management may be an effective alternative management scheme for appropriating the value of local ecosystem services. One possibility is to build on communal institutions created to solve other resource management issues. Such a group may be able to internalize the indirect benefits of local ecosystem services or serve as a means of negotiating with other groups that may be receiving these benefits without incurring the costs of conservation measures.

International actions to ensure the supply of global values from developing country wildlands, such as the projects being developed under the aegis of the Global Environmental Facility, are likely to emphasize the creation and upgrading of protected areas. However, the open access status of many wildlands in developing countries means that it may be futile to try and simply "protect" valuable ecological functions of wildlands by excluding local users. Since ecosystem services are congestible, encroachment does have a negative impact on the ensuing level of benefits. A better approach would capitalize on the synergies between local sustainable management and global values by integrating efforts at developing sustainable and appropriable local uses with attempts to subsidize the provision of global ecosystem service and existence values.

Unfortunately such efforts can be precluded by the terms of reference of international efforts. For example, the mandate of the Global Environmental Facility is to fund projects that supply global external benefits, but that would not ordinarily be funded owing to unattractive rates of return. Funding for projects that yield local benefits – and therefore yield acceptable rates of return – are precluded from consideration. Clearly, if conservation of global benefits and local sustainable management must go hand in hand such myopic emphasis by donors on global benefits – however admirable in intention – may be misguided in practical terms.

Genetic resources

Genes are the basic unit of heredity. Each gene contains a code sequence made up of nucleotide components, for the construction of a single protein from amino acid building blocks. The number of genes per organism varies from 1,000 in bacteria, to 100,000 in mammals and 400,000 in flowering plants and some animals (Wilson, 1988). As a result the aggregate genetic information contained in a single strand of DNA is enormous.

> If we magnified it [DNA] until its width equalled that of wrapping string, the fully extended molecule would be 960 kilometres long. As we traveled along its length, we would encounter some 20 nucleotide pairs or "letters" of genetic code per inch (Wilson, 1988: 7).

Biologists draw a distinction between the genetic coding and its physical expression. The term "genotype" refers to the hereditary information contained in a particular set of genetic material, while "phenotype" is used in referring to the actual manifestation of these genetic characteristics. The importance of this distinction lies in the fact that some of the genetic information in each organism is unused or suppressed. Thus organisms with identical phenotypes can have different genotypes, but organisms with identical genetic make-ups must have the same physical characteristics. Physical (or social) interaction between organisms may alter the phenotype of an organism, but will not directly influence the underlying genotype. Only through its indirect influence on reproduction does the interaction with the environment contribute to change at the genetic level.

Biological resources differ from genetic resources because of this genotype-phenotype distinction. Historically, the economic value of genetic resources originated from the use of genetic variability in improving the characteristics of existing phenotypes. Humans have engaged in "genetic engineering" for centuries by domesticating and breeding wild species. The simple act of harvesting wild plant and animal species also exerts a selective pressure that influences the evolution of phenotypic traits. More recently, advances in biotechnology have enabled scientists to derive valuable products directly from germ plasm. The value of genetic resources thus stems from the manipulation of genetic material to produce products – from simple proteins to entire organisms – of value to human beings.

Genetic improvements to domesticated species have long been instrumental in increasing crop yields. Over the past fifty years, the use of genetic resources in US agricultural research has contributed approximately 50 per cent of long-term increases in yield gains from major crops (Duvick, 1986). Genetic improvements in wheat and rice respectively added $2 billion and $1.5 billion per year in Asia during the Green Revolution (Walgate, 1990). While it is difficult to trace through the impact of wild genetic stock relative to that of cultivated varieties, traditional land races or stored germ plasm, plant breeders have shown a preference for avoiding "weedy relatives or wild species unless absolutely necessary" (Duvick, 1986). This is attributed to the chance of inadvertently introducing undesirable characteristics from species that have not been carefully selected for cultivation.

At the same time, genes from wild ancestors linger in "non-wild" crop varieties providing a hidden source of genetic diversity. In addition, it is acknowledged that major advances in crop breeding often come from the introduction of exotic genotypes. For example, Iltis and Ungent collected a "weedy tomato" in the Peruvian Andes in 1962 which significantly raised the sugar content of commercial tomatoes. The market value of this wild tomato is estimated at $8 million per annum (Iltis, 1988). Many such examples of improvements made by wild genetic stock exist, but there is no systematic record of wild versus domesticated contributions to agricultural production. More importantly, there is no evidence that the economic contribution of these resources were ever appropriated by the managers of the wildlands from whence they came.

In the future, crop breeding may return to a heavier reliance on wild species. New biotechnologies – of which genetic engineering is one specific branch – have all but eliminated the species barrier that in years past often limited the range of experimentation that farmer breeders could undertake. New cell and tissue culture technology enabling rapid cell propagation, the development of biochemical methods useful in detecting genes or the individual proteins they produce, and recombinant DNA technology allowing manipulation of DNA implies that it will not be long before the genes from wild species may be used to improve the characteristics of any and all species. These biotechnological advances will also increase the ability of scientists to test and manufacture products *in vitro* or even in living animals or micro-organisms that are derived from wild genetic resources. The long list of anticipated products includes vaccines, diagnostic tests, medicines, bacterial plastics, waste digestion, disease vector controls, fungicides, etc.

The importance of plant genetic resources in both traditional and modern medicine is well known. Plotkin (1988) calculates that Amazonian Indian tribes use over 100 species for medicinal purposes. Oldfield (1989) reports that in 1973 half of the world's medicinal compounds were derived or obtained from plants and one-quarter of prescription drugs in the US contained essential active ingredients from higher plants in 1973. Plant-based retail drug sales in OECD countries – including both prescription and over-the-counter drugs – totalled $43 billion in 1985 (Principe, 1987). How much of these uses actually involved the manipulation of genetic material is difficult to determine, but genetic engineering techniques will have an increasing impact on the products produced by the rapidly growing biotechnology industry.

As Flint (1990) points out, the retail value of products derived from genetic resources vastly exaggerates the economic value of the genetic resources in the wild. Seed and pharmaceutical industries are big businesses; seed company sales in 1988 approached $15 billion and those of pharmaceutical companies registered $120 billion in 1987 (Hobbelink, 1991). The revenues of such businesses, however, reflect the need to recoup large expenditures on, amongst other things, research and development (R&D). Genetic resources represent just one input into the R&D budget of seed and pharmaceutical companies. The cost of research, development and product testing to meet US regulations for a single product may reach upwards of $100 million (*Businessweek*, quoted in Principe, 1987).

Research and development expenditures on biotechnology were estimated to be $4 billion in 1985 and $11 billion in 1990 (Hobbelink, 1991). Of the 1985 investment figure only 7.5 per cent took place outside of OECD countries. India has an ambitious biotechnology program aimed at generating $1.5 billion in products per year by 1995, but the total amount invested so far comes to just $120 million (Walgate, 1990). This compares poorly with Monsanto and DuPonts" joint program of R&D slated to cost $390 million per year (Hobbelink, 1991). The exact value of genetic resources back in the wilds is relatively unknown and unresearched. Ruitenbeek (1989) took an industry average of £5,000 per patent as representative of the value of research discoveries in his calculation of genetic values in the Korup rainforest. Brown and Swierzbinski (1988) point out that because species contribute to the production of knowledge the value of genetic resources will depend on the size of the R&D budget. Too little in the way of R&D means that genetic resources will be undervalued and underprovided by society. This highlights the importance of the ongoing debate over whether R&D in biotechnology – and hence production of useful products – should be rooted in the private or public sector. Brown and Swierzbinski suggest that appropriating the value of R&D is difficult if the end products are "pure" public goods. On the other hand, they also demonstrate that even a market structure will undervalue genetic resources.

The evolved institutional norm treats genetic resources as public goods. The collection of plant samples, for example, is unrestricted in most countries. Material from plant genetic seed banks – whether national or international – is freely reproduced and shared. The policy advanced by the International Agricultural Research Centres and followed by researchers around the world of free exchange of germ plasm means that genetic resources are non-exclusive. Genetic material is also non-rival by nature. The consumption of germplasm by one researcher does not impinge on the ability of another breeder to obtain the germplasm and conduct additional research.

This strong case for considering genetic resources as public goods has weakened as pharmaceutical and seed companies have become the dominant investors in biotechnology R&D. Private companies currently account for between 66 per cent and 75 per cent of biotechnology spending – but much of the remaining public portion of biotechnology spending goes directly to industry. The increasing ability of companies in the developed world to seek patent protection for manipulated genetic material and genetic engineering processes has gone hand in hand with the increasing dominance of R&D by private – in most cases multinational – companies.

The issue of patent protection has major ramifications for the appropriability of genetic resources originating in developing countries. Patenting allows companies to exclude others from the new and rival products they create – they be purchased in the marketplace. By making not only genetically altered material, but also the technologies themselves, into private goods, developing countries feel that multinationals are effectively preventing them from participation in the biotechnology field. Developing countries must now not only buy the technologies that are so crucial to producing competitive products but they must also buy germplasm – germplasm that often originated in the South. Thus, free access to genetic material is increasingly being denied as companies exert pressure to establish patent rights with which to guard their "property".

Consternation in developing countries over this one-way flow of germ plasm is inspiring calls for retaliation. At the extreme, developing countries could refuse to recognize patents granted in developed countries or assert sovereign control over their genetic resources. Developing countries are in a quandary over these choices. If they do not agree to protect intellectual property rights the transfer of biotechnologies from developed countries is likely to be curtailed. Obtaining this technology may be crucial to research efforts aimed at producing products appropriate to the needs of developing countries as seen by themselves, not as construed by multinationals.

If developing countries jettison the common understanding and treatment of genetic resources as freely available public goods, they may also lose the benefits of public sector R&D provided by the International Agricultural Research Centres (IARCs). With financial assistance from the developed world, the IARCs have been instrumental in promoting the storage and free exchange of germ plasm, as well as producing the high yielding varieties of the Green Revolution. However, the Green Revolution is increasingly being criticized for its negative impacts not only on the environment, but also on genetic diversity itself. By encouraging hybrid mono-cultures in place of intercropping, past IARC research and crop breeding has actually led to genetic erosion (Hobbelink, 1991; Haugerud and Collinson, 1990). While IARC research methods and practices will no doubt improve, these past failures raise additional questions about the viability of the present system.

None the less, the outcome remains unclear. The question is whether or not the free exchange of germ plasm and the system of international crop breeding research is inferior to a market structure based on the investments of multinational companies and the enforcement of sovereignty over genetic resources by developing countries. Deliberations over this issue are currently underway in a host of fora: the Keystone Dialogue on Plant Genetic Resources, FAO's Intergovernmental Commission on Plant Genetic Resources, the meetings of the NGO Genetic Resources Action International (GRAIN), the intergovernmental group preparing the draft Convention on Biological Diversity, etc.

The key issue for developing countries comes down to appropria-tion – if mechanisms are not in place to appropriate the value of genetic resources the full value of wildlands will not be appreci-ated and the depletion of genetic stocks will continue. Increas-ing research into methods for appropriating the value of genetic resources will assist in devising effective solutions. One novel approach, underway at the Instituto Nacional de Biodiversidad (INBio) in Costa Rica, is to begin appropriating the value of research and development within the country of origin. By developing a comprehensive database of information on native Costa Rican species INBio hopes to be able to capture an increasing amount of the value represented in the end products of pharmaceutical and other industries.

Conclusion

The discipline of environmental economics is rapidly expanding our knowledge of the economic value and importance of species and habitat existence, ecosystem services and genetic resources. While illustrating the magnitudes of these economic values is useful, it is of equal importance to understand the factors that determine why these particular values of wild resources are so difficult to appropriate. For this reason, this chapter has emphasized an analysis of the public good characteristics of each of the three types of wild resources. In so doing, the reliance on the conventional economic concepts of "pure" public goods and private goods is shown to be insufficient for clearly distinguishing between different types of intangible values produced by wildlands.

Species and habitat existence prove to be the most amenable to classification as public goods. Efforts to transfer resources from developed to developing countries in order to account for unappropriated existence values will need to confront free-riding in order to initiate broad-based co-operative action at the international level. Ecosystem services deviate from the characteristics of a "pure" public good, showing evidence of congestibility and falling into the same category as many other wildlife resources – that of common pool resources. The menu of management options for ecosystem services will vary from communal management, to upgrading public sector management and using international mechanisms to provide for both the sustainability of local uses and the protection of "global" values. Finally, genetic resources defy a concrete characterization. Treated as public goods for many years recent developments indicate that they may also be characterized as exclusive goods. In the years ahead, developing countries may see fit to keep a tight grip on sovereign resources such as their genetic stock, as the international system turns to an allocation of genetic resources driven by the agenda of multinational biotechnology companies and based on the principle of market power.

References

Barbier, E.B., "The Contribution of Environmental and Resource Economics to an Economics of Sustainable Development", *Development and Change* 20: 429-459, [1989a].

Barbier, E.B., *The Economic Value of Ecosystems: 1 – Tropical Wetlands*. LEEC Gatekeeper Series GK 89-02.[London: International Institute for Environment and Development (IIED), 1989b].

Brookshire, D.S., L.S. Eubanks and A. Randall, "Estimating Option Prices and Existence Values for Wildlife Resources", *Land Economics* 59: 1-15, [1983].

Brown, G.M. Jr. and J. Swierzbinski, "Optimal Genetic Resources in the Context of Asymmetric Public Goods", *Environmental Resources and Applied Welfare Economics: Essays in Honor of John V. Krutilla*, V.K. Smith (ed.), 91-118 [Washington, DC: Resources for the Future, 1988].

Duvick, D.N., "Plant Breeding: Past Achievements and Expectations for the Future", *Economic Botany* 40: 289-297, [1986].

The Economist, "Sparing a Dime", 17 August, 1991.

Ehrlich, Paul R., "The Loss of Diversity: Causes and Consequences", *Biodiversity*, E.O. Wilson and F.M. Peter (eds), 21-27, [Washington, DC: National Academy Press, 1988].

Flint, M.E.S., "Biodiversity: Economic Issues", unpublished paper for the Overseas Development Administration, London, [1990].

Haugerud, A. and M. Collinson, "Plants, Genes and People: Improving the Relevance of Plant Breeding in Africa", *Experimental Agriculture* 26: 341-362, [1990].

Hobbelink H., Biotechnology and the Future of World Agriculture. [London: Zed Books, 1991].

Iltis, H.J., "Serendipity in the Exploration of Biodiversity: What Good are Weedy Tomatoes?", *Biodiversity*, E.O. Wilson and Frances M. Peter (eds), 193-9, [Washington, DC: National Academy Press, 1988].

Krutilla, J.V., "Conservation Reconsidered", *American Economic Review* 57: 777–86, [1967].

Majid, I., J.A. Sinden, and A. Randall, "Benefit Evaluation Increments to Existing Systems of Public Facilities", *Land Economics* 59: 377–92, [1983].

McNeely, J.A., *Economics and Biological Diversity: Developing and Using Economic Incentives to Conserve Biological Resources*, [Gland: IUCN, 1988].

Munasinghe, M., *Managing Water Resources to Avoid Environmental Degradation: Policy Analysis and Application.* World Bank Environment Working Paper No. 41 [Washington, DC: World Bank, 1990].

Nordhaus, W., "To Slow or Not to Slow: The Economics of the Greenhouse Effect", [Department of Economics, Yale University, 1990].

Oldfield, M.L., *The Value of Conserving Genetic Resources*, [Sunderland, Massachusetts: Sinauer Associates, 1989].

Pearce, D.W., *An Economic Approach to Saving the Tropical Forests*, LEEC Paper DP 90-06, [London: IIED, 1990].

Pearce, D.W. and A. Markandya, "Marginal Opportunity Cost as a Planning Concept in Natural Resource Management", *Environmental Management and Economic Development*, Gunter Schramm and Jeremy J. Warford (eds), 39-55. [Baltimore: Johns Hopkins University Press, 1989].

Plotkin, M.J., "The Outlook for New Agricultural and Industrial Products from the Tropics", *Biodiversity*, E.O. Wilson and F.M. Peter (eds), 106-16. [Washington, DC: National Academy Press, 1988].

Principe, P.P., *The Economic Value of Biological Diversity Among Medicinal Plants*, [Paris: OECD, 1988].

Randall, A., "The Problem of Market Failure", *Natural Resources Journal* 23: 131-47, [1983].

Ruitenbeek, H.J., "Appendix 13: Korup National Park Social Cost Benefit Analysis", in World Wide Fund for Nature, *Republic of Cameroon, Korup Project: Plan for Developing the Park and its Support Zone*, [London: WWF, 1989].

Samples, K.C., J.A. Dixon and M.M. Gowen, "Information Disclosure and Endangered Species Valuation", *Land Economics* 62: 306-12 [1986].

Walgate, R., *Miracle or Menace? Biotechnology and the Third World* [London: The Panos Institute, 1990].

Walsh, R. G., J.B. Loomis and R.A. Gillman, "Valuing Option, Existence and bequest demands for wilderness", *Land Economics* 60: 14-29 [1984].

Wilson, E.O., "The Current State of Biological Diversity", *Biodiversity, E.O. Wilson and F.M. Peter (eds), 3-18. [Washington, DC: National Academy Press, 1988].*

Notes

1. In the case of species and habitat existence it is the continued existence of species and habitats that is defines as the resource – not their continued use for production or harvesting purposes. Thus, this chapter considers the non-use values of species and habitats.

2. Appropriation is defined as the ability to capture the full benefits of a wild resource by the person or group managing the resource.

3. It may even be the case that the value of a wild resource accrues in full to someone entirely different than the manager of the wildland from which it originated. Such values are not appropriated at all and there is no incentive whatsoever for the manager to conserve the resource.

4. The provision of law, order and security from external threat are often cited as fundamental public goods that justify the creation of the nation-state by *laissez-faire* economists. Clearly even these fundamental public goods ar not necessarily available to all – this is particularly true in terms of equal access to the provision of internal law and order.

5. Because it is difficult to separate the non-use component from the use component the results of the Samples et al. study are not included in Box 3.4

6. A privileged group is a subset of the individuals that value a particular public good. A privileged group values the public good highly enough that the benefits they receive outweigh the costs of conversation. As they can only stand to gain from the unilateral provision of public goods, privileged groups will go ahead and unite such action.

7. A joint project of the World Bank, the United Nations Development Programme and the United Nations Environment Programme.

4

THE ROLE OF WILDLIFE UTILIZATION AND OTHER POLICIES IN BIODIVERSITY CONSERVATION

Timothy M. Swanson

The problem of biodiversity conservation is to determine policies that will effectively transfer value that exists in the developed world (i.e. funds) to those developing countries that harbour substantial quantities of diversity, and to do so in such a manner as will create incentives to maintain these reserves into the foreseeable future. That is, this is one international environmental problem where the focus is upon *national* resources, i.e. resources that fall within national boundaries. Unlike many other international problems, e.g. ozone depletion or atmospheric and marine pollution, the conservation of biodiversity hinges mainly on the proper management of resources within the borders of a given nation. There are three very difficult, interrelated problems to be solved in this context: the development of a framework for selecting the "optimal amount of diversity"; the valuation of some important but intangible goods and services; and the creation of incentive-based transfer mechanisms across international boundaries. Any one of these is very difficult to solve; taken together, they constitute a nearly intractable international environmental problem.

The choice of the optimal amount of diversity is a very difficult subject to address, on account of the ethical implications of choosing which species are to survive and which are not. However, this is not a choice that can be avoided; the choice will either be made knowingly or out of ignorance and neglect. Humans now have the technological capacity to choose precisely how many, and which, species will continue to share the earth with them. To ignore this fact, and to avoid taking the decision explicitly, simply acts to confer extinction upon a wide range of species through wilful ignorance. Over the next few decades we must make a clear-cut decision on the species that will continue to exist.

It might seem to be the easiest route to simply grant existence rights to all species; that is, it might be held to be an "absolute" that all species have the right to exist, and that humans have the responsibility to respect these rights.[1] However, this is not likely to be a realistic policy, even over the medium term. The human species currently appropriates about 40 per cent of the produce of the earth's ecosystems, which means that one species (out of the 3 to 10 million species that exist) is already taking nearly half of all that is available (Vitousek et al, 1986). Furthermore, the human population is projected to double in size once again over the next century, or sooner; even given drastically reduced population growth rates, this doubling is not likely to be avoidable given current demographic characteristics (Western, 1989). Extrapolating these facts into the future, given current technology and living standards, it appears that the human species may be appropriating about 80 per cent of the earth's produce in less than 100 years' time. And, since 85 per cent of the world's population will then be living in the developing world, where the pressure is for living standards to increase, not remain stagnant, it is possible that this represents a lower bound on the proportion of resources that will ultimately be appropriated by humans.

The prospects for sufficient resources being made available for all of these human needs and also for those of other species is zero. It is contrafactual to assume that human rights will be sacrificed in the name of other species. Therefore, in the next 100 years, there will be tremendous pressures placed upon the resource base previously made available to other species. Difficult choices will have to be made, and there will inevitably be a much lower number of species; the question is not whether such a reduction will occur, but whether it will be conducted out of complete ignorance and neglect, or not.

To a large extent, the outcome of this decision will almost certainly provide for the continued existence of those species that humans have enjoyed using. This is not a normative prescription; but simply an observation on the way that the process is currently operating. There are less than 1 million elephants but 100 million cattle on the earth not because of intrinsic worthiness, but because of developed usefulness. The cattles' use of the earth's resources is translated into human use of the same when humans use the latter. Therefore, the use of the resource base by these species falls under the "human" side of the account; their use is our use.

This is not the case for under-utilized species and, when human resource requirements expand, these species find themselves "undercut". Humans meet their expanding needs by placing greater demands upon the resource base; we technologically "enclose" more and more of the earth's resources, disallowing other species access to the resources they have historically relied upon for their existence. Humans will in this way indirectly extinguish a large portion of the world's species over the next century, and nearly all of these will come from the "under-utilized" category (Diamond, 1989). This simple observation underlies the logic of a policy of wildlife utilization: "use it or lose it" appears to be the moral of recent evolutionary history.

However, this is not the full story; it is a far more complicated picture in total. This is because some of the most important values of biodiversity are not easily captured through the simple process of utilization; this simple economic logic is only a starting point, not a complete policy. Therefore, it is very important to understand the basic economic nature of the problem of inappropriable values, and to consider their solutions as well in this context. Conservation of biological diversity will require a simple policy of wildlife utilization in combination with policies that address these other, more complex, values.

The economic nature of the problem of biodiversity supplies

Most goods are supplied in proportion to the costliness of their production and the demand for their consumption, i.e. the current menu of choice in society results from what people have chosen in the past from the range of goods and services that could possibly be produced from the existing resource base. Goods that are not in demand will not, in general, remain on the menu of choice. When irreversibilities are involved, these goods, once removed, will never be available again. Therefore, the constructive use of the demand for some of the diverse products of natural habitats is an essential force in maintaining these species on the current menu of choice.

However, certain types of goods and services cannot be supplied through this process. In particular, the intangible services flowing from natural habitats (e.g. options, existence, information, general ecosystem services) are very difficult to provide for in this way. On account of their amorphous and intangible nature, it is not easy to bill others for their use, and thus it is difficult to induce potential suppliers to invest in keeping them on the menu. A policy of utilization alone will not assure an adequate supply of these sorts of goods and services on account of these inadequate incentives to investment.

This is precisely what we now observe regarding biological diversity. The developing countries have huge stocks of this wealth, in comparison to the developed, and the flow of services is very much from South to North. (That is, the uses of biodiversity are very often appropriated almost exclusively in the North, e.g. biotechnology patents, and when more evenly distributed, e.g. existence values, they are usually more highly valued there in any event.) Yet, much of this flow of services goes entirely uncompensated; therefore, there are few, if any, incentives to invest in maintaining the current stock of diversity.[2]

These intangible services of natural habitats are examples of so-called "public goods", and the policy problem of biodiversity provision is in part a problem of providing for international public goods. Such goods are difficult enough to arrange for in the domestic context. The basic problem there is one of "free riders", i.e. the services flow to all persons, irrespective of whether compensation has been paid, and hence there is little incentive to pay for those services. However, in the international context the supply of public goods is much more complex, on account of irreversibilities and fixed borders.

If one country desires to provide internally for a flow of biodiversity services, it might do so by itself investing in a stock of natural habitat. This is not possible with respect to biodiversity in the developed world because it is not possible to re-create either the diversity that once existed here or the diversity that presently exists in the South outside of its niche. This is the problem of irreversibilities; investments in biological assets, once foregone, are often lost for ever.[3]

It is therefore necessary to invest in biodiversity resources where they currently exist. It is difficult to extract that payment from the developed world because of the aforementioned free rider problem, but, supposing that such a payment was forthcoming, would this then assure the future supply of the international public good?

To a large extent, the problem of supplying biodiversity services is not solved in this way, the bargaining leverage is merely reversed. Once the North's payment for a given stock of natural habitat is received in the South, there is no greater incentive for investment in this public good. In this situation, it would now be the South's turn to free ride on the North. They could now keep the payments received while investing at their desired level in natural habitat stocks. The existence of fixed borders, and the incapacity to transfer property rights across them, means that the free rider problem must continue to exist (whether the free rider is the developing or the developed country). And, in either case, the undersupply of biodiversity services is assured.

In short, there are no static solutions to this problem; there is no one-off quick fix that will guarantee the continued supply of biodiversity services. It is not possible to transfer stocks of biodiversity across international boundaries. What is required is a system of "dynamic reciprocity", i.e. a system of reciprocity where, on a period-by-period basis, the supply of biodiversity *services* is expressly compensated for by the transfer of payment. The provision for a sequence of such payments provides the mutual incentive to invest at the beginning of each period (one state "invests" by making a transfer and the other by maintaining a stock of natural habitat), and it also affords the prospect of an enforcement mechanism at the end of each period should the other party elect to free ride. In the international context, it is only such a dynamic relationship that is capable of solving the problem of the provision of international public goods.

The instrument of wildlife utilization has the earmarks of such a system of dynamic reciprocity, albeit not for the less tangible goods of natural habitats (Swanson, 1991). With utilization, the investing country comes to link the flow of future revenues with the maintenance of stocks of the species within its country, and this provides the ongoing incentives to invest in their provision. For example, each year's cull of elephants in Zimbabwe could provide the funds that warrant the maintenance of a stock of some 50,000 of them in that country. Likewise, the prospect of payment by Japanese consumers of some $10 million dollars for this ivory would encourage the Zimbabweans to continue to invest in supplying elephants (Swanson and Pearce, 1989). A given stock of a species is maintained because it represents a worthwhile investment by its resident country; otherwise, it will be replaced by one with demonstrated investment potential, e.g. cattle.

The problem of biodiversity conservation policy-making requires the implementation of a generalized process for conserving the optimal number of species. In principle, this will require giving effect to the values existing in the North and transferring these to the South, in a dynamic and interactive fashion. A simple policy of wildlife utilization is effective at accomplishing this with regard to the more tangible values of biodiversity; however, other options must be explored with regard to the transference of the other, more intangible, values.

A variety of approaches to conserving diversity

The general object of this chapter is to ascertain the effectiveness of the existing and proposed policies for biodiversity conservation, as viewed from within the framework developed in the section above. Can the international community solve the problem of providing a *dynamic* mechanism that will encourage investments in the full range of biodiversity services? Four distinct approaches have been attempted: listing, funding, property rights and trade regulation. Each has its role to play either in conjunction with, or as a component of, a global wildlife utilization policy.

First, a very basic method for providing mutual assurance over time is reciprocity *in kind*, i.e. the establishment of a mutual commitment to the maintenance of natural habitat by "listings" on a common "noticeboard". The 1971 Convention on Wetlands of International Importance, known as the "Ramsar" convention, was the prototype of this genre. Probably the most extensive set of listings has derived from the UNESCO Man and Biosphere programme, initiated in 1976. There are also listing arrangements developed under numerous regional conventions as well: the Western Hemisphere Convention, the Berne Convention (for Europe), and the ASEAN Convention (for Southeast Asia).

This "listing" approach to natural habitat conservation is very effective for certain shared regional resources, e.g. a shared lake, river or wetland. It operates by providing that each of the states with an interest in the common resource should provide an express commitment to its conservation, by listing a preservation site. All states have an interest in taking part, in order to encourage the others to do likewise; the listing operates as a barter mechanism – each state compensates the others in kind for their respective listings.

Such an approach is very effective for true "shared resources", where equal access allows for equal sacrifices to be made. It is not very useful in the case of resources that are distributed very unevenly, as are biodiversity assets. In this case, there is little that the developed North has to offer the developing South in the way of in kind compensation. Nearly all of the biodiversity resources are located in the South, and therefore the North must compensate the South with some asset other than biodiversity. Very likely, the compensation will take a monetary form, in order to allow developing countries to choose their own preferred assets in which to invest (such as the health or education of the population).

Therefore, an in kind approach to compensation is not operable where the international resource involved is unevenly distributed. In these cases, it will be necessary to construct mechanisms for the flow of financial assets from the concerned to the conserving states. Even then, there are a number of different approaches to consider: direct funding, new property rights and trade controls.

The term "funding mechanism" here refers to what are essentially attempts at constructing an international tax and transfer system. That is, such mechanisms are developed to identify and utilize an international tax base for the funding of international public goods. The best example of such a mechanism is still the first, i.e. the World Heritage Convention (1975). Recently, however, there have been a number of multilateral aid programmes developed with more specifically biological objectives, such as the Tropical Forestry Action Plan (1983) and the Global Environmental Facility currently being installed at the World Bank. It is possible that many people consider these to be further attempts at "funding" the conservation of natural resources in the developing world, but it is important to understand in what fashion they do operate as funding mechanisms. In addition, some long-standing conventions with previously non- funding systems are attempting to extend into the funding arena, e.g. the recent development of the Ramsar Trust Fund. Finally, the most ambitious attempt at a tax-and-transfer system to date has been the Proposed Convention on the Conservation of Biological Diversity, formulated for discussion at the 1992 United Nations Conference on Environment and Development. All of these institutions are addressed below in the section on funding mechanisms.

Some of the most fascinating policies developing recently have involved "property rights" based approaches; so-called debt-for-nature swaps and various forms of biotechnology rights being the principal forms of this type. Of course, the simple policy of wildlife utilization also falls within this category, because the unifying principle in a property rights regime is that persons pay for the product at the time that they receive express (and exclusive) rights in it. The more innovative attempts at using property rights, and their impact on biodiversity conservation, are surveyed in the section below.

Finally, there are the more complicated forms of wildlife utilization policies that are represented in the wildlife trade regulation schemes. The Convention on International Trade in Endangered Species, CITES (1973) was the prototype for this manner of policy, and the Bonn Convention on the Conservation of Migratory Species (1979) followed in its wake. The next step in the evolution of these regimes came not with a new convention, but in the context of the meetings of the Conference of the Parties to CITES. In this context, there have evolved a series of producer quota systems that indicate the potential for a new direction in biodiversity conservation. These movements are discussed below in the section on trade regulation.

Each of these forms of biodiversity conservation policy has a specific role to play in the economic framework of the biodiversity problem. The remainder of this chapter is meant to indicate what that role might be, and also to indicate the capacity of the existing institutions to fulfil it.

Funding mechanisms for biodiversity conservation

Probably the most straightforward means of supplying public goods is through general taxation and public supply. This is usually the way that many of the most common domestic public goods, for example a public library, are supplied. Citizens are taxed, usually on some basis corresponding to ability to pay, such as income, and then the public goods are purchased from this fund and made available for all to use. In the domestic context, the public library represents a store of public information – made available for all to use – much like the information represented by the biodiversity contained within the natural habitats of the developing world.

There are two general problems regarding the use of such funding mechanisms in the supply of biodiversity, one that applies to all public goods supplied by this method and one that is attributable to the international character of biodiversity. First, it is not easy to ascertain, through general taxation methods, the extant demand for publically supplied goods, and therefore it is difficult to know whether the right amounts of the goods are being supplied.

This is known in economics as the problem of "demand revelation", and it is, once again, another aspect of the free rider problem. In this context, each citizen to benefit from the supply of the public good can be asked how much he or she values its provision, but since everyone will have its use (so long as it is supplied) irrespective of the value revealed, there is no incentive to tell the truth. And, if there is any concern that a value expressed will be interpreted as a "bid", thereby resulting in a tax charge corresponding to the bid, there will in fact be an incentive vastly to understate the true valuation.

So long as a person can be persuaded that the actual provision of the good (or the amount of the good that will be provided) depends upon the values given by every taxpayer, it is possible to create incentives for persons to reveal their true willingness to pay. However, this is obviously more difficult when the good is increasingly "public" in nature (so that its supply is clearly available to all and unlimited in quantity) and it is clearly a complicated procedure to undertake. The determination of the amount of a public good to provide through this method is not a straightforward, and sometimes not a very feasible, task.

Nevertheless, numerous economic studies have demonstrated the application of techniques of demand revelation in the provision of public goods. The methods utilized range from surveys to implicit valuation by reference to surrogate markets (e.g. the value of a neighbourhood's amenities may be assessed by reference to the differential value of housing in the area, to which the amenities are attached, although not separately priced) (Pearce, Markandya and Barbier, 1989). Clearly, one of the more difficult tasks to achieve, when public goods are supplied through general taxation, is to determine the public's "optimal amount" of that public good.

The second problem raised by general taxation in the financing of biodiversity conservation is its international character. The tax for biodiversity would have to be levied primarily on the developed countries, who have the greater ability to pay and are also the primary users of the services. But the fund, once accumulated, would then have to be transferred almost entirely to the developing world, where the investments in the supply of these services are required. Importantly, since the supply of biodiversity is an ongoing process, the tax and transfer mechanism would have to be ongoing as well; that is, it would have to be dynamically interactive, compensating countries continuously for their investments in each period.

The primary difficulty with international taxation is its unstable and uncertain character. To date, contributions to international bodies have been largely voluntary in nature, and many countries have often been dilatory and neglectful in making their contributions. Such "voluntary" payment mechanisms create tremendous uncertainties regarding the ongoing status of the international fund, and render the institutions unstable and insecure.[4]

Since investment in biodiversity by developing countries is wholly dependent upon the perception of a flow of revenues over future years generated by that investment, the uncertainties implicit in international funding mechanisms make those investments decidedly shaky. Reliance upon other countries' "voluntary" contributions is not the first choice for an investment strategy in most countries. Countries wish to invest in a manner that will allow them to escape from "aid dependency", not to ensure their reliance on it.

Therefore, there are substantial problems with the general funding approach to biodiversity conservation. Nevertheless, it is an important component in the overall schema, and one of the most longstanding international conventions in the arena – the World Heritage Convention – nicely illustrates this approach. It is worthy of consideration, with these limitations in mind.

The World Heritage Convention

The Convention Concerning the Protection of the World Cultural and Natural Heritage was adopted within the General Conference of UNESCO in 1972, making it one of the first international environmental laws in place (Lyster, S., 1985). Its fundamental importance lies in laying the groundwork for the development of an internationally recognized interest in the management of domestic resources. It applied the doctrine of the "common heritage of mankind" not only to unowned resources, such as the sea or space, but also to some of those which were clearly the property of individual states.

Previously, the import of international law was that domestic resource management was the sole concern of the state concerned. For the majority of resources, this makes good sense in an economic framework; secure ownership rights encourage investment in resources. However, it also makes perfect sense economically to speak of all resources as being the common heritage of mankind. That is, in an economic framework, all "ownership" is only an artifice by which the individual (or state) is given the correct incentives for the proper management of the "owned" resources for the benefit of all society (or societies). Ownership is not a license to degrade or destroy, but, it is hoped, an incentive system to encourage stewardship and investment in resources.

Applying the "common heritage of mankind" doctrine to domestic resources in the context of the World Heritage Convention serves two purposes. It recognizes this ultimate, overriding interest of world society in domestic resources; that is, domestic resources are only domestic because it serves the entire *world's* interest that they should be so. Second, it recognizes that situations exist in which the assignment of certain resources to exclusively domestic management can break down as a management system, and then the global interest in managing those resources must be reasserted.

The existence of trans-boundary pollution was one of the first instances in which the overriding international interest in domestic management was asserted.[5] The World Heritage Convention probably represents the second context in which international interests were deemed pre-eminent, and this time it was asserted in order to address the public good problem discussed above. Essentially, the world community was asserting its interest in various cultural (e.g. the pyramids, the Taj Mahal) and natural resources, and recognizing the responsibility then incumbent upon it to participate in the payment for the management of these resources.[6]

The World Heritage Convention operates as a funding mechanism through the workings of the World Heritage List [Art. 11] and the World Heritage Fund [Art. 15]. The World Heritage List has been developed by a committee of delegates from 21 of the states party to the convention (elected at each meeting of the conference of the parties). It is composed of various areas submitted by their host states as potential World Heritage Sites, and, if accepted by the Committee, they are then eligible for funding from the World Heritage Fund.

The World Heritage Fund has been established by making compulsory donations of one per cent of the states' UNESCO contribution. Since UNESCO contributions are derived from a general United Nations' formula based upon ability-to-pay, the fund is similar to an income tax on the states that join the convention.

Box 4.1 Funding available under the World Heritage Convention

| | | | (thousand US dollars) | | |
Type	1983	1984-85	1986-87	1988-89	1990-91
Voluntary	2,278	805	1,082	1,260	633
Mandatory	1,842	1,842	931	1,442	2,110*
Total	4,110	2,647	2,113	2,702	2,743*

*Assessed but not yet received.

Source: World Heritage Commission.

The World Heritage Convention broke much new ground. Besides developing the first income tax system for assisting countries in the management of domestic resources for the global good, it also created express obligations for states to do just that[7] and it provided the incentive system – the fund – for the enforcement of those obligations. In meeting the model of the sort of policy instrument required for the supply of international public goods, it fits very well.

Its limitations are primarily financial. The amount of funding - about $2 million per annum – provided for the purposes of this convention are miniscule. As a result, the World Heritage List represents only a very small portion of the world's natural and cultural capital.[8] More importantly, there is no provision within the scheme, or within the budget, for any manner of dynamic interaction. The funding available is insufficient to provide the basis for long-term commitments for all of the important sites. Hence, most sites are funded on a one-time project basis, which provides little incentive for the long term conservation of the area.

With these specific limitations noted, the World Heritage Convention remains an excellent example of funding mechanism-based conservation.[9] There would be much worse ways to finance biodiversity conservation than the amendment of the convention to provide for an increase of contributions to five or ten per cent of the UNESCO contribution.

Other funding

The difference between a "funding mechanism" and simple funding is the presence of a system of incentives that directs that funding into the supply of public goods. The World Heritage Convention accomplishes this object through its list and fund, and thus qualifies as a funding mechanism for the supply of global public goods.

Aid without incentives relies more upon a state's good intentions, and is distinct from a mechanism for supplying global public goods. Much of the international development assistance that flows to the Third World does so without a dynamic framework of incentives, and therefore does not provide much incentive for long-term investments in international resources that primarily benefit global welfare.

An example is the Tropical Forestry Action Plan, initiated by the World Resources Institute and then joined by the World Bank, FAO and the UNDP in 1985. This plan has attracted substantial funding from the developed world; about $180 million was committed in 1990, with a further $140 million pledged. In total it has been estimated that about $1 billion per annum was being spent on development assistance for tropical forestry projects, and that these contributions could be projected to increase each year through the middle of this decade (IIED, 1990).

Although these are tremendous sums of money, relative to the World Heritage Convention budgets, the programme does not at present have the structure to channel these funds into the provision of international public goods. It awards funds to countries that submit research proposals regarding forestry policy and evaluation, but is doing little to recognize the need for funding to flow to these countries on a continuing basis in recognition of their provision of global goods.

Of course, there is much to be gained from the construction of rational forest utilization policies.[10] Forest utilization, as with all "wildlife utilization", is a necessary component of a strategy for biodiversity conservation. The distinction being made here is the difference between a funding mechanism for public good provision and technical assistance for more rational wildlife utilization. To date, the TFAP has functioned exclusively in the latter role. This is an important role to fulfil, but it should then be analysed from the perspective of its contribution to the rationalization of wildlife use policies.

Another new mechanism for funding biodiversity conservation is the Global Environmental Facility recently initiated at the World Bank. This fund has been established by World Bank donors in order to allow a three-year programme in environmental projects to be considered. The facility consists of Bank Special Drawing Rights in the amount of $1.2 billion, of which approximately $500 million is to be allotted to biodiversity conservation projects (UNEP, 1991).

Again, there is little, if any, dynamic incentive structure surrounding this very substantial amount of funding. However, the terms on which the funds are to be allocated expressly recognize the importance of allowing compensation to countries for externally supplied benefits. That is, the GEF provides that the funds are to be allotted to projects where the internal benefits would not warrant the project, but the inclusion of benefits flowing to other countries would provide a reasonable return to the investment. Clearly then, this allows for the payment of compensation to countries that devise "projects" that contain public goods as a significant component of their product. However, there is no provision for ongoing compensation for those public goods, and so there is no incentive to provide for their existence beyond the time horizon of the funded project.

Furthermore, the development of further capital intensive "projects" may be more a part of the problem, than the solution, in regard to biodiversity conservation. This is because the fundamental idea behind project-related funding is the investment of financial resources in capital goods, which then yield a return over time to both banker and debtor. However, in the context of biodiversity, the "capital goods" already exist – they are the sum of the resources found in natural habitats. The problem in this instance is not the absence of capital, but the absence of a *flow* to that *natural capital*. Sometimes, the investment of financial resources in man-made capital goods allows for the development of natural resources, so that a flow of revenues is then flowing to both. Many multilateral investment projects are based on this idea, i.e. to invest in the development of the raw or natural material sectors of developing countries. In general, this can be very helpful for these countries, as their comparative advantage often lies in their differential natural endowments.

In the case of biodiversity, however, investments in man-made capital goods do not often lead to the development of a flow of revenues to biodiversity services, and in fact often lead to a reduction in the amount of biodiversity capital stock.

The former is true because man-made capital goods usually go hand-in-hand with commitments to specialization in production, not diversity. Capital goods are justified when production of any one good is to occur on a large enough scale to warrant developing a fixed system of production. Thus, for example, most machinery of any scale is calibrated to a very narrow range of product. Diversity in production requires heterogeneous and flexible methods, that can be applied to everything from rubber tapping to lizard harvesting in the context of a forest. This sort of flexible system of production is not really compatible with the fixed system corresponding to large-scale capital goods; therefore, investments in man-made capital are not very conducive to the generation of revenues to diverse natural materials.

More importantly, it is very possible that the introduction of man-made capital can actually result in the deterioration of the natural capital stock, either directly or indirectly. The fragmentation of natural habitat is as destructive of diversity as is wholesale conversion, and thus the introduction of large-scale "projects" into former wildlands can directly result in diversity destruction. The greater danger is that the introduction of large-scale investments in man-made capital can indirectly result in damage to natural capital, by the encouragement of increased rates of incursion and conversion. For example, much of the loss of the Brazilian Amazonian rainforest has followed in the wake of large road improvement schemes to link the urban districts with the interior. Clearly, such man-made capital projects have resulted in huge losses in natural capital.

It is important to treat with great caution the strategy of project-based investments in biodiversity conservation. To the extent that these investments are based on traditional development models based on the generation of returns to combined man-made/natural capital goods, they are probably inapplicable in the context of biodiversity capital and they are possibly inconsistent with it as well. The idea of biodiversity conservation must be the generation of a flow of revenue to the existing natural capital base *without the introduction of large-scale man-made capital goods*.

The purpose for including these aid programmes in this analysis of biodiversity conservation has been threefold. It was intended to document the substantial amount of funding that is beginning to flow towards biodiversity conservation; the forestry-related funding under the primary aid programmes, TFAP and GEF, alone constitute commitments in excess of $1.5 billion per year over the next few years. This clearly reveals the developed world's desire to avoid some large part of the mass extinctions foretold by the current rates of deforestation.

Second, this section was intended to demonstrate the difference between funding mechanisms for the supply of global public goods and funding for technical assistance. They are two very different things, and it is not a solution to the former problem to supply funding for the latter. Despite the general level of funding, there is still the need for a mechanism that will channel the money into the provision of the intangible goods and services of natural habitat.

Third, it was important to identify the basis on which aid for biodiversity conservation must proceed, in order for there to be a constructive impact. Creating an international fund for biodiversity resources is only a necessary condition for their conservation, not sufficient in itself to guarantee a positive effect. It is important that such aid, once gathered, be routed in a way that will provide incentives for diverse production in natural habitats, i.e. to generate a flow of revenue to the existing (natural) capital base rather than to create a distinct capital base. The traditional development model may in some cases be inconsistent with this necessity, and thus it is very important to look closely at the ways in which this substantial amount of funding should be applied.

The Draft Convention on the Conservation of Biodiversity

The Proposed Convention on the Conservation of Biological Diversity and for the Establishment of a Fund for that Purpose has been the focus of international debate over the means for funding biodiversity conservation into the future. It is on the agenda for the 1992 United Nations Conference on Environment and Development in Rio de Janeiro. While this convention is laudable for its attempts to establish a self-standing fund through non-voluntary contributions, it misconceived the problems of biodiversity conservation and therefore inadvertently created incentives that detracted from its conservation.

The Draft Convention once again builds upon the "common heritage/common burden" theme also found in the World Heritage Convention.[11] In Article 2, it states as its fundamental principle that the costs of conserving biological diversity "should be shared equitably by all", while the benefits of such "should be available to all". This implicitly recognizes the importance of the public good components of biodiversity, and also recognizes the necessity of international funding to compensate their suppliers.[12]

Again, similar to the World Heritage Convention, the convention is intended to operate through a listing mechanism and fund. There is provision for the listing of any area of sufficient biodiversity consequence, by an "Advisory Committee" (made up of delegates from elected parties). When such an area is listed, there is then an express obligation to conserve that area placed upon the host state (Art. 5).

The first, important difference between this convention and the WHC is that these listings can occur without any action or acquiescence by the host state; the obligation to conserve a listed area may be imposed upon a state by the Advisory Committee. This is a necessary component of a cost-effective mechanism for providing international public goods. There is no way of assuring that the most important terrain will lie within party states, and thus the most effective agreement will be one where the parties agree to act together to conserve the most important sources of global benefits, whether they lie within a party state or not. This represents another significant step closer to the rational provision of global public goods, much like the initial steps taken by the World Heritage Convention.

A substantial difference between this draft convention and the WHC is the method of funding. Whereas the WHC is income-based, the draft convention attempts to raise funds through a "user fee" system. That is, Article 26 of the draft convention provides that taxes should be levied in each party state on the users of "specified biomaterials", both individually and in relation to their rate of use. The specified biomaterials mentioned in the convention are to be listed in an Annex to the treaty by the conference of the parties, but the commentary to the draft treaty indicates that the drafters foresee taxation of "users of animal or plant products obtained from the wild".

Such a "users' fee" system, when applied to biodiversity conservation, is wholly misconceived. First, the convention states that it is intended (and the international need is most severe) for the development of financing for the public good components of biodiversity. This financing is sorely needed. However it is impossible to provide it through a system of user fees. This is because every person on earth is, by definition, a user of the public good characteristics of biodiversity. A public good, such as the value of the oxygen or carbon fixing provided by the forests, is available to all, or none; there is no in-between. This is why an income-based tax is most appropriate for financing pure public goods; it implicitly recognizes that every individual is necessarily a user, and then provides for individual contributions based on the ability to pay. Therefore, focusing a biodiversity tax only on the users of the products of natural habitats entirely misconceives the appropriate tax base, and unnecessarily limits contributions to the fund to a very small subset of the total group of users (i.e. everyone).

If the subset of users to be taxed under the draft convention were arbitrarily selected (e.g. all persons whose surnames begin with "A"), the potential damage done by this funding mechanism would be reduced. However, in selecting the products of natural habitats as the focus for the tax, the convention creates the possibility of very substantial harm to the mechanisms in place for the conservation of the tangible products of biodiversity in the process of attempting to provide funding for the intangible ones.

There already are "users' fees" assessed to the users of the tangible goods and services of natural habitats; these are the "prices" that these persons pay for these goods and services in the market. As explained previously, the receipt of these payments, and the expectation of future receipts from future flows of goods and services, provides the incentives for developing countries to continue to invest in natural habitats. The prices charged in the market for these tangible goods and services can be increased through the assessment of additional taxes, but this will necessarily result in a loss in efficacy of the wildlife utilization policy.

The benefits of the fund developed under the draft convention, (and the potential dynamic incentive system that it might develop for encouraging investments in natural habitat), is coming at the expense of the discounting of the incentives that already exist within the wildlife utilization system. To some extent the fund will be developed simply by shifting funds from one system to the other. Even worse, the tax will also result in the disappearance of some funds from the wildlife utilization system without any compensating flow into the convention fund. In the best case, the draft convention will result in the transference of funding already in the system from less developed countries to the "Advisory Committee". In the worst, the draft convention will result in a net loss of revenues available for biodiversity conservation.[13]

There is indeed a role for a "wildlife utilization" regulation policy, perhaps even one involving a tax on wildlife trade; however, this should be developed with the object of maximizing the return to sustainable natural habitat production in Third World countries, not diverting their revenues elsewhere. The nature of such an optimal wildlife utilization policy is discussed in greater detail below. The draft convention clearly was not developed with the

object of creating an optimal wildlife utilization system; to a large
extent it runs head-on into the system that already exists.

Figure 4.1 The biodiversity convention tax wedge

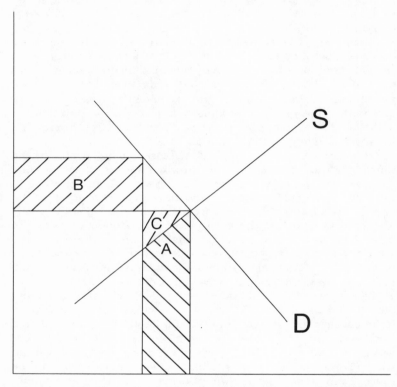

The proposed biodiversity convention proposes to fund the public good
aspects of biodiversity through the taxing of the tangible aspects of the
same goods and services. Such a system simply acts to transfer some
of the funding already available for investing in natural habitats from
the developing country to the international fund (area A once flowed
to developing countries, now area B instead flows to the fund), and
it acts to eliminate other funding completely (area C). In essence, the
fund is being established at the expense of the potential contribution
from wildlife utilization; it is very possible that there could be a net
loss in natural habitat funding, depending on just how poorly the tax
is implemented.

The draft convention is simply trying to establish an ongoing international fund to be administered by the Advisory Committee, supposedly for the purpose of encouraging the supply of biodiversity public goods. However, a tax for the purpose of providing a fund for the compensation of suppliers of the "public goods" of biodiversity (information, options, existence, etc.) cannot, by definition, be a "users' fee" unless it is assessed to everyone. It is the confusion of the drafters on this count that has led to the unnecessary conflict between the convention and wildlife utilization policy. For this reason, the proposed biodiversity convention should evolve to incorporate an income based tax, along the lines of the World Heritage Convention but much more substantial. Otherwise, it runs the risk, even if it succeeds in developing a funding mechanism for biodiversity conservation, of doing more harm than good.

Property rights based regimes

The wildlife utilization policies discussed in this chapter are all examples of property rights based regimes. Such regimes are based on the principle of "users fees". The prospect of being able to charge such fees provides the incentives to invest in supplying goods amenable to property rights regimes.

There are other instances in which it is very difficult to use property rights, but this manner of mechanism has been attempted in any event; examples in the context of biodiversity are: debt-for-nature exchanges to transfer "development rights" internationally, and biotechnology rights to provide a system for compensating genetic information.

Development right transfers

One means by which developed countries might invest in biodiversity is to attempt to do so directly, i.e. to attempt to purchase natural habitats within the borders of other countries. In general, the notion of a property title in the territory of a state does not transfer across national boundaries. This is because property titles merely represent the state's promise to enforce the rights of a given individual to the use of the indicated resources, to the exclusion of all other individuals. As with all ownership, it is a mechanism that is allowed for the advancement of society's interest, by the use of incentives to motivate the individual.

However, if a given owner's interest in the use of land comes to conflict with that of society's, it is generally accepted that the state has the right to retake some or all of the owner's rights in the property. This is precisely what happens in cases of planning, or zoning, in most countries; the state is asserting its pre-eminent right to dictate land use as against the owner's interests. Usually, this involves restricting the owner's rights of development, when the owner's incentives are such that the property would be developed more intensively than the community would prefer.

International transfers of land titles are just the reverse of this situation. Here, the developed nations would like to purchase "development rights" in developing nations in order to preserve a substantial part of the still existing natural habitat. Given existing rates of exchange and land prices, it is now possible to purchase titles in quite substantial chunks of Third World real estate. Then, with the rights to develop these lands carefully salted away up North, the natural habitat can (so the argument goes) be preserved for ever. This is the motivating force behind much of the debt-for-nature movement taking place today. About a quarter of a billion dollars worth of debt has been converted into such property rights thus far.

Box 4.2 Debt-for-nature exchanges in the Third World

(Property rights purchased in terms of debt face value – millions of US dollars)

Country	Exchanged	To be exchanged
Costa Rica	79.25	34.25
Dominion Republic	.80	79.42
Ecuador	10.00	50.00
Argentina	0.00	60.00
Peru	0.00	10.00
Madagascar	2.10	5.90
Zambia	2.27	0.00
Phillipines	0.39	1.61
Sudan	0.80	0.00
Bolivia	0.65	0.00
Total	96.26	241.18

Source: Dogse (1990).

However, this strategy fails to recognize that, in the upcoming century, the interests of these societies are likely to diverge considerably from that of these land owners. As population pressures become more and more intense, the development decisions of these absentee landlords will come to look increasingly at odds with the public interest in these states. Then these development rights will be worth virtually nothing. Once it is recognized that property rights cannot be exercised in a fashion that clearly conflicts with state interests, then it also becomes clear that the strategy of transboundary transfers of property rights cannot have any real long-term impact on state decision making regarding resource development. In this sense, international "title transfers" are essentially equivalent to one-time payments to countries in exchange for a promise not to develop a specified habitat. These sorts of mechanisms have no dynamic incentive structure to them, and therefore they must fail over time as internal pressures for development increase.

An alternative to international transfers of title, which is currently being exercised by some conservationist groups, is the transfer of development rights to groups within the country. For example, some of these debt-for-nature exchanges have been organized around a local conservation group, which is then vested with the management or development rights regarding the real estates. Of course, national governments need not honour the property rights of internal groups any more than external, when their rights clearly conflict with the social interest. However, it does present a far more interesting scenario.

In effect, the transfer of these significant sums of money and resources to an often previously nonexistent, or insignificant, conservation group is to build a power base within the country whose objectives are consistent with the external interests. It is something akin to the development of an internal pressure group, and their empowerment with hard currency. It may take place through the mechanism of property rights, but it is largely brought about by pressure group politics. It may be as effective an instrument as is available to provide these public goods, but this will be a function of each state's political system and remains to be seen.

Biotechnology right transfers

Much of the intangible value of biodiversity is represented by the specific chemical and genetic structures present there. During the course of this century intellectual property right regimes have been developed that make it possible to claim property rights in specific types of chemical and genetic structures. Given that the vast majority of the world's natural genetic wealth exists in the Third World, it might be expected that these countries would also be the holders of the majority of these new types of property rights. However, nothing could be further from the truth.

Clearly, this is one of the primary contributing factors to the continuing depreciation of genetic capital. Since the holders of the capital stock are not vested with many compensatable rights, there is very little incentive to undertake substantial investment programs in maintaining that stock.

Box 4.3 The distribution of biotechnology rights

Although the bulk of the world's genetic wealth resides in the less developed countries, nearly the entirety of the world's biotechnology patent rights are held by the developed countries. An example is provided by examining the distribution of European versus Latin American biotechnology patents.

Citizenship of recipients of:

Europatents granted	Latin American patents granted
United States 36%	Developed countries 89%
EC States 32%	Latin American countries 11%
Japan 23%	
Rest of world 9%	
(0% to Latin Americans)	

Sources: Howard, N. (1991); Hobbelink, H. (1991). Data are for the first quarter of 1990.

This bias exists on account of clearly drafted laws which discriminate against naturally occurring genetic capital in favour of human altered varieties. For example, Article 53(b) of the European Patent Convention states that no protection is available for "plant or animal varieties or essentially biological processes for the production of plants or animals." Similarly, in the landmark US decision, *Diamond* v. *Chakrabarty*, which established the first rights to patents in live organisms, plants and animals in 1980, the court stated that the basis for awarding a patent in a living organism was that: "the patentee has produced a new bacterium with markedly different characteristics than any found in nature . . . His discovery is not nature's handiwork, but his own; accordingly, it is patentable subject matter under patent law."

These selections provide an indication of the extent of the bias that exists in favour of rights in genetic structures when altered by human intervention, and against similar structures if developed by nature. In essence, the legal system has contrived to treat the informational products of nature as "open access", and thus the only appropriable genetic information is that which results from human intervention.[14] Again, such a bias actively discourages any investment in the maintenance of the stocks of natural genetic capital. It must be one of the single most important factors in the continuing decline of this very valuable capital stock.

In fact, the open access status of the raw genetic material has been enshrined in the programme that has been devised to preserve it (Juma, 1989). The International Board for Plant Genetic Research (IBPGR) has oversight responsibilites with regard to the world's system of International Agricultural Research Centres, where substantial quantities of germ plasm from hundreds of thousands of plant varieties are stored. There are three factors in the administration of this programme that have clearly damaged the incentives to invest in the maintenance of these and other species in the wild. First, these varieties were nearly always taken without any compensation to the host country. Second, a substantial number of these gene banks have been established in the developed world, while being filled with varieties taken from the developing. Third, the IBPGR has a policy of "free access" to its holdings; any person may receive a sample of germ plasm for research purposes without payment. All of these charactertics have essentially disenfranchized the host countries from their genetic assets; there is no possibility of significant investments in genetic capital stocks in the face of these policies.

Of course, there has been controversy concerning these policies, leading to various calls for reforms; however, not all of these would correct the current imbalance. First, the 1985 FAO Undertaking regarding Plant Genetic Resources attempted to proclaim all plant genetic resources "freely available", from the raw natural germ plasm to the marketed synthesized varieties. This simply makes the worst case worse, by proclaiming all genetic resources "open access" and hence unworthy of investment. Happily, the undertaking has made little progress toward general acceptance as there were no incentives within it to encourage the developed countries to accept it.

A more useful attempt at reform was the call at the 1987 FAO meeting of the Commission on Plant Genetic Resources for "Farmers Rights", i.e. a call for the recognition of the right to compensation of the source states for donated germ plasms. This right has been recognized now through the development of an international fund for the compensation of source countries. Consultations are still occurring on the issue of how to extract contributions for the fund, but the idea of taxing seed companies had been mooted.

In general, a much more serious attempt at reforming biotechnology law is necessary in order to allow the ready patenting of naturally occurring useful genetic varieties. This would be the first-best approach to inducing investments in the genetic stocks maintained in the wild, and it would not be that much more difficult (than the already incredibly complicated world of biotechnology law) to implement or enforce. Probably the single most fundamental policy modification that can be instituted to create broad-based incentives for biodiversity conservation is the reform of the laws on biotechnology rights.

Wildlife trade regulation

As has been emphasized, a policy of wildlife utilization provides on-going incentives for the investment in natural habitat, in order to generate a future supply of the tangible products of the habitat. For this reason, wildlife utilization is an important policy to pursue in order to encourage the supply of the tangible products of biodiversity.

However, there are two important limitations to this policy. One, as stressed previously, is its lack of application to the less tangible facets of biodiversity; to the extent that these are present, there necessarily will be underinvestment in the supply of biodiversity, since these values are largely inappropriable through a policy of utilization. Secondly, it is often the case that the management of natural habitat utilization is both difficult and costly to control. Some of these difficulties are relatively easily remedied, by devolving the habitat from state to local community control systems (as discussed in chapter 5); however, these problems can remain costly none the less, on account of the less intensive techniques used for control and appropriation (e.g. lack of fences). In some instances, the switch from natural habitat production to more intensive techniques will occur simply on account of these cost considerations, despite the higher value of the products of natural habitat.

An optimal, but more complicated, policy of wildlife utilization will take these two factors into consideration, and develop mechanisms that address both. The demand-side considerations (concerning the inappropriable values of natural habitat) can be addressed through revenue maximizing policies. The supply-side considerations (concerning the costliness of natural habitat control systems) can be addressed through selective purchasing policies. Together, these more complex mechanisms for wildlife utilization policy are able to provide some funding for the full range of products of natural habitat, and its appropriate management (Swanson, 1989).

Demand side management

Revenue maximising is achieved through the control of the price at which the tangible products from natural habitats are sold. All goods have a certain price at which revenue maximization occurs, and if there are not good substitutes for them, that price can often be considerably higher than that which exists in the market. This is known as "demand inelasticity". The fact that natural habitats are becoming more scarce, and are expected to become even more so, contributes to the relative scarcity of its products, and this makes its revenue maximizing prices (and the total revenues potentially appropriable from them) even higher. In short, one of the conseqences of centuries of conversions of natural habitat to more specialized production systems is to increase the inelasticity of the flow of goods from the former (as supplies of these goods and their closest substitutes become more restricted) and to decrease the elasticities of the goods from the latter (as their supplies flood the market) (Swanson, 1991).

This is the basis for the expectation that the demand for the tangible products of increasingly scarce natural habitats will usually be inelastic. This was found to be the case in a recent study of the demand for African elephant ivory, for example, where it was found that an increase of 100 per cent in the price of ivory in Japan would result in a 30 per cent increase in the total revenues flowing to its suppliers, while reducing the quantities of ivory required to be supplied by 70 per cent. (Barbier, et al 1990).[15] Therefore, there is both a theoretical and an empirical basis for the expectation that revenues from the sale of the products of natural habitats can be significantly enhanced through carefully orchestrated price controls.

Why would a policy of price supports be desirable with regard to the tangible products of natural habitats? In general, it is believed that market prices reflect the world's willingness to pay for any given goods, and for their continued supply. According to economic theory, attempts to distort this market equilibrium would only result in the creation of incentives to invest in the supply of *more* of the tangible products of natural habitats than the world's expressed preferences would justify. In other words, one of the primary advantages of a utilization-based policy is supposed to be its capacity to determine the quantity of the utilized goods that the world wants; orchestrated distortions simply act to negate this important positive attribute of this policy.

However, when it is clear that there are important positive, inappropriable, external benefits to the provision of a tangible good, there is good reason for society to increase the reward to the tangible good in order to provide an implicit return to the intangible one. That is, when these products come jointly (tangible/intangible) but it is only possible to price one of the two goods (because the other is of the nature of a "public good"), then it can be the optimal "second best" policy to provide price supports to the tangible good in order to foster the incentives to invest sufficiently in the joint supply of both (Swanson, 1990).[16]

There are three theoretically equivalent mechanisms for implementing these price supports: consumer state taxes, producer state taxes, or joint producer supply restrictions. That is, once the revenue maximizing price is determined, it can be installed by collecting the difference between that and the market price at the consumer state, or in the producer state. Equivalently, if all producers of the good agree on the correct limit to the supply to be placed on the market, then this will also result in revenue maximization.

So long as the revenue maximizing price/quantity combination is implemented in one of these fashions, the optimal demand side wildlife utilization system is in place.

Supply side management

The control of access to natural habitats can be very problematic, and the increasing value of natural habitat products is making this even more so. Freedom of access makes control difficult often leading to population reductions and consequent increases in prices, which simply increases the incentives to obtain illegal access to the species.

Optimal demand side policies will not stop these situations where they are already in place. The price supports will even increase the incentives to attempt to evade controls over the natural habitat. This means that a supply side policy must be implemented in combination with a demand side policy. Such a policy must be constructed in such a way as to reduce the costliness of controlling access to the species.

In general, it is inconsistent to speak of intensive controls over natural habitats. One of the primary attributes of such habitats are their unregimented nature; this is what allows diversity to flourish. Therefore, one of the requisites of an effective supply side policy will be its capacity to control supplies without intervening drastically in the habitat (by the use of fences, massive patrolling, etc.) The best means of controlling access to natural habitat products would be through a policy of selective purchasing. Under such a scheme, it is possible to reduce incentives to illegally harvest in natural habitat through a consumer commitment to purchase only from the properly designated controller. There is no incentive to engage in unauthorized harvesting if there is no market for the produce.

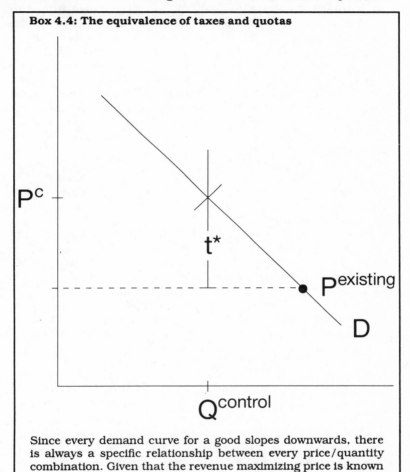

Box 4.4: The equivalence of taxes and quotas

P^c

t^*

$P^{existing}$

D

$Q^{control}$

Since every demand curve for a good slopes downwards, there is always a specific relationship between every price/quantity combination. Given that the revenue maximizing price is known (Pc), the supply of the optimal quantity (Qc) is precisely equivalent to the charging of the optimal tax (t*). Both result in the price/quantity combination (Pc,Qc).

There are always "black markets" that undermine such controls; however, the extent of an illegal market is largely determined by the method of implementation and the consistency between the objectives of the controller and those being controlled. With regard to the latter, it is very likely that the vast majority of the ultimate consumers of many wildlife products reside in developed countries, where there is a widely expressed demand for more effective controls over natural habitat production. This has been demonstrated in the case of the recent ivory trade controls implemented by the primary consumer states (the EC, the US and Japan), where the consumers effectively shut down the trade by refusing to purchase ivory products. However, this is not meant to imply any support for consumer-led "bans" as a means of controlling access to natural habitats; we are simply noting that consumers have already indicated their capacity to regulate wildlife markets, and we believe that this capacity could also be put to constructive effect by the enforcement of revenue maximizing (rather than revenue minimizing) prices.

Even with a "designated supplier", however, there still remain incentives for the excessive exploitation of natural habitat. This is because each supplier has no incentive to turn away supplies derived from natural habitats other than that for which he is the designated supplier. These incentives, when applied across all suppliers, can result in a situation where each is purchasing all of the wildlife product that it is offered (irrespective of whether it fits within the supplier's management plan) because each knows that another supplier will do so if it does not.

The solution to this dilemma is for consumers to refuse to purchase quantities from a designated supplier, unless they correspond to the quantity that would issue from the rational management of that supplier's own habitat, i.e. a consumer-enforced system of individual quotas. In this fashion, the supplier has absolutely no incentive to look elsewhere for supplies, as the correct management of its own lands will satisfy its quota. In addition, given that the same system is applied across all other designated suppliers, there is no longer any incentive for any of them to pursue others' supplies. Each supplier's habitat is secured because the size of its market is secured; cross-boundary excursions cannot increase the size of that market and so there is no longer any incentive to undertake them.

Such a system could be implemented effectively through a number of different mechanisms. Individual quotas could be set by committee, and then enforced through the issuance of "coupons" or the construction of an "exchange". Coupons essentially take the place of the regulated commodity in the market. Once a given number are printed, then the consumers enforce the regulatory system by refusing to admit the regulated good without a coupon. When the coupons are distributed to the designated suppliers, the task of controlling access to the species becomes one of controlling access to the coupons instead, which is usually a far less costly proposition (Swanson, 1989).

Alternatively, the consumer states could instead construct an "exchange", which is a mechanism for assuring that goods on the market are "exchanged" only between consumers and designated suppliers. An exchange operates by allowing certified trade to occur only within its walls, while consumers enforce the exchange mechanism by refusing entrance to any goods other than those traded through the exchange. Again, the exchange would have to establish and enforce individual quotas for each designated supplier, disallowing sales within the exchange beyond the annual quota. Swanson and Pearce (1989).

Demand and supply side management combined

Any of these supply-side methods effectively controls the costliness of natural habitat utilization by means of controlling access to the markets. In combination with a demand side management policy, the essence of an optimal wildlife utilization policy becomes apparent. The revenues from wildlife utilization can be maximized and the costliness minimized by a policy that combines an effective demand/supply side management programme.

The natural combination of the two halves is a producers' association with joint revenue maximizing quotas being enforced by a consumer-led exchange (or, if the good concerned is not so significant in individual value, then a coupon). Since any supply side system will require consumer-enforced quotas imposed on suppliers, there is no additional cost in constructing these quotas in order to make them jointly revenue maximizing. This then provides an additional incentive for all producers to attempt to join in the association. It also avoids the extra expense, burden and uncertainty associated with tax transfers across borders.

Therefore, an optimal (but decidedly more complicated) wildlife utilization policy should move towards consumer-enforced producer commodity associations. This will increase the returns to particular tangible goods of natural habitat (and implicitly compensate investments in the supply of related intangibles as well) plus it will also decrease the costliness of natural habitat production. This is definitely an objective worth pursuing for the compensation of developing countries' supply of biodiversity services.

The Convention on Trade in Endangered Species ("CITES")

The CITES convention was signed in March 1972 and came into force three years later. It provides the primary international control structure for the trade in wildlife products. Initially, it was drafted with little attention to the concept of constructive utilization of the trade; it focused instead on the identification of endangered species and the withdrawal of the demand for those. Recently, however, the Conference of the Parties has been taking steps towards a more constructive approach, with the attempted development of various sorts of quota systems. Although these are in still in their formative stages, they represent important steps toward a rationalized international control structure.

The convention as a trade regulation mechanism[17]

As drafted, the CITES convention provided little in the way of a constructive trade utilization mechanism. It functions primarily through the operation of two "Appendices", on which potentially endangered species are listed. Appendix I is supposed to contain those species currently threatened with extinction, while Appendix II contains species for which there is some indication that they might become threatened. The Conference of the Parties to CITES makes these determinations at its biennial meetings.

Once a species is listed on either of the CITES Appendices, it becomes subject to the permit requirements of the convention. An Appendix I species may not be shipped in the absence of the issuance of an "export permit" by the exporting state; this permit may not be issued, under the terms of the convention, unless both the exporting state certifies that the export will not be detrimental to the species and the importing state certifies (by the issuance of an import permit) that the import will not be used for commercial purposes. Therefore, an appendix I listing acts as an effective "ban" on the trade in those species and, even if exporters wish to continue the trade, the importing states have the duty to deny all non-scientific imports.

An Appendix II listing, however, leaves the decision on trade control to the discretion of the exporting state. That is, there is no role for the importing state, other than to ensure that an export permit is issued for each specimen. These permits are issued so long as the exporting state certifies that the export will not be detrimental to the survival of the species.

The other important responsibility of member states is to provide annual reports to the CITES Secretariat on the amounts of trade in listed species. The Secretariat also acts as the intermediary between exporting and importing states, to confirm the authenticity of trade documents for example.

The history of the CITES convention has witnessed one species after another progress from Appendix II to Appendix I, as potentially unsustainable trade levels raise concerns about the viability of the species. Most recently, this has occurred in the well publicized case of the African elephant, for which a 12 year listing on Appendix II ended in 1989 with its "uplisting" by the Conference of the Parties.

Such a progression from "potentially threatened" to "endangered" is very predictable, given the structure of the CITES convention. This is because an Appendix II listing gives little in the way of a wildlife trade framework; that is, it does nothing to manage either supply or demand pressures in the manners set forth above. Instead, it leaves each range state operating independently, with no international assistance to perform the additional monitoring tasks that are required. In most respects, an Appendix II listing accomplishes little whatsoever.

What an Appendix II listing certainly does accomplish is to publicize the potential rarity of the species, thereby increasing current speculative demand pressures. Since most wildlife species exist in unmanaged circumstances, it is usually difficult to handle the existing, let alone any increased, pressures. Thus, the progression of species from listing on Appendix II to "endangered" status is not unforeseeable; for many species, it is entirely predictable.

An Appendix I listing promises much more in the way of international co-operation; however, the efforts are put to no constructive effect. That is, once the regulated species completes the progression from virtually uncontrolled Appendix II species to endangered Appendix I species, the international community then launches into concerted action to "ban the trade". Of course, for some species (such as the rhinoceros) there is little other option by this stage in the proceedings; however, for the vast majority of endangered species, the withdrawal of value from the products of wildlands merely hastens its elimination. The situation has gone from bad to worse; with the uplisting, the traded species is protected from short-term extinction from over-exploitation, while simultaneously hastening the medium-term extinction of its habitat. Now what is lost is not only the single species generating consumptive value, but also many of the related species and systems whose shared habitat could be subsidised by this value.

Therefore, CITES as drafted provides for a peculiar sort of international regime of trade controls. For traded wildlife species it initially provides little more than a global notice of "potential rarity value" (with the posting of an Appendix II listing), while following that with the withdrawal of developed world purchases of the wildlife product (via an Appendix I ban) when the population then comes under even greater pressures. As a mechanism for transfering value from North to South for the conservation of wildlands and the wildlife they contain, the CITES system fails miserably as traditionally practised.

The convention – recent attempts at innovation

As early as 1979, the delegates from developing countries brought the anomoly of "indirect extinction" to the attention of the Conference of the Parties. In San Jose, Costa Rica, they argued (as do we here) that there must be an economic benefit from controlled species if they were to be able to justify protecting their habitats from development. These concerns gave rise to the first step towards the reform of CITES, with the adoption of Conference Resolution 3.15 at the New Delhi Conference of the Parties in 1981. This resolution provides for the downlisting of certain Appendix I populations for the purposes of sustainable resource management. The criteria that specify how Appendix I species may be utilized in order to procure compensation for their habitat are known as the "ranching criteria", and each Conference of the Parties usually sees a large number of such proposals for review and possible acceptance. The first ranching proposal accepted involved the transfer of the Zimbabwean population of Nile crocodile to Appendix II in 1983.

Ranching proposals tend to be focused on a particular state, or operation, and do not constitute mechanisms for the constructive control of the entire trade. In essence, they continue the "ban" while allowing very limited, individual operations to recommence. While being of some utility, they do not constitute attempts at harnessing the value of any particular species.

In 1983, a species-based approach was first adopted with regard to the exploitation of the African leopard. Although listed on Appendix I, it was recognized in Conference Resolution 4.13 that specimens of the leopard could be killed "to enhance the survival of the species". With this, the Conference of the Parties approved an annual quota of 460 specimens, and allocated these between the range states. In 1985 this quota was then increased to 1,140 animals, and in 1987 to 1,830.

This approach to trade management was then generalized in 1985 with Resolution 5.21, which provided for the systematic downlisting of populations where the countries of origin agree a quota system that is sufficiently safe so as to not endanger the species. Under this resolution, five different species have been subject to quota sytems: three African crocodiles, one Asian crocodile, and the Asian boneytongue a fish much admired by the Japanese as a wall hanging).[18]

Finally, the third avenue of innovation under CITES, and the most concerted effort thus far, has been the creation of a Management Quota System for the African elephant populations under Resolution 5.12. This system represented a step forwards and two or three steps backwards in the continuing evolution of a workable trade control system. It represented a step forward in its basic scheme of linking quotas to populations on an ongoing basis. However, the implementation of this principle was lost in the failure of the system to provide for adequate controls on the forces of demand and supply. The Management Quota System failed to utilize the incentives for cooperation that exist between range states; predictably, each range state acting independently was insufficient to manage the forces of demand for the whole. Secondly, the system relied on the good faith of the range states and trading states for its implementation (rather than the evidenced abilities of final consumers); predictably, the good faith of these persons was insufficient to manage supply pressures. Finally, the Management Quota System failed as a consequence of these clear inadequacies, resulting in a complete collapse of public confidence in the capacity for trade controls to work – this loss of confidence represents a very substantial backwards step (Barbier, E., et al, 1990).

The importance of all of these developments is that they represent a search for the "middle ground" between Appendix I and Appendix II regimes. Although that search is only just beginning, its existence is demonstrative of the parties' awareness of the needs that the CITES system does not satisfy. CITES must continue to evolve to provide for an effective trade utilization regime, rather than continue to act as the recorder of the process of species' evolution from Appendix II to Appendix I status. In order to do so effectively, there must be a clear target provided, otherwise the fiasco of the Management Quota System will only be repeated again and again. The control of wildlife trade is a potentially important instrument for the conservation of diversity, but CITES must develop a very different control mechanism if it is to contribute to the harnessing of these values.

Conclusion

The global problem of diversity conservation requires a range of approaches because there is a spectrum of different products associated with natural habitat. Adequate investments in the maintenance of some of these products are readily provided for with a simple policy of wildlife utilization; however, there are other facets (information, options, existence) that require a much more complex approach to policy.

This chapter has attempted to canvass the possible international approaches to the conservation of the entire range of biodiversity services. These are not simple or straightforward policy prescriptions, because the nature of the problem itself is complex and multi-faceted. The public good nature of the products, and the need to transfer substantial values in a systematic fashion from North to South is the essence of the problem. The essence of the solution is a system of dynamic reciprocity, whereby ongoing investments in diversity in the South are compensated year-by-year by payments from the North. A good start would be a well-regulated, and much more complex, wildlife utilization policy, in combination with some mechanisms for compensating specific intangible services from natural habitats. Finally, there can be little doubt that the entire system of genetic resource rights requires a complete overhaul; this merely represents the international recognition of the right to compensation for the conservation of these primary resources. If the international community wishes to preserve this diversity, it must pay for it, and these are the mechanisms for payment that are most promising for wildland and wildlife conservation.

References

Barbier,E., J. Burgess, T. Swanson, and D. Pearce, *Elephants, Economics and Ivory* [Earthscan: London, 1990].

Diamond,J., "Overview of Recent Extinctions", in "Population, Resources, and Environment in the Twenty-first Century", in Western, D., and Pearl, M., *Conservation for the Twenty-first Century*, [Oxford. Oxford University Press,].

Dogse,P. and B. von Droste, *Debt-For-Nature Exchanges and Biosphere Reserves: Experiences and Potential, MAB Digest 6* [Paris: UNESCO, 1990].

Hobbelink,H., *Biotechnology and the Future of World Agriculture* [London: Zed Books, 1991].

Howard,N., *Legal Protection of Biotechnology within the European Community with Reference to Environmental Protection*, unpublished dissertation, University of London [1991].

Juma,C., *The Gene Hunters*, [London: Zed Books, 1989].

Lyster,S., *International Wildlife Law*, [London: Grotius, 1985].

Pearce, D., A. Markandya, and E. Barbier, *Blueprint for a Green Economy*, [London: Earthscan, 1989].

Prescott-Allan,R. and C. Precott-Allan, *Genes from the Wild*, [London: Earthscan, 1983].

Repetto, R. and M. Gillis, *Public Policies and the Misuse of Forest Resources* [Cambridge: Cambridge University Press, 1988].

Swanson, T. and D. Pearce, "The International Regulation of the Ivory Trade – The Ivory Exchange", paper prepared for the International Union for the Conservation of Nature [London: Gland, 1989].

Swanson, T., "Policy Options for the Regulation of the Ivory Trade", in Cobb,S. (ed.), *The Ivory Trade and the Future of the African Elephant*, [Oxford: Ivory Trade Review Group, 1989].

Swanson,T., "A Proposal for the Reform of the African Elephant Ivory Trade", London Environmental Economics Centre DP 89-04 [London: International Institute for Environment and Development, 1989].

Swanson,T., "Conserving Biological Diversity", in Pearce, D., *Blueprint 2: Greening the World Economy, [London: Earthscan, 1991].*

Swanson,T. *"The Economics of Wildlife Utilization", Paper presented at the Workshop on Wildlife Utilization, General Assembly of the International Union for the Conservation of Nature, Perth, Australia [1990].*

Swanson, T., *"International Regulation of Wildlife Utilisation", Report to the CITES Secretariat, 1991.*

Swanson,T., *"Wildlife Utilization as an Instrument for Natural Habitat Conservation: A Survey", London Environmental Economics Centre DP 91-03 [London: International Institute for Environment and Development, 1991a].*

United Nations Environment Programme, "A Note on Options for a Financial Mechanism to Meet the Requirements of a Convention on Biological Diversity", Ad Hoc Experts Group on Biological Diversity: Madrid [1991].

Vitousek,P., P. Ehrlich, A. Ehrlich, and P. Matson, "Human Appropriation of the Products of Photosynthesis", Bioscience, vol. 36(6), pp. 368-373 [1986].

Western,D., "Population, Resources, and Environment in the Twenty-first Century", in Western, D., and Pearl, M., *Conservation for the Twenty-first Century* [Oxford: Oxford University Press, 1989].

Wijnstekers, W., *The Evolution of CITES*, Secretariat of the Convention on International Trade in Endangered Species: Lausanne.

Notes

1. This is what the Endangered Species Act in the United States has done. It disallows any public actions that may extinguish a threatened species.

2. One means of investing in maintaining a stock of an asset is simply not to make withdrawals regarding it. This is a primary form of investment currently being requested of the developing countries, ie the creation of preserves and conservation areas is asking for uncompensated investments just as much as if the payment of hard currencies were involved.

3. For this reason I am one of the few economists supporting the EC Common AGricultural Policyk and similar such agricultural subsidy schemes in the developed world. These schemes maintain a long obsolete agricultural industry within the developed world, rather than allowing it to migrate "offshore" to the developing where the same outputs could be produced much more cost effectively. However, this would result in the perverse situation, conservation-wise, of increasing incentives to invest in natural habitats in the North while decreasing those incentives (by increasing the opportunity costs) in the South. On account of irreversibilities, the North cannot transform itself into the *in situ* keeper of the world's biodiversity. Therefore, I am a supporter of the CAP; for as long as this hopelessly inefficient scheme can be kept going, it provides some time for better means of maintaining natural habitat to be devised and implemented.

4. This has been the case throughout the life history of the Secretariat for the Convention on International Trade in Endangered Species, for example. One of the primary activities of each year must be the acquisition of the funding necessary to accomplish its range of tasks (C. Huxley, pers. comm.).

5. The early *Trail Smelter* case, where the US sued Canada for the emissions of a plant near the US Canadian border, was the first instance in which the international interest in controlling domestic management was universally recognized.

6. Article 6(1) of the World Heritage Convention provides that: "While fully respecting the sovereignty of the States on whose territory the cultural and natural heritage . . . is situated, and without prejudice to the property rights provided by national legislation, the States Parties to this Convention recognize that such heritage constitutes a world heritage for whose protection it is the duty of the international community as a whole to co-operate."

7. Article 4 of the Convention obligates the parties to do "all that it can . . . to the utmost of its resources" to conserve listed sites.

8. Of course, by the nature of the mechanism (ie income taxation), it is difficult to know if this shortfall in funding is attributable to a lack of international demand for the supply of more of these sites, or whether it is attributable to problems of free riding, ie the lack of incentives for any state to step forward and volunteer to pay more unilaterally. This is the general problem with taxation based provision of public goods.

9. It is now being replicated to an extent by the development of International Trust Funds within the context of other international regimes. For example, the Ramsar convention, discussed

in Section D below, has recently established a Trust Fund for the compensation of wetland sites listed in developing countries.

10. One of the primary factors contributing to the loss of biodiversity is the existence of state policies that encourage deforestation, even when it is clear that this is not the economically (or financially) use of the land (Gillis, 1989). The TFAP makes an important contribution to the creation of sustainable wildlife utilization regimes when it puts public policies on a more rational footing.

11. The Article numbers refer to the IUCN Draft 6 of the Biodiversity Convention, one of the last drafts to contain an explicit form of funding mechanism. Current drafts of the Convention speak very broadly to this point.

12. A small, but fundamentally important, misstatement in the convention is the use of the phrase "should be available to all" in regard to the benefits of biodiversity. This implies that there should be open access to all facets of biologically diverse goods and services. However, the public good components of biodiversity simple *are* available to all, on account of their inappropriable nature. It is on account of this characteristic that they are in danger of bieng undersupplied. When the benefits of biodiversity are appropriable, this must be encouraged in order to provide incentives for investment in their supplies. To the extent that the convention is implying that all facets of biodiversity should be rendered non-appropriable, this is merely making the problems afflicting some of the components unnecessarily infect the others.

13. In terms of economics, the determination whether the draft convention will result in a net loss of funding or not depends on the relative eleasticities of demand and supply of the taxed commodites. For a small tax, with relatively equal supply and demand effects, the net effect of the convention is likely to be small, resulting only in a transfer of funds from the Third World to the international panel.

14. There are "Plant Breeders Rights" that confirm a breeder's rights in a particular variety of plant, even when it has been produced through a selective biological process. However, the requirements under these laws (eg uniformity of variety) are still based upon the human synthesized genetic variety, only in this case the synthesis occurs through selective breeding rather than direct genetic manipulation. These rights do not afford much, if any, protection to the supplier of the raw natural materials of genetic variety.

15. That is, the demand eleasticity of ivory in Japan was calculated to be -·70. This is, of course, a point estimate and therefore its application across a range of demand as broad as a doubling in the price of ivory is purely speculative. However, it is clearly the case that other products with similar demand eleasticities (eg petroleum at -·50) have been found to be inelastic over a broad range of prices, at least in the short run.

16. This has been shown to be precisely the function of an intellectual property rights system. A society awards a monopoly (a form of a price support) to an investor in supply of a new product, precisely because the newness of that product implies information, which is a public good and therefore unpriced. In order to induce the investment in such information, or innovation, the society elects to support the price of the related tangible product, because this creates incentives to continue to invest in new information in the neighbourhood of the previous investment (Swanson, 1990).

17. Much of the following discussion derives from a report constructed for the CITES Secretariat in the course of a review of the international reptile skin trade (Swanson, 1991b).

18. At the Seventh Conference of the Parties, in Resolution 7.14, this scheme for developing quota systems was made time limited, so that no quota system could continue beyond two Conferences of the Parties. The argument was to encourage the movement away from general quota systems, and towards specific ranching regimes; however, for best natural habitat conservation, the preferred movement should be in the opposite direction.

5

COMMUNITY-BASED DEVELOP-MENT IN AFRICA

Edward B. Barbier

The current interest in community-based wildlife management and wildlands development in Sub-Saharan Africa must be viewed within the context of evolving approaches to natural resource preservation.[1]

The initial approach, which has its roots in the Western environmentalist movements and ideology of the past century and still predominates today, saw the establishment of large areas of national parks and reserves as the foremost priority for African conservation. Ownership, control and management of these preserved areas and resources were to be vested in the government. The main objective of national policy towards these "public" resources was, in the first instance, to protect them as part of the "national" heritage on behalf of all citizens, and wherever possible, to develop and reap the potential benefits from tourism, hunting, culling and other revenue-earning activities. For most African countries, the policy was a direct legacy of the colonial era; for others, it appeared to be a "successful" approach to wildlife management worth adopting. Coordination and control of these protected areas and parks was usually centralized in one or more government agencies, such as a national parks and wildlife department or a forestry department. In some countries, this approach was further replicated at regional level (e.g., state or province).

Unfortunately, establishment of many of the protected areas frequently worked against the direct economic interests of local communities. The abrogation of the wildlife and wildlands by the state meant that many communities no longer had access to resources that they had traditionally exploited for years, perhaps centuries. More often than not, the gazetting of land for these "preserved" areas led to the displacement or enforced relocation of rural communities with little real compensation for the loss in traditional livelihoods or resources. Any subsequent harvesting, hunting or other use of the land and wild resources from these areas was deemed illegal, yet at the same time, many neighbouring communities had to bear the full brunt of crop and other economic damages arising from marauding wildlife or their frequent migration. The result was that rural communities not only lost their traditional management and use rights to local wild resources but also saw little incentive, and indeed a major cost, in conserving them.

The situation has worsened in recent years under the combination of rising rural populations, scarcity of arable land and increased urbanization. Direct land-use conflicts over protected areas and their resources are now the norm in many parts of Africa. With poverty endemic in many rural areas, illegal encroachment, hunting and harvesting in wildlife and wildland parks and reserves is often the only available means of securing subsistence and income. Local people may not necessarily be directly involved in these activities, but their complete alienation from or disinterest in wildlife conservation frequently translates into little opposition to or concern for the depletion of local wild resources by others. Where there is a local interest in maintaining these resources, the breakdown of traditional common property management regimes into virtual open access exploitation leaves rural communities with little means of enforcing sustainable management. With the limited financial resources, trained manpower and equipment at their disposal, the national and local authorities responsible for protecting and maintaining these preserved areas are often powerless to control the problem. Low morale and wages can lead to government officials and park employees to participate in, and in some cases, even instigate the lucrative, illegal exploitation of protected resources.

In addition, Africa has always had large populations of wildlife outside of national parks and reserves. Although these wildife populations were found on privately owned and communal (tribal) lands, government policies have often made it illegal to exploit these populations and market wildlife products. In the absence of legal markets, land owners and occupiers have no incentive to maintain or allow wildlife to remain on the land. Instead, wildlife is seen as a nuisance and barrier to more profitable and pressing uses of the land.[2]

These problems arising from past conservation policies and increasing economic pressures on wild resources have led to a rethinking of wildlife management strategies in Africa. In some instances, de-gazetting of some reserves and parks has been advocated. For example, Malawi suffers from extreme rural poverty and increasing scarcity of arable land, yet 11 per cent of the country's land area is set aside as protected area – the third largest share in Africa after Botswana and Tanzania and well above the world average of 4 per cent. It has been argued that small increments of Malawi's protected areas with low wildlife population densities could be safely de-gazetted and redistributed to local communities for agricultural use without seriously affecting the return from tourism or hunting safaris or damaging environmental benefits such as protection of watersheds, preservation of key species and protection of fisheries (World Bank, 1991). Clearly, however, there is a limit to how much land currently under protection fits these criteria in Malawi or in other African countries.

A more direct, and possibly more widely applicable, approach to reconciling rural development and conservation has been advocated through *community-based wildlife management*. A number of projects emphasizing this approach have been established in recent years, and many more are currently being set up. The following chapter discusses the economic potential of community- based wildlife management in Africa as the "new phase" of conservation-led development. Two examples, the CAMPFIRE programme in Zimbabwe and the Luangwe Integrated Resource Development Project (LIRDP) in Zambia, are discussed to illustrate some of the potential as well as the problems of such schemes.

Community-based wildlife management

In a recent review of existing community-based wildlife utilization and management schemes in Africa, the World Bank noted the potential of the approach in promoting overall rural development through increases in local incomes, improved standards of living, strengthening local community structures and human resources, and generally empowering local communities to manage their own natural resources with minimal external input or control (Kiss, 1990). At the very least, such schemes seek to engender the co-operation of local communities in wildlife conservation through ensuring that a sufficient share of the benefits gained from wildlife management and utilization will accrue to communities to compensate for any costs imposed on them.

There are several ways in which this sharing in the benefits can occur:

● *revenue-sharing* with the local community of any proceeds from wildlife-related activities, such as tourism, safari hunting, commercial culling, and so forth.
● *employment or income generation* through the development of

rural development programmes or activities in the protected area or in surrounding buffer zones, local job creation in tourist, wildlife and park services or in commercially run cropping or hunting schemes and creation of markets for local handicrafts and produce.

● *infrastructure investment* in schools, roads, hospitals, clinics, water supply and other much needed public infrastructure works required by rural communities.

● *direct utilization* of wild resources, through reserving hunting quotas and licenses for local communities, establishing user rights and buffer zones for limited resource exploitation, controlled culling operations by local people for subsistence, pest damage control or profit, facilitating private, commercially oriented wildlife operations, such as game ranching, and other means of increasing the direct economic benefits to local communities from wild resources.

Community-based wildlife management and utilization schemes usually have one or more of the above means of sharing benefits with local communities. As argued by Cumming (1990a), the important economic potential of wildlife resource utilization is the variety of uses it can support; for example, in the case of rangeland (animal) species, potential options include:

(a)   game viewing and photographic safari;
(b)   safari and trophy hunting of wild populations;
(c)   combinations of game viewing and trophy hunting;
(d)   cropping wild populations for meat and other products;
(e)   cropping confined or fenced populations (game ranching),
(f)   combinbations of sport hunting and cropping wild populations;
(g)   intensive management of confined populations of one or two species (game farming);
(h)   running cattle, or cattle and other domestic stock, with wildlife under options (a) to (f) (multi-species systems).

Thus wildlife utilization and management schemes have many income-earning opportunities from which to choose, and have some flexibility to adopting the right option suitable to the economic needs, institutional setting (e.g., private or communally owned land, market conditions and infrastructure, etc.) and ecological conditions facing local communities.

Besides increasing benefits to local people, community based wildlife projects also have some commitment to increasing local participation and "empowerment". This ranges from involving local communities in project planning and design to training and skills development in project activities to actual community-run management of culling operations, tourist services, anti-poaching operations and other project activities.

However, with the exception of privately run commercially oriented pojects, in most schemes actual ownership of the protected areas and wildlife remains in the hands of the state, and many of the important decisions regarding use rights still remain with central authorities or their local representatives. This is also true of many of the management schemes outside of protected areas, where government decisions concerning land use planning and zoning is crucial to determining which areas are open to greater wildlife resource exploitation, which areas are still to have "protective" status, and which areas are open to other forms of land use. A good example of this approach is the development of Wildlife Management Areas (WMAs) in Botswana (Lawson and Mafela, 1990). Land in Botswana is zoned either as Commercial Farming Areas, Communal Farming Areas and Reserved Areas, which comprise land reserved for people with a few cattle and those reserved for alternative uses. Twelve WMAs are planned in seven districts, comprising some 21 per cent of Botswana's total land area. As special reserve areas set aside for multiple wildlife uses with community participation, WMAs will be subject to district land use plans requiring approval by local and national authorities. Although not all community-based schemes in Africa are so formal in their implementation, the need to implement these projects in conjunction with carefully planned land use strategies is seen to be a top priority by most governments – effectively putting an "upper limit" on the role of local community participation in many important implementation, planning and management decisions.

CAMPFIRE, Zimbabwe

The Communal Area Management Programme for Indigenous Resources (CAMPFIRE) is a fairly recent development in the evolution of wildlife management policy in Zimbabwe. During the past fifty years, there has been a steady increase in the land set aside for the protection of wildlife in national parks and reserves, which now occupy around 12.5 per cent of total land area in the country (see Table 5.1). Since the 1960s, farmers with privately owned commercial land were also encouraged to develop game ranching and safari hunting, and more recently, forest lands have been utilized for safari operations.

However, until recently, occupiers of communal lands – which comprise approximately 50 per cent of total land area – have had little economic incentive to maintain wildland or wildlife. Increasing population fuelled demands for more agricultural land for crop production and livestock rearing, and the eradication of many tsetse infested areas "opened up" new areas for these purposes. As result, wildlife on communal lands was viewed increasingly by local inhabitants as a threat to crops and human safety and a competitor to cattle for grazing (Martin, 1984).

Table 5.1: Land areas (km²) used for wildlife conservation and utilization in Zimbabwe

Year	National parks	Safari areas	Forest areas	Communal lands	Commercial farms	Total	% of Zimbabwe
1930	17,500	0	0	0	?	17,500	4.48
1940	10,583	0	0	0	?	10,583	2.71
1950	11,075	0	0	0	?	11,075	2.83
1960	11,800	0	0	0	350	12,150	3.11
1970	26,073	7,494	0	0	30,000	63,567	16.26
1980	22,799	18,576	5,541	3,356	30,000	80,272	20.54
1990	22,799	18,576	4,963	12,806	27,000	86,144	22.04

Source: Cumming (1990d)

The 1975 Parks and Wildlife Act maintained the status of wildlife as state property, but permitted landholders to make use of wildlife populations subject to sustainable management. Although private landowners now had the incentive to exploit wildlife on their own land for their own benefit, the lack of a readily identifiable landholder on communal lands meant that many local inhabitants saw little benefits from wildlife management and utilization (Jansen, 1990). Moreover, management of wildlife on communal lands was still vested in the state.

Initial attempts at sharing the wildlife revenues obtained from communal land operations with local communities were also not proving very successful. Trophy hunting fees were paid by operators to the central government, which were to be returned to districts to fund "approved" projects, such as schools, clinics and other public infrastructure investments. However, only 57 per cent of the nearly Z$6 million earned from wildlife in the communal areas between 1980 and 1987 had been returned to the districts by the end of 1987. The communal lands of the Zambezi valley generated wildlife revenues of Z$2.1 million between 1981 and 1986 but by 1987 only 44 per cent had been returned to the districts (Jansen, 1990).[3]

Initiated in 1978, Operation WINDFALL (Wildlife Industries Development for All) was an attempt to distribute meat from elephant culling in national parks to neighbouring communities and return the proceeds from safari hunting to local district councils. However, WINDFALL largely failed to achieve its objectives, as little meat found its way back to local communities, only a small proportion of the revenues were returned to the district councils let alone the local communities and there was a lack of local participation in decision-making and any sense of local proprietorship. Any revenues that were reimbursed to local communities were regarded largely as government handouts, failing to engender any sense of the relationship between the revenues and wildlife management (Murphree, 1990).

Building on these earlier attempts and hoping to improve upon them, the government of Zimbabwe launched Project CAMPFIRE in 1984 specifically to address "the problems of communal resource ownership by a more equitable allocation of natural resources and by placing a value on them which has hitherto been absent for the communal land resident" (Martin, 1986). The project arose from the regional land use plan for the Sebungwe Region of north-west Zimbabwe, where it was recognized that, on the one hand, communities were suffering extensive crop losses due to wildlife which was being heavily poached, while on the other, ecological and economic conditions appeared more suitable for maintaining and exploiting some wildlife resources, even after tsetse fly eradication (Martin, 1984). Unlike its predecessors, however, CAMPFIRE aimed to involve communal area residents directly in wildlife management and to enable them to receive readily identifiable benefits from those resources. As a consequence, it was hoped residents would perceive wildlife as an economic asset, protect it from illegal hunting and regard its management as a financially attractive land use option (Jansen, 1990; Martin, 1986).

As originally conceived, the CAMPFIRE approach was to be based on a "system of group ownership" with well-defined rights of access to natural resources for the communities resident in the target areas. This would involve the creation of locally based natural resource co-operatives, concerned with management not only of wildlife but also grazing, forestry and water resources. Each co-operative would function with essentially the same rights and obligations as a privately owned commercial ranch, with all inhabitants of the community being co-operative shareholders. Profits could be allocated at the discretion of the community either for communal benefit or to individual inhabitants (shareholders). To assist communities in acquiring legal proprietorship of wildlife and other resources and to provide them with the necessary technical and financial assistance for developing the required management

Figure 5.1: CAMPFIRE IN ZIMBABWE

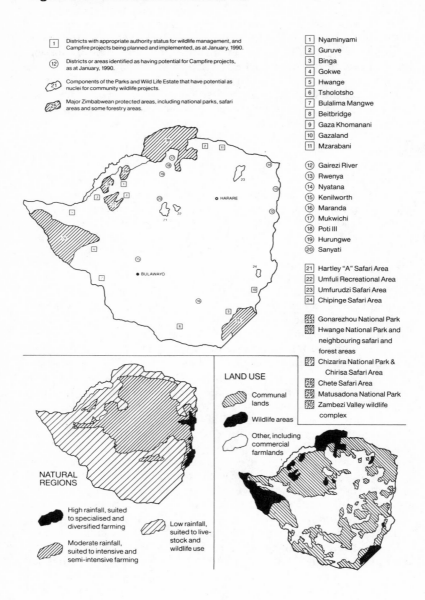

Source: **Zimbabwe Trust et al. (1990)**

structures, strategies and skills, CAMPFIRE also recommended the establishment of a governmental implementing and technical support agency (Martin, 1986; Murphree, 1990).

However, over four years passed after the CAMPFIRE initiative was announced before it was actually implemented. The main stumbling block appears to have been the lack of funding for an implementing agency within the Department of National Parks and Wildlife Management, possibly reflecting conflicts of interest and skepticism at high levels about wildlife development as an alternative to agriculture or livestock raising (Murindagomo, 1990). Instead, with the support of a local NGO (Zimbabwe Trust, or ZimTrust) and the Centre for Applied Social Sciences (CASS) at the University of Zimbabwe, Nyaminyami and Guruve District Councils in the Zambezi Valley received permission in January 1989 to initiate CAMPFIRE activities. Wildlife management projects were launched in the Omay and the Kanyanti/Gache Communal Lands of Nyaminyami and in Dande Communal Lands of Guruve. Nine other district councils have since received approval for similar management programs, and a further nine have been identified as potential CAMPFIRE sites (see Figure 5.1).

After the first full year of operation, an assessment of the Nyaminyami and Guruve districts' early experiences with CAMPFIRE was conducted by Jansen (1990). The following summarizes the results of this analysis.

Nyaminyami District

The Nayaminyami District Council formed the Nyaminyami Wildlife Management Trust (NWMT) with the objective of administering and managing the wildlife resources of the area for the benefit of local inhabitants. District councillors who are members of the NWMT are the chairmen of Ward Development Committees, and decisions regarding wildlife operations and distribution of revenue and other benefits is made on behalf of their ward constituents by these councillors.[4] In its first year of operation, the Trust established hunting and culling quotas for wildlife, instigated problem animal control (PAC) and anti- poaching activities, developed two impala cropping operations, licensed two safari operators and paid out compensation for economic damages. Table 5.2 summarizes the 1989 financial balance sheet for the NWMT.

A total of Z$319,353 was earned in 1989 (Z$2.1 = US$ 1 in 1989), of which around 85 per cent came from concession and trophy fees from safari hunting and the remainder from sales of meat, hide and skins through the culling and PAC operations. In addition,

Table 5.2: Nyaminyami Wildlife Management Trust: 1989 income and expense statement

		Of which: NWMT [Zimbabwe $]	Zimtrust	Notes
1. Revenue				
1.1	Buffalo Range Safaris	148,349		Concession fee and trophy fees
1.2	Astra Wildlife	117,790		Concession fee and trophy fees
1.3	Mashonaland Hunters	6,048		Gatche Gatche
	Sub-total Safari Hunting:	$272,187		
1.4	Cropping I	11,554		Meat, hide and skin sales – impala
1.5	Cropping II	24,356		Meat, hide and skin sales – impala
	Sub-total Cropping:	$35,910		
1.6	PAC meat & skins	11,256		
1.7	Kapenta fishing	0		To begin in 1990
	Total revenue	$319,353	$0	All receipts for expenditures are available
2. Recurrent expenditure		Of which: NWMT	Zimtrust	
2.1	Cropping costs I	6,478	3,766	
2.2	Cropping costs II	13,848	4,756	
2.3	Staff T & S	2,932	539	Includes camping and cycle allowance
2.4	Staff salaries	12,096		
2.5	Casual wages	811		This includes PAC and buffalo cropping labour
2.6	Transport & equipment hire	636		
2.7	Wildlife compensation	26,681		
2.8	Kapenta licenses	2,400		

2.9	Advertising, publications		208	2,185	
2.10	Vehicle fuel, oil, maint. & repair			114	This may include some non-vehicle
2.11	Vehicle insurance			5,507	fuel and oil
2.12	Kapenta boat operation				
2.13	Ammunition			2,156	
2.14	Stationary & printing		176		
2.15	Equipment & stores		223		
2.16	Bank charges/sundries			1,070	
2.17	Uniforms				
	Total recurrent expd.	$86,581	66,488	20,093	
3. Net revenue		$232,772	$252,865	($20,093)	Revenue less recurrent expenditure
4. Capital expenditure					
4.1	Motor vehicle			57,186	
4.2	Equipment (cropping, camping, W.M.)			53,717	No depreciation in 1989
4.3	Radios			17,037	50% deposit; no depreciation
4.4	Kapenta boats X			43,650	
	Total capital expenditure	$171,590	$0	171,590	
5.	**Total expenditure**	$258,171	$66,488	$191,683	
6.	**Nyaminyami Craft Centre Contribution**			$10,250	
7.	**Surplus (Deficit)**	$61,182	$252,865	($201,933)	Revenue less recurrent & capital costs
8.	**ODA Co-financing**			($100,967)	
	(½ of Total Expenditure)				
9.	**Zimtrust deficit after ODA co-financing**			($100,967)	
	(Zimtrust Cash Contribution)				

Table 5.2: (Continued)

		Of which: NWMT	Zimtrust	Notes
10. Allocation of NWMT funds available		% Distribution:		
10.1 Capital & operating reserve	$29,579	12%		Including depreciation reserve
10.2 District Council Levy	$25,287	10%		10% of NWMT surplus
10.3 Dividends to Wards	$198,000	78%		$16,500 for each of 12 wards
Total	$252,865	100%		
Surplus distributed to each ward:	$16,500			One-twelfth of line 10.3
Estimated no. of households in district:	2,000			
Dividend to each household	$99.00			

Notes: 1 Zimtrust's total expenditure excludes the cost of providing the general manager, and related support services.

Source: Jansen (1990)

ZimTrust financed Z$20,093 of recurrent expenditure as well as Z$191,683 of capital expenditure. This enabled NWMT to run a surplus of Z$252,865; without ZimTrust's support the surplus would have been only Z$61,182.

The surplus of Z$252,865 was divided among distributions to ward level (78 per cent), a reserve fund for capital expenditures (12 per cent) and levies retained by the district council (10 per cent). Each of the 12 Wards received approximately Z$16,500, which were earmarked for a number of small projects ranging from footbridges to a nursery, a clinic, housing for nurses and teachers, a butchery and a beerhall. With approximately 2000 households in the entire district, the total of Z$198,000 distriubted to ward level translates into Z$99 per household, or approximately 15-25 per cent of annual household incomes.

However, other direct benefits also resulted from the programme. First, compensation amounting to Z$27,681 was paid to local inhabitants for crop and animal damage and loss of human life. Such compensation is a major accomplishment as it represented the first legal monetary reward received from wildlife by local residents, and for the first time, saw actual remuneration to offset a "cost" of wildlife conservation. Second, meat from cropping and PAC operations were sold locally at a subsidized price (Z$1 per kg compared to Z$3-5 if transport costs of bringing it to the area are included). The meat sales provided not only nutritional benefits but also represented additional, direct benefits to local inhabitants from wildlife resources.

Guruve District

As the government agency responsible for wildlife management in communal lands, the Department of National Parks and Wildlife Management set up a Guruve District Wildlife Committee and Ward Wildlife Committees along lines similar to the NWMT in Nyaminyami. The assistance of ZimTrust was also obtained in Guruve in implementing CAMPFIRE in the western wards of the district. Activities in 1989 consisted of developing a district- council run safari operation and licensing a private safari hunting concessionaire. No monitoring of or compensation for wildlife damage was instigated.

Table 5.3 indicates the accounting balance sheet and distribution of revenues. The district-council run safari operation (DCSO) earned a net revenue of Z$67,614 from daily charges and trophy fees. However, as ZimTrust's subsidy for recurrent expenditures amounted to Z$98,432, net revenue from the DCSO increased to

Table 5.3: Guruve District Council — wildlife account

	[Z$]	[%]
1. Net revenue		
DC Safari Operation (DCSO)	$67,614	29
Zambesi Hunters	$168,600	71
Total	$236,214	100
2. Allocation of revenue from DCSO		
Net revenue	$67,614	
Plus Zimtrust recurrent cost subsidy	$98,432	
Equals funds available for distribution:	$166,046	100
Distribution to date:		
1. Kanyurira Ward	$47,310	28
2. Chisungo Ward	$4,030	2
3. Chitsunga Ward	$10,000	6
4. Chapota Ward	$0	0
5. Matsiwo Ward	$0	0
6. Neshangwe Ward	$0	0
7. Chiriwo Ward	$0	0
Sub-total funds distributed to wards:	$61,340	37
District council levy	$19,925	12
Reserve Capital Fund	$33,209	20
District Management Fund	$11,291	7
Sub-total: funds retained at D.C. level:	$64,425	39
3. Allocation of revenue from Zambezi Hunters		
Payment to District Council	$168,600	
Distribution to date:		
1. Kanyurira Ward	$0	0
2. Chisunga Ward	$0	0
3. Chitsungo Ward	$0	0
4. Chapota Ward	$0	0
5. Matsiwo Ward	$0	0
6. Neshangwe Ward	$0	0
7. Chiriwo Ward	$0	0
Sub-total: funds distributed to wards:	$0	0
Sub-total: funds retained at D.C. level:	$168,600	100
Memorandum items:		
Value of quotas: [Quota × Govt Z$ Fees]		
D.C. Safari Operation [DCSO]	$94,690	
Zambesi Hunters	$128,975	

Source: Jansen (1990)

Z$1660,046. Added to this are the trophy and concessions fees of Z$168,600 from the private safari operator (Zambezi Hunters).

Only 37 per cent of the revenue from the DCSO was distributed to three wards – Kanyuria, Chisunga and Chitsungo – and none of the revenue from Zambezi Hunters was distributed. The remaining revenue was retained by the district council as a council levy, a "reserve fund" and capital expenditure financing. The council claims that most of the latter revenue has been allocated for building four schools and two clinics in the district. Of the Z$47,310 it has received, Kanyurira Ward will pay each of its 86 households a cash dividend of Z$200, use Z$7,000 to purchase furniture for a newly built classroom block, allocate Z$15,000 to assist construction of a clinic and place the remaining Z$8,110 in a reserve fund. However, both Chitsungo and Chisunga Wards received shares too small to allocate to households (Z$10,000 and Z$4,030 respectively), and will instead use the money for capital projects decided by residents – e.g., a block of toilets for the secondary school in Chitsungo.

Conclusions on the Campfire schemes

The early experiences of the the Nyaminyami and Guruve CAMPFIRE schemes can be assessed both in terms of their *economic* and *participatory* benefits. The primary economic objective is to increase local inhabitants' share of benefits from wildlife so that it is viewed as an economic asset. The primary participatory objective is to increase local communities' control and management over wildlife and wildland resources in the locality.

Jansen (1990) suggests that the Nyaminyami scheme fared well in its first year in achieving its economic objective but less well in fostering community participation. However, ward councillors do appear to be playing an increasing role in determining policy, and communication with households is facilitated by frequent visits by the wildlife manager and game guards who have been informing inhabitants about the wards' wildlife dividends. Nevertheless, in a recent survey most villagers still indicated that they believed that the wildlife belonged to the NWMT and not to them. The next stage in participatory development is the development of management and economic units at the ward and village level that can improve on local management and share in economic benefits from the scheme.

Jansen (1990) argues that the first year of operation at the Guruve scheme was less successful both in economic and participatory terms. Only one ward out of the seven participating in the scheme actually distributed money directly to inhabitants;

four wards received no funds at all. The high retention of funds at the district level does not allow individual residents to feel that they are receiving any benefits from wildlife management in their areas. Except in Kanyurira Ward, the Ward Wildlife Committees were largely ineffectual in representing their constituents.

The establishment of a district-run safari operation also proved to be costly, and only yielded sufficient revenue to be distributed because of the subsidy from ZimTrust. Jansen calculates that, if the DCSO had been equally as efficient as the private operator, it would have yielded revenues of Z$124,000 instead of Z$67,614 – assuming that the revenue from the DCSO is in the same ratio to the value of its quota as was that of Zambezi Hunters. A joint venture with an experienced safari operator, with the district council providing the quota, camp and anti-poaching services would have been a less costly way of initiating safari operations.

In sum, the two schemes are good illustrations of both the pitfalls and the promises offered by CAMPFIRE in Zimbabwe. As several assessments have noted, the main obstacles to be overcome are:

(i).   improving the economic and financial viability of projects, so that they are self-sustaining in the long term;

(ii).   encouraging district councils to devolve genuine authority for wildlife management to wards and villages, particularly concerning the distribution and application of revenues;

(iii). changing perceptions of policy makers and external donors to promote community-based wildlife management where it is economically and ecologically more attractive than conventional agriculture, livestock and even state-run wildlife schemes.[5]

Luangwa Integrated Resource Development Project, Zambia

Whether a CAMPFIRE-like approach can be modified for and adopted in other areas of Africa remains to be seem. As discussed above, other community-based wildlife schemes do exist elsewhere in Africa. Two illustrative examples are in Zambia, the Luangwa Integrated Resource Development Project (LIRDP) and the Administrative Design for the Management (ADMADE) of Game Management Areas (GMAs), which both grew out of the Lupande Development Project (1985-7) in the Luangwa Valley (see Figure 5.2).

ADMADE is strictly a wildlife utilization programme operating in the Lower Lupande hunting block of the valley, with replications beginning in 15 of the remaining 31 GMAs throughout Zambia.

Figure 5.2: LIRDP project location

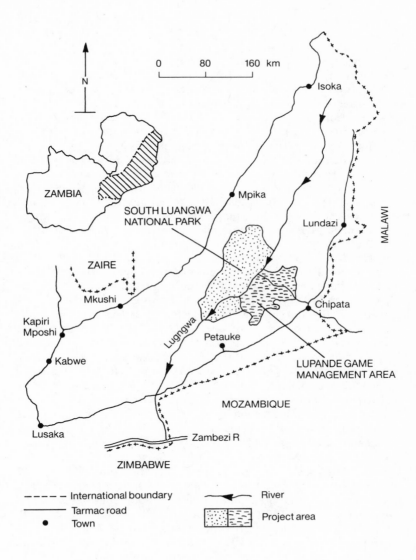

*Source:*Dalal-Clayton (1988)

LIRDP is in contrast supposed to be a multi-sectoral programme for economic development, covering the South Luangwa National Park and the entire Lupande GMA (c 35,000 people) (Lewis, Mwenya and Kaweche, 1989; Lungo, 1990). In addition to wildlife management LIRDP includes programmes in agriculture, forestry, fisheries, water resources and infrastructure, but in practice revenues are virtually dependent on wildlife utilization (currently 60 per cent of total), principally safari fees (50 per cent of total). Other sources of wildlife revenue include park entry fees and guard charges for tour companies, resident hunting permits and sales of meat and other products from culling schemes. ADMADE can obtain revenues from safari hunting fees, any culling schemes and local right-to-hunt fees but not district or national hunting licenses.

Both schemes involve a revolving fund, whereby a proportion of revenues are returned to the local communities. Under ADMADE, 35 per cent of revenues are disbursed to community projects within the GMA; 40 per cent to wildlife management and enforcement programmes within the GMA, mainly the Village Scout Programmes; 15 per cent to national park management; and 10 per cent to the Zambia National Tourist Board. Local employment is directly generated through the Village Scout Programmes and any culling operations, and indirectly through community projects. Local communities have access to meat from culling and from right-to-hunt fees. Under LIRDP, 40 per cent of revenues go to community projects in the Lupande GMA, selected by a local leaders' sub-committee, and 60 per cent are for LIRDP project management and operating costs. LIRDP generates similar employment and consumption benefits as ADMADE. In addition, a local leadership sub-committee (LLS) decides the allocation of off-take quotas for each wildlife species, ensuring that district game licenses for local hunting are equally divided among the six GMA chieftainships.

Success in elephant conservation and reducing poaching has been claimed by both programmes. This has been particularly noticeable with regard to controlling elephant poaching. In the South Luangwa National Park and its adjacent GMAs, a 40 per cent decrease in elephant populations occurred from 1979 to 1985 – principally from illegal hunting. However, the number of elephant carcasses found in a 55 sq km monitoring zone in Lower Lupande has declined from 0.09 per sq km in 1985 to 0.01 in 1987-8, whereas elephant density has increased from 0.07 per sq km to nearly 2 per sq km (Lewis, 1989). LIRDP reports close to 500 illegal hunting arrests and nearly 400 firearms confiscated, with much assistance from local communities in aiding enquiries into illegal hunting activities (LIRDP, 1989).

As both ADMADE and LIRDP operate in the same area (Luangwa

Valley), it is difficult to tell which programme is having an impact on reducing poaching; it is also too early to tell which should be the more relevant model for replication – not just in Zambia but elsewhere in Africa where wildlife is threatened. However, an evaluation of LIRDP was recently conducted (IUCN, 1989), which included an economic assessment of the project's benefits. The following summarizes the results of that assessment.[6]

As noted above, LIRDP was conceptualized and built upon initiatives by the Department of National Parks and Wildlife Services (NPWS) in the Lupande Development Project. Actual implementation of the LIRDP programmes is the hallmark of Phase 2 (1987-92), which seeks to link wildlife resource utilization to the broader objective of integrated resource development of the project area. Specifically, LIRDP seeks to:

(i)   increase revenue earning from sustainable utilization of wildlife resources;

(ii)   channel revenues and other benefits from wildlife exploitation to the local communities;

(iii)   to reduce the conflicts between the management and utilization of wildlife and other forms of land and resource use; and,

(iv)   by the above means reduce the incentives for illegal use of wildlife and thereby in the long run lower the costs of law enforcement.

Thus LIRDP sees itself as as an "experiment" that "extends the approach of the Lupande Development Project to the Lupande Game Management Area as a whole and to the South Luangwa National Park...with a view to applying the extended approach to rural development in other parts of the country" (LIRDP 1987, p. 119).

In essence, the whole economic rationale behind LIRDP is to create the incentives for local communities in the project area to conserve and manage sustainably their resources, especially wildlife resources. In the past revenues from all legal forms of wildlife utilization – hunting, safaris and tourism – accrued to the Government of the Republic of Zambia (GRZ). Little revenue was retained by local communities to be directed to the investments that these communities desired. Moreover, direct exploitation of the wildlife resources for meat and other products by local people became illegal activities, or at least were heavily discouraged through the bureaucratic process of applying for the appropriate licences. This abrogation of traditional rights to exploit wildlife resources coupled by the lack of locally retained revenues from legal wildlife-related activities meant that local people had little incentive to support these activities and every incentive to hunt illegally. Legal, sustainable management of wildlife was no longer an economic option. The long-term aim of LIRDP is to revive this option.

Although early project documents refer to and actually calculate the potential gross revenues to be earned from all forms of wild-life utilization in the South Luangwa National Park (SLNP) and the Lupande Game Management Area (GMA), no feasibility study involving some form of cost-benefit analysis of this economic potential has ever been conducted.[7] The project nevertheless has demonstrated that significant revenues can at least be made from safari hunting, and regularly reviews the revenue-earning potential from wildlife utilization (see Table 5.5, below).

Table 5.4 shows actual and estimated expenditures for LIRDP and their breakdown by programme activity in its first years of operation. Spending from LIRDP's own generated resources is excluded. Late funding of the project (September 1988) meant that LIRDP did not spend all the money allocated for 1988.

LIRDP expenditures appear fully in line with the original project proposal (LIRDP, 1987). The highest categories of expenditure are for the road development programme, the wildlife management pro-gramme, the agricultural programme and headquarters' develop-ment. In 1988/9 the project was forced to spend around US$45,000 of its funds on emergency repairs on the Chipata–Mfuwe road, even though this is currently outside of the project's sphere of responsibility.

Figures supplied by LIRDP staff indicate that in 1988/9 capital expenditures accounted for around 65 per cent of total actual expenditures. This is again in line with proposed spending plans. From the project proposal document (LIRDP, 1987), it is clear that most capital spending will be complete by 1992, and recurrent expenditures will dominate – i.e., they will comprise over 90 per cent of total expenditures in that year. This suggests that at the end of Phase 2 LIRDP annual expenditures will be at least US$2 million just to keep programmes and staff functioning.

Table 5.5 indicates actual revenues accrued by LIRDP over the 1988-9 period. Revenues from wildlife utilization, and particularly safari hunting, overwhelmingly dominate. For example, wildlife accounts for well over 60 per cent of all revenues received to date. Safari hunting appears to contribute to over 50 per cent of total revenues; however, this figure may not be a true representation of the full contribution. As Table 5.5 records the actual receipts of revenue by LIRDP, the contribution of safari hunting might be under-represented, as not all revenues have been recovered from the Wildlife Conservation Revolving Fund. The restructuring of the

Table 5.4: Actual and estimated expenditures of LIRDP (in US$)

Exchange rates: 1988 and 1989: US$ 1.00 = Z$8.00   1990: US$ 1.00 = Z$ 16.00

Activity	1988 Allocation a/	1988 Expenditure a/	1989 Expenditure b/	1990 Expenditure c/
LIRDP HQ Development	296,750	241,992	584,625 d/	350,000 e/
Road Development Programme	547,500	100,648	366,375	750,000
Manpower Development Programme	34,750	1,870	103,125	100,000
CBRU Organizations f/	0	0	50,000	10,000
Small Scale Enterprises	0	0	40,000	100,000
Tourism Development Programme	0	0	0	20,000
Hunting Development Programme	0	0	0	30,000
Agricultural Research Programme	57,500	45,305	41,000	100,000
Agricultural Extension Programme	195,750	229,330	224,625	425,000
Soils Survey and Erosion Study	20,375	7,324	45,625	7,000
Electric fencing	18,250	0	18,250	10,000
Tsetse Control Programme	42,500	21,581	15,250	10,000
Womens' Programme	37,500	11,987	55,375	33,000
Co-operative Programme	23,750	17,323	14,750	5,000
Forestry Programme	51,000	30,216	93,500	110,000
Fisheries Programme	11,875	0	12,500	30,000
Water Development Programme	11,875	0	18,750	50,000
Wildlife Management Programme	734,750	392,014	729,375	500,000
Works and Supply Unit	150,375	119,769	98,750	75,000
Monitoring and Evaluation Unit	32,125	28,874	25,625	35,000
Community Projects g/	6,625	24,451	0	0
Total	**2,273,250**	**1,272,682**	**2,537,500**	**2,750,000**

a/ Actual expenditure less than allocated expenditure in 1988 because of late disbursement of funds (September 1988).
b/ Expected expenditure for 1989.   c/ Budgeted expenditure for 1990.
d/ Includes Mambwe headquarters construction of $40,000.   e/ Includes Mambwe headquarters construction of $100,000.
f/ Community based Resource-use Organizations.   g/ After 1988 community projects funded by LIRDP own resources.

Source: Author's calculations for IUCN (1989).

safari hunting industry by the Ministry of Tourism in 1989 also resulted in losses of revenues owing to delays.

Table 5.5: Actual revenues of LIRDP (in US$)

Exchange rates
1 January to 31 Dec., 1988: US$ 1.00 = Z$8.00
1 January to 31 May, 1989: US$ 1.00 = Z$ 9.00
1 June to 31 August, 1989: US$ 1.00 = Z$ 11.00 b/

Activity	1988 (1/1-31/12)	1989 (1/1-31/5)	1989 (1/6-31/8)	Cumulative revenue
Wildlife	31,522	45,823	21,865	99,210
Safari hunting	30,272	41,793	11,119	83,184
Culling schemes	1,250	0	1,250	2,500
Park entry fees	0	2,303	8,730	11,033
Other c/	0	1,727	765	2,493
Fisheries	0	40	0	40
Forestry	0	0	0	0
Agriculture	2,467	8,276	19,429	30,172
Loan recoveries	1,444	57	0	1,501
Sale of maize/mealie-meal	1,022	7,944	19,429	28,395
Other	0	276	0	276
Works and Supply Unit	0	40	0	40
Other d/	7,752	15,071	5,722	28,544
Total	41,740	69,250	47,016	158,006

a/ Based on actual revenue receipts as of September 1989. Sums may not add due to rounding.
b/ Average over three months.
c/ Includes resident hunting permits and guard charges.
d/ Interest credited to LIRDP account.

Source: Author's calculations for IUCN (1989).

The direct revenues to LIRDP from tourism through National Park entry fees, are relatively small, with a very minor additional contribution through guard charges. In addition to instituting guard charges, LIRDP would like to increase revenues from tourism further through a non-resident entry fee of US$5.00 per day and a tourism levy on lodges and operators (LIRDP, 1989). The local tourist industry, as represented by the Hotels and Catering Association of Zambia, Luangwa Branch, has expressed concern over the impact of such measures on the competitiveness and economic viability of their industry. The Association is even more alarmed over the failure of LIRDP to consult and work with the industry on designing an appropriate and economic system of levies. For its part, LIRDP has expressed willingness to improve liaison with the industry, yet as a net subsidizer of tourism (through road grading, escort scouts, anti-poaching costs, etc.) LIRDP insists that it must effectively increase cost recovery from tour operators to avoid the collapse of services when external funding to the project ends (LIRDP, 1989). However, further problems and confusion have been created through the imposition by the Ministry of Tourism of a non- resident entry fee of US$8.00 in January 1989 without prior notification of LIRDP or tour operators.

Sales of meat and other products from culling schemes are a current and potential source of revenues. The Nyamaluma scheme, after five years of operation, is currently earning sufficient revenue to cover recurrent costs but not expected future capital requirements. The new scheme at Kamwenje in Nsefu has just begun selling meat only. Establishing culling schemes as viable commercial enterprises is often difficult. The success of Nyamaluma may be due to special factors, such as low human population density compared to high wildlife species density, which may not be so favourable elsewhere.[8] A study from Tanzania indicates that the profitability of culling depends on successful exploitation of both meat and other products (e.g., skin), and that there are no economies of scale in such operations (ITC, 1989).

After wildlife, agriculture is the next main revenue contributor. Most agricultural revenues are mainly from sales of maize and mealie meal, with loan recoveries also significant. Thus the agricultural programme is "developing in the direction of an area-based parastatal authority co-ordinating all aspects of resource use and production, and recycling of all revenues, i.e. from credit service charges" (LIRDP, 1989). Hence, sales of maize and mealie meal, as well as loan charges, are an attempt by LIRDP to recover some of the costs of credit, supply of inputs, purchase, storage, transport, and marketing and/or processing.

Revenues from fishing, forestry and works and supply (i.e., workshop charges for private customers) are currently insignificant. The project has high hopes that substantial revenues can be raised through licence and concession fees for forestry and the sale of honey and wax, but timber exploitation must proceed with care until the ability of forest resources to sustain increased exploitation is assured.

In sum, it is clear that wildlife utilization, and particularly safari hunting, will continue to be the major contributor to LIRDP revenues in the near future. These revenues are expected to be expanded through further development of safari hunting and the establishment of LIRDP's own hunting company. Hunting licenses will make a greater contribution as wildlife recovers. Revenues from tourism can also be expected to increase, subject to successful resolution of differences with the Ministry of Tourism and the industry. Sales of meat and other products from culling schemes are also anticipated to raise revenues, subject to the economics of culling. Agriculture can also make a contribution to the cost recovery of its extension programme. Fishing revenues might provide a very modest source of revenues. It is anticipated that revenues from forestry will develop slowly, until the economics of sustainable exploitation are determined.

A cashflow analysis of the LIRDP programme is presented in Table 5.6 to indicate the financial position of the project. The analysis must be considered provisional, as the analysis was conducted when the project was effectively only in its first years of operation. Thus only costs in year one are based on actual expenditures, and given the delays in revenue receipts, the revenues for years 0 and 1 are based on expected earnings suggested in a recent progress report (LIRDP, 1989). Costs and revenues for the other years are therefore based entirely on projections.

Three scenarios are projected in Table 5.6. All three assume the same cost streams, whereby future costs after 1992 are assumed to decline by 5 per cent in real terms due to the success of wildlife management and anti-poaching activities, completion of some programmes and improved efficiency. The difference in the scenarios, therefore, lies in the rate of growth of revenues in *real terms*, i.e. after allowing for inflation since 1988/9.

In terms of *financial sustainability*, the analysis shows that even with real growth of revenues of 5 per cent, the project will not be self-financing before its 15th year (Scenario 1). An extremely high real rate of growth of revenues of 20 per cent must be sustained in order to achieve self-financing by the 10th year (Scenario 3), which is well after Phase 2 ends. A middle projection achieves financial sustainability by the 12th year (Scenario 2).

Table 5.6 also includes calculations of the net present worth (NPV) at a 10 per cent discount rate, and of the financial rate of return (IRR) for each scenario. These calculations indicate how LIRDP compares as a financial investment. Thus only Scenario 3 compares favourably. However, LIRDP should by no means be judged solely as a financial investment; its purpose is not just to raise revenues but to increase incomes and other economic and social benefits in the area. Thus the NPV and IRR results in Table 5.6 are less important for assessing LIRDP's performance.

Table 5.6: Cash flow analysis of LIRDP (in thousand US$ at 1988/9 prices)

	Scenario 1			Scenario 2			Scenario 3		
Year a/	Cost b/	Revenue c/	NetRevenue	Cost b/	Revenue c/	NetRevenue	Cost b/	Revenue c/	NetRevenue
0	2228	130	-2098	2228	130	-2098	2228	130	-2098
1	2538	200	-2338	2538	200	-2338	2538	200	-2338
2	2750	400	-2350	2750	400	-2350	2750	400	-2350
3	2370	600	-1770	2370	600	-1770	2370	600	-1770
4	2370	800	-1570	2370	800	-1570	2370	800	-1570
5	2251	840	-1411	2251	880	-1371	2251	960	-1291
6	2138	882	-1256	2138	968	-1170	2138	1152	-986
7	2032	926	-1105	2032	1065	-967	2032	1382	-649
8	1930	972	-958	1930	1171	-759	1930	1659	-271
9	1833	1021	-812	1833	1288	-545	1833	1991	157
10	1742	1072	-670	1742	1417	-325	1742	2389	647
11	1655	1126	-529	1655	1559	-96	1655	2867	1212
12	1572	1182	-390	1572	1715	143	1572	3440	1868
13	1493	1241	-252	1493	1886	393	1493	4128	2634
14	1419	1303	-116	1419	2075	656	1419	4953	3535
15	1348	1368	20	1348	2282	935	1348	5944	4596
16	1280	1437	156	1280	2511	1230	1280	7133	5852
17	1216	1509	292	1216	2762	1545	1216	8559	7343
18	1156	1584	428	1156	3038	1882	1156	10271	9116
19	1098	1663	565	1098	3342	2244	1098	12326	11228
20	1043	1746	703	1043	3676	2633	1043	14791	13748
	37461	22002	-15458	37461	33768	-3695	37461	86074	48614

Scenario 1	Scenario 2	Scenario 3
NPV(10%): -10738	NPV(10%): -8266	NPV(10%): 1810
IRR: -14.68%	IRR: -1.95%	IRR: 11.38%

a/ Year 0 is October 1988 to September 1989.   b/ Costs in year 0 are actual 1988 allocations less Chipata–Mfuwe road maintenance ($45,000): costs in years 1-2 are the 1989 and 1990 budget estimates: costs in years 3-4 are the remainder of the NORAD grant of $12.3 mn: costs in years 5-20 are assumed to decline by 5% annually.   c/ Assumes $200,000 increases in years 2-4 and 5% real growth after year 4.   d/ Assumes $200,000 increases in years 2-4 and 10% real growth after year 4.   e/ Assumes $200,000 increases in years 2-4 and 20% real growth after year 4.

Source: Author's calculations for IUCN (1989).

In conclusion, financial sustainability of LIRDP by the end of Phase 2 is not a realistic proposition. After 1992, the project will either have to receive additional external funding and/or substantially reduce its expenditures, most likely through rationalization of some programmes.

In addition to the revenues raised, the *total economic* benefits of the project include:

(i)   the "narrow" *economic* (e.g., income and production), *environmental* (e.g., resource rehabilitation and improvement) and *social* (e.g., health, education and nutrition) benefits generated by LIRDP programmes in the project area;

(ii)   the economic, environmental and social benefits generated by the Local Leaders' Sub-committee re-investing its 40 per cent share of LIRDP revenues in community projects; and,

(iii)   the "external" benefits (e.g., accruing outside the project area or to parties other than the intended beneficiaries) of both of the above forms of investment. Examples of these would be the increased profits of tour operators, savings by the government of Zambia on famine relief to Luangwa, increased wildlife in adjacent GMAs and so forth.

Ideally, the generation of these total benefits must be weighed against their costs. As noted above, a financial or economic analysis is the best method of assessing the total net benefits of LIRDP to the area. If the discounted net benefits are positive, then LIRDP has succeeded in its objective of *economic sustainability.* In the absence of such an analysis and given that the project is in its early stages, it is too early to determine whether LIRDP or any of its component programmes will be economically sustainable.

An important point to note is that although some of the total economic benefits will involve directly marketed goods and services (e.g., meat sold from culling schemes, sales of hybrid maize and vegetables, and so on), other benefits are not marketable (own consumption of hunted meat, food grown for subsistence, etc.). The latter set of benefits may actually be extremely important, especially in the context of overall "sustainable" development of the area. The inter-relationships among benefits in the form of project revenues, marketable economic benefits to the community and non-marketable benefits are therefore crucial.

Greater attention appears to be paid to these inter-relationships in some LIRDP programmes as opposed to others. For example, in wildlife utilization, the quota system yields project revenues from safari hunting, district licences and sales of culled meat. But by allocating district licences to local hunters, as well as quotas for crop protection and special celebrations the system is also catering for local income and meat consumption needs. And, of course, 40 per cent of the revenue generated is returned to the community through the revolving fund. The issue of whether the distribution of these benefits is correct, of course, needs to be examined further. But the system does at least recognize the inter-relationships among the different types of benefits and appears to be flexible enough to allow for change in the distribution of benefits. For example, a new system of pricing and distributing culled meat has recently been suggested by the Local Leadership Sub-committee to ensure that local communities have better access to this benefit.

In contrast, the credit, marketing and processing activities of the agricultural programme seem to have been conducted with little attention given to the impact on farmers' incomes, food requirements, soil erosion, water use, allocation of labour and other important economic, environmental and social impacts. Basic information on labour and resource use, production costs and returns seem not to be routinely consulted, even though such information is collected and the project's monitoring and evaluation unit produced a report on crop surveys and a report on the impact of horticultural schemes (Kalyocha, 1988a and 1988b).

For example, the report on horticultural schemes (Kalyocha, 1988a) noted problems of:

(i)   over-supply of one or two commodities at one time and at one place;
(ii) lack of transport to take commodities to high demand areas;
iii) generally lack of marketing know-how by the majority of the scheme members;
(iv) crop damage by wildlife; and
(v)   water shortages in the dry season.

In sum, despite impressive efforts to raise revenues – especially from wildlife utilization – LIRDP is unlikely to be self-financing by the end of Phase 2. Additional external financing and/or reducing costs by rationalizing programmes will be required.

However, LIRDP is not just about maximizing project revenues. Its primary objective should be furthering economic sustainability by maximizing the total *net benefits* to the area of LIRDP activities. It is premature to conclude whether or not LIRDP is succeeding in this objective.

In general, efforts by the project to increase net revenues from wildlife utilization have been admirable. However, efforts to increase

revenues by either increasing overall utilization or by increasing the
share of revenue-earning wildlife uses (e.g., safari hunting, culling)
should proceed cautiously. In this regard, a project progress report
correctly identified four points that need to be emphasized (LIRDP,
1989 p. 27):

(i)   the objective of sustainable use must remain paramount and
       political pressures to increase quotas must be resisted;
(ii)   the technical capacity to estimate quotas through survey work
       must be improved, particularly to avoid over-harvesting key
       species such as buffalo, and to avoid under-harvesting com-
       mon species such as warthog;
(iii) conflicts between safari hunting, district license hunting and
       culling must be reduced by liaison and co-operation between
       the various participants; and,
(iv)   conflicts between wildlife utilization in the GMA and tourist
       use of the park must be resolved by research and liaison
       between the various parties and clear zonation of use.

The same approach must be firmly established with regard to
other revenue-raising initiatives, such as in forestry and fishing.
In particular, timber exploitation must proceed with care until
the ability of forest resources to sustain increased exploitation
is assured, the economic benefits and costs of exploitation are
established and proper account is taken of benefits derived from
use of minor forest products and other local uses of forests.

Agricultural activities should by all means be encouraged to
recover costs, but it should be kept firmly in mind that the objective
of agriculture is not simply to raise revenues or even to perform
marketing and credit functions but to improve the economic,
social and environmental benefits to the local community through
improved farming sytems and opportunities.

To date, the main achievements of LIRDP have been the reduction in commercial poaching; strengthening the effectiveness of
game patrols and scouts; the concern and action of food security in an area of chronic shortage; the decentralized decision-
making structure; and the mechanism for retention of revenues
in and for the local community. However, LIRDP cannot afford
to be complacent that, by distributing 40 per cent of its revenues to local leaders to disburse, the project is automatically
fulfilling its task of ensuring economic sustainability as well as
greater community participation. People's participation in the
project could be further strengthened by focusing on the ward
level and co-operative development, as well faciliating the role of
the Local Leaders' Sub-committee as a body truly representative

of local communities. The objectives of greater local co-operation and reduced poaching could also be simultaneously encouraged through using the skills within the project as active managers and monitors of wildlife populations, and not simply as informers (IUCN, 1989).

Conclusion

The ultimate aim of community based wildlife utilization is to improve the co-operation of local communities to participate in the conservation of wildlife resources. The rationale is simple: local people are the most familiar with the area and the wildlife within it; the failure to ensure their co-operation will make them indifferent and perhaps hostile to conservation efforts, which they will see as being "imposed from outside". What's more, most communities claim a traditional right to exploit their local wildlife resources. Hunting wildlife for meat is one of the most important of these "rights", not only because the meat may be the only source of supplemental protein but also because hunting is a culturally significant craft – often with mystical links to tribal ancestors. Local hunters in the community often have an important social function and status.[9]

The supression of a community's rights to some exploitation of the local wildlife, or a share in any of the proceeds resulting from wildlife utilization, may actually encourage local people to hunt illegally or to support outsiders engaged in these activities. Illegal hunting for meat may particularly become widespread for poorer communities or in areas where livestock rearing is difficult (e.g. owing to tsetse fly infestation). The alienation of communities from their local wildlife may lead to direct conflicts. Large migratory animals may increasingly be seen as a costly "nuisance", inflicting extensive crop damage and occupying potentially arable land. Local communities may view wildlife conservation as asking them to put up with these costs with little benefit or compensation in return.

The history of wildlife conservation efforts in Africa has been dominated by a universal approach of divorcing local communities from any control or rights of exploitation of their wildlife coupled by law enforcement efforts by the central and local authorities (notably the national parks and wildlife departments) to "protect" the wildlife. Wildlife "utilization", except perhaps for tourism and limited safari hunting, has been discouraged, and any safari and tourist revenues have gone to the state, not to local communities. The state's objective is to manage wildlife for the benefit of the whole nation, whereas the local communities are denied access to protected areas and even to the right to hunt in areas neighbouring them. The incentives for the local population to engage in or assist poaching increase, while their incentives to co-operate in reducing poaching or aiding conservation efforts decrease.

Community-based wildlife development represents an important departure from this approach. However, as the two case studies in this chapter have shown, the economic and participatory benefits of these schemes need to be carefully developed and continuously monitored in order to succeed in the twin objectives of ensuring that local communities begin viewing wildlife as an economic asset worth maintaining and that they have sufficient control over decisions to manage the resource and the income it generates.

This requires greater understanding both in national and international policy debates over the role of community based wildlife management. In national policy debates, the potential economic role of wildlife and wildland resources and their value to local communities must receive careful consideration alongside more conventional rural development options such as agriculture and livestock raising. As both the Zambian and Zimbabwean experiences show, a commitment by national policy makers to community-based wildlife management and de-centralization of control over revenues is a key condition for success. Similarly, in international policy debates decisions to control or ban trade in wildlife products should not be implemented without taking into account the implications for national and community-based wildlife development in Africa. For example, one reason cited by Zimbabwe, Zambia and other Southern African countries in opposing the decision by the Convention on International Trade in Endangered Species to ban all trade in elephant ivory is their fear of the implications to manage their elephant populations sustainably through community-based development schemes.[10]

In sum, as argued by Bell (1984), the whole approach of community-based wildlife development should be to reconcile conservation goals of species and natural system preservation with the individual aspirations of the people concerned by integration, negotiation and participation. Economic and political commitment to this approach at all levels is essential if it is to succeed.

References

Barbier, E.B., J.C. Burgess, T.M. Swanson, and D.W. Pearce, *Elephants, Economics and Ivory*, [London: Earthscan, 1990].

Bell, R.H.V., "Traditional Use of Wildlife Resources in Protected Areas", in R.H.V. Bell and E. McShane-Caluzi (eds.), *Conservation and Wildlife Management in Africa*, Proceedings of a Workshop Organized by the US Peace Corps, Kasungu National Park, Malawi, October [Washington, DC: US Peace Corps, 1984].

Bell, R.H.V. and E. McShane-Caluzi, E. (eds.) *Conservation and Wildlife Management in Africa*, Proceedings of a Workshop Organized by the US Peace Corps, Kasungu National Park, Malawi, October [Washington, DC: US Peace Corps, 1984].

Child, B. "Assessment of Wildlife Utilization as a Land Use Option in the Semi-Arid Rangeland of Southern Africa", in A. Kiss (ed.), *Living with Wildlife: Wildlife Resource Management: Wildlife Resource Management with Local Participation in Africa*, Technical Paper No. 130 [Washington, DC: The World Bank, 1990].

Cummings, D.H.M., *Communal Land Development and Wildlife Utilisation: Potential and Options in Northern Namibia*, Project Paper No. 14, WWF Multispecies Project, Harare [1990a].

Cummings, D.H.M., *Developments in Game Ranching and Wildlife Utilization in East and Southern Africa*, Project Paper No. 13, WWF Multispecies Project, Harare [1990b].

Cummings, D.H.M., *Wildlife Conservation in African Parks: Progress, Problems & Prescriptions*, Project Paper No. 15, WWF Multispecies Project, Harare [1990c].

Cummings, D.H.M., *Wildlife Products and the Market Place: A View from Southern Africa*, Project Paper No. 12, WWF Multispecies Project, Harare [1990d].

Dalal-Clayton, B., *Wildlife Working for Sustainable Development*, Gatekeeper Series No. SA9, Sustainable Agriculture Programme, [London: IIED, 1988].

International Trade Centre, *Report on Development and Promotion of Wildlife Utilization*, Ministry of Lands, Natural Resources and Tourism, Government of Tanzania, Dar Es-Salaam [1989].

IUCN, *First Review Mission – Luangwa Integrated Resource Development Project* [Switzerland: IUCN, Gland, 1989].

Jansen, D.J., *Sustainable Wildlife Utilization in the Zambezi Valley of Zimbabwe: Economic, Ecological and Political Tradeoffs*, Project Paper No. 10, WWF Multispecies Project, Harare [1990].

Kalyocha, G.C.K., "An Examination of the Impact of Horticultural Schemes and Women Clubs under Luangwe Integrated Resource Development Project", *mimeo.*, Monitoring and Evaluation Unit, LIRDP, Mfuwe, Zambia [1988a].

Kalyocha, G.C.K., "Report on the 1988 Crop and Plot Management Survey", *mimeo.*, Monitoring and Evaluation Unit, Mfuwe, Zambia [1988b].

Kiss, A. (ed.), *Living with Wildlife: Wildlife Resource Management:*

Wildlife Resource Management with Local Participation in Africa, Technical Paper No. 130 [Washington, DC, World Bank, 1990].

Larsen, T. and F.B. Lungu, *Preparation Report on the Luangwa Integrated Resource Development Project (LIRDP)*, LIRDP, Chipata, Zambia [1989].

Lawson, D. and P. Mafela, "Botswana Wildlife Managment Areas" in A. Kiss (ed.), *Living with Wildlife: Wildlife Resource Management: Wildlife Resource Management with Local Participation in Africa*, Technical Paper No. 130 [Washington, DC, World Bank, 1990].

Lewis, D.M., A.N. Mwenya, and G.B. Kaweche, "African Solutions to Wildlife Problems in Africa: Insights From a Community Based Project in Zambia", *mimeo.*, ADMADE Project, National Parks and Wildlife Service, Government of Zambia, Lupande [1989].

LIRDP, *Luangwa Integrated Resource Development Project: The Phase 2 Programme*, LIRDP, Chipata, Zambia [1987].

LIRDP, *LIRDP Progress Report: October 1988-September 1989*, LIRDP, Chipata, Zambia [1989].

Marks, S.A., *The Imperial Lion: Human Dimensions of Wildlife Management in Central Africa*, [Boulder, Colorado: Westview Press, 1983].

Martin, R.B., "Communal Area Management Plan for Indigenous Resources (Project CAMPFIRE)" in R.H.V. Bell and E. McShane-Caluzi (eds), *Conservation and Wildlife Management in Africa*, Proceedings of a Workshop Organized by the US Peace Corps, Kasungu National Park, Malawi, October [Washington, DC, US Peace Corps, 1984].

Martin, R.B., *Communal Areas Management Programme for Indigenous Resources (CAMPFIRE)*, CAMPFIRE Working Document No. 1/86, Department of National Parks and Wildlife, Government of Zimbabwe, Harare [1986].

Murindagomo, F., "CAMPFIRE Programme (Dande Communal Lands) - Zimbabwe", in A.Kiss (ed.), *Living with Wildlife: Wildlife Resource Management: Wildlife Resource Management with Local Participation in Africa*, Technical Paper No. 130 [Washington, DC, World Bank, 1990].

Murphee, M.W., "Decentralizing the Proprietorship of Wildlife Resources in Zimbabwe's Communal Lands", *mimeo.*, Centre for Applied Social Sciences, University of Zimbabwe, Harare [1990].

World Bank, *Malawi – Economic Report on Environmental Policy*, Southern African Division [Washington, DC: World Bank, 1991].

The Zimbabwe Trust, The Department of National Parks and Wildlife Management and The CAMPFIRE Association *People, Wildlife and Natural Resources – The CAMPFIRE Approach to Rural Development in Zimbabwe*, The Zimbabwe Trust, Harare [1990].

Notes

1. For reviews of this history, see Bell and McShane (1984); Cummings (1990c and 1990d); and Kiss (1990). For an in-depth study of the history of a particular region, e.g. Luangwa Valley

in Zambia, see Marks (1983).

2. There are notable exceptions to this attitude by African governments. As noted by Cumming (1990d), for the last 30 years Zimbabwe's policy has sought to increase the value of wildlife as an economic asset to land holders outside of the national park and reserve system. The approach to communal lands will be discussed in the case study of campfire, below. Economic aspects of the Zimbabwean policy towards encouraging privately owned commercial game ranching operations as a viable alternative to livestock raising is discussed by (Child, 1990; Cumming, 1990b; and Jansen, 1990a). In recent years, both approaches have been increasingly adopted by Zambia, Botswana, South Africa and now other Southern AFrican countries.

3. Over the period of 1980–7 the value of the Zimbabwean dollar fell from Z$0.643 to Z$1.661 per US dollar.

4. In Zimbabwe, each district is subdivided into approximately 10–20 wards with around 5–10 villages per ward. An average village contains about 100 families.

5. For recent reviews of these issues see Jansen (1990); Murphree (1990); and Zimbabwe Trust et al (1990).

6. The assessment was conducted by the author for IUCN, 1989.

7. In some cases, the lack of any proper financial analysis (see 1. above) has led to misleading statements in earlier documents. For example, Larsen and Lungu (1985 p. 46) state that "if we invest between $0.5 and 1 million per year in anti-poaching and wildlife research management in SLNP and Lupande GMA, we will get a return which is almost tenfold . . . between $5.7 and 7.5 million." However, the authors fail to add in the additional costs of expanded tourist facilities (including roads), administration and logistics, which are essential to achieving these maximum revenue benefits. More importantly, whereas the majority of these costs are capital items and weighted towards the early years of the project, as LIRDP has discovered, it takes a significant period of time to build up wildlife utilization revenues to the maximum level suggested by Larsen and Lungu. A simple financial analysis, with appropriate discount rates would have given a more accurate picture of the situation. In the absence of such an analysis, statements such as "the large increase in revenues alone justifies investments of the size proposed in this document" (Larsen and Lungu, 1985) are presumptuous, and give a false impression of the actual economics of the project.

8. Even so, the Nyamaluma scheme initially experienced substantial losses in income through the breakdown of vehicles and an outbreak of anthrax.

9. For an extensive study of the cultural significance of local hunting see Marks (1983).

10. For a review of the economic issues surrounding the ivory trade and the CITES ban, as well as the implications for community-based wildlife management, see Barbier et al, 1990.

6

WILDLIFE TOURISM

J. Barnes, J. Burgess, D. Pearce

Wildlife-based tourism is a non-consumptive means of using wild resources to benefit human populations. Sensitively managed, wildlife tourism offers a nation the chance to develop a high value-added industry that simultaneously protects wildlife by removing, or reducing, the incentive to develop land for agriculture or other uses and/or exploit wildlife for consumptive uses. There are four important caveats that are required for "sensitive management" of wildlife tourism:

(i)   the management of wildlife tourism needs to be sensitive to the *scale* of tourism, which can both threaten wildlife and give rise to stress in animal populations. In addition, the *type* of tourism can threaten wildlife: birdwatchers tend to be less obtrusive than watchers of animals. The effect of the foreign cultures introduced, and the capital derived from, wildlife tourism on local populations also needs to be considered;

(ii)   incomes from tourism need to filter down to local people whose land and interests are affected in one way or the other. This is necessary in order to create adequate incentives for local populations to protect lands and wildlife. Whilst significant financial capital is generated by tourism, most is normally spent on transportation, lodging, food and supplies, with little accruing to local economies in and around tourist sites. "Rent seeking" and "rent dispersion" are common problems within the wildlife tourism industry (Barbier et al., 1990). However, indirect benefits from tourism – while a relatively small share of the total value of tourism – can have significant beneficial impacts on the local economy. These indirect benefits may take the form of wages from employment, compensation fees, or development of local social services;

(iii) where wildlife tourism occurs on reserve lands, the goals of the park management must be furthered by the economic gains from the tourist industry and not counteracted by tourist activity in order for the park management to support this use of wildlife;

(iv)   to ensure the long-term success of wildlife tourism in developing countries, the tourism industry needs to be sensitive to the wide range of potential tourists. Wildlife tourism needs to be accessible to visitors from a wide range of economic status and regions, and not just confined to the rich or foreign (Robinson and Redford, 1991).

In contrast to most consumptive uses of wildlife resources that lead to small commercial or subsistence economies, a well managed wildlife tourist industry can lead to relatively high returns – often rivalling other major sources of national income, especially in developing countries. International tourism offers substantial returns for developing nations that place a high premium on earning foreign exchange. Estimates of the expenditures for wildlife tourism are difficult to come by. The World Tourism Organization estimates the annual expenditure from all international tourism at around $195 billion (United Nations Environment Programme, 1991). Domestic tourism -i.e tourism within a nation by resident nationals – is probably of the order of $1.5 *trillion*. Swanson (1991) estimates that 11 per cent of the exports of Sub-Saharan Africa come from tourism; 13 per cent in Latin America and 9 per cent in south and east Asia. What proportion of these revenues is accounted for wildlife and natural habitat- based tourism (ecotourism) is not known, but it is significant that "special interest" tourism – tourism linked to some specific purpose such as wildlife or adventure – is estimated to be growing at some 10-15 per cent per annum (p.a.) compared to the 8 per cent p.a for mass tourism (Dixon and Sherman, 1990).

Table 6.1 shows figures of visitors to countries where wildlife is a major attraction. The table shows that Kenya attracts some 500,000 overseas visitors a year. Some part of this total will reflect business visitors but most are tourists. Particularly significant in Table 6.1 is the high visitor number for Kenya compared to the very low figures for Tanzania, Malawi and Uganda, even though species availability and diversity is as great if not greater than in Kenya. The implication is that the three former countries are forgoing substantial foreign exchange receipts through underdevelopment of their wildlife based tourist industry. Wildlife tourism generates around $400 million p.a in Kenya, the second largest source of foreign exchange. In Ecuador, around 100,000 people (national and international) visit Cotacachi-Cayapas Ecological Reserve, compared to some 33,000 who go to the Galapagos Islands. Tourism is Ecuador's second largest foreign exchange earner.

**Table 6.1: Numbers of international visitors to
countries with major wildlife attractions**

(1985, 000s)

Reference/Country		Rank
Spain	43,235	1
Botswana	327	78
Cameroun	130	109
Costa Rica	262	84
Ecuador	238	92
Kenya	541	67
Malawi	44	138
Malaysia	2,906	24
Tanzania	59	129
Uganda	14	164
Zambia	144	144
Zaire	35	146
Zimbabwe	320	79

Source: United Nations Environment Programme 1991, Table 7.9.

This chapter investigates the economics of the wildlife tourist industry, using the example of Botswana. The value of wildlife attractions is often highly significant, as demonstrated in three additional case studies – the viewing value of elephants in Kenya, the value of ecotourism at a tropical rainforest site in Costs Rica and the "recreational value" of Khao Yai National Park, Thailand. The value of ecotourism can have important implications for the relative attractiveness of non-consumptive use of wildlife resources compared to alternative consumptive uses of wildlands and animals. The general thesis of this chapter is that wildlife tourism offers both a major economic potential for developing countries, even allowing for the necessary investment in infrastructure, and an opportunity to manage sustainably wildlife resources.

Wildlife tourism in Botswana

The macroeconomic importance of wildlife tourism

Surprisingly few studies exist of the wildlife tourist industry in terms of its macroeconomic importance. Table 6.2 shows the results of a detailed analysis of the industry in Botswana. Most of Botswana's wildlife resource tends to be concentrated in the nation's national parks and game reserves, which occupy some 17 per cent of the surface area of the country. A further 21 per cent of the land area is covered by "wildlife management areas" (WMAs) where wildlife may be managed as an economic resource. The wildlife regions have fairly well defined geographical divisions: the Kgalagadi region, representative of the south-west arid biome; the Okavango/Chobe region containing a rich fauna with Central African elements; the Makgadikgadi region, and the Limpopo region which contains south-east lowland faunal elements.

Table 6.2: Wildlife tourism in the macroeconomy of Botswana 1986

(Million Pula 1990)

	Current investment	Gross output	Gross value added
Game viewing:			
mobile safaris	1.3	3.6	1.3
lodges/ camps	13.6	23.2	8.5
motels	0.5	0.8	0.4
Hunting:			
safari hunting	1.4	9.2	5.0
Support services:	5.6	15.6	3.2
Total	21.4	52.4	18.4

Source: Barnes 1990a, 1990b

The wildlife industry has several distinct components of which tourism comprises two:

● game viewing tourism;
● safari hunting tourism;
● subsistence and licensed hunting;
● commercial wildlife production;
● secondary trade and processing of wildlife products.

The tourist component has an estimated value-added of some Pula

18 million (around $10 million) out of a GNP of some $2500 million, i.e. about 0.4 per cent of GNP (see Table 6.2). It has been suggested that a multiplier of 1 might be applied to this figure to capture the second and further round impacts of this expenditure, bringing actual GNP contribution to perhaps 0.8 per cent. This is an estimate of the *actual* rather than the *potential* contribution. A detailed assessment of profitability of the industry (FGU-Kronberg, 1988) suggests that wildlife tourism could be increased by a factor of five before profitable opportunities were exhausted. This allows for the necessary investment in infrastructure. In the unlikely event that all other contributions to GNP stayed the same, the wildlife tourism sector could therefore contribute some 2 per cent of GNP directly and 4 per cent overall.

The FGU-Kronberg (1988) study was based on operator returns and may understate the real value of tourism because of the various incentives for operators to understate income. Another study on the economic impacts of wildlife-based tourism in northern Botswana (Borge, et al., 1990) surveyed both operators and tourist. Responses indicated that tourists had paid an estimated Pula 141 million (around $78 million) for Botswana safari company services in 1989. But safari companies reported having received gross income of only Pula 35 million (around $19 million) in the same period. This suggests a significant income leakage and that Botswana is failing to capture a large proportion of the value of its wildlife tourism.

The game viewing industry is supplied by some 67 companies offering game viewing services to tourists, with around half of them providing permanent facilities in the form of lodges and camps. Safari hunting is supplied by some 14 operators and is dominated by three of these. Hunting visitors are few but with prices charged are very high. Table 6.2 shows that game viewing tourism contributes around twice the GDP of safari hunting. Within the category of game viewing, fixed facilities (camps and lodges) are around six times more important in terms of GDP than mobile safaris. Some other indicators of significance are:

- in terms of employment, wages and salaries comprise around 13 per cent of the mobile safari gross output, 20 per cent of game viewing and 32 per cent of safari hunting;
- the government "take" of gross output in 1986 was 5 per cent of mobile safaris, 3 per cent of game viewing lodges and camps, and 11 per cent of safari hunting.

If employment creation is important, then, safari hunting appears to be efficient. The government rent capture is very low, but the fari hunting.

If employment creation is important, then, safari hunting appears to be efficient. The government rent capture is very low, but the figures for the current (1991) take are probably much higher since the Botswana government was effectively subsidizing the industry in 1986, since when fees and licence costs have been increased.

The microeconomics of wildlife tourism

Table 6.3 looks at the economics of game viewing from the stand-point of a potential investment in a tourist lodge in Ngamiland, Botswana. The evaluation is carried out for the *financial* rate of return and the *economic* rate of return. The difference between the two arises because financial costs and revenues are often not repre-sentative of the true economic values to a country. As an example, the ruling exchange rate may not reflect the true scarcity value of foreign exchange. Similarly, if labour would otherwise be unem-ployed, then the economic value of that labour is below the wage rate that would be paid to it in the project. That is, the "opportunity cost" of the labour is less than the actual wage rate. An economic, as opposed to a financial, assessment therefore works with measures of *shadow prices* i.e. economic values that reflect more accurately the true opportunity cost of the resources in question.

Table 6.3 shows that game tourism is both financially and economically attractive in Botswana. The internal rate of financial return of around 17 per cent may be compared with real rates of return of some 12 per cent in the private sector, i.e. it pays private enterprise to invest in such schemes. The economic rate of return is considerably higher, so that if the private sector rate of return of 12 per cent is used as a discount rate for government, there is an additional rate of return of some 20 per cent. Another way of looking at the issue is in terms of returns to land. In many African countries, despite their geographical size, land is often a scarce input. This is true of Botswana where cattle grazing certainly competes with other uses of land. Table 6.3 shows that financial rates of return of some 17 per cent can be achieved on an area of 21,500 hectares. As Box 2.2 in Chapter 2 shows, this compares more than favourably with cattle grazing where internal rates of return are only 6 per cent.

The value of wildlife tourism

There have been few attempts to estimate the value of wildlife tourism in developing countries. This is partly due to the limited availability of data, but also because alternative valuation tech-niques have only recently been applied in developing countries

Table 6.3: Illustrative economics of a tourist lodge development Ngamiland, Botswana

(Time horizon 10 years, Discount rate 6%)

Financial analysis

Extent of concession	21,500 hectares
Concession stock	715 large stock units (LSU)[1]
Initial capital outlay	Pula 1.32 million
Revenues	Pula 1.53 million p.a

less

Operating costs	Pula 1.02 million p.a.
Gross profit	Pula 0.51 million p.a
Internal Rate of Return[2]	17.5%
Net Present Value[3]	Pula 1.3 million

Economic Analysis

Capital outlays	Pula 1.41 million
Revenues	Pula 1.69 million p.a.

less

Variable costs	Pula 0.87 million p.a
Gross economic benefit	Pula 0.82 million p.a
Economic rate of return[4]	35.3%
Net present value	Pula 3.5 million

Sensitivity of NPVs to different assumptions about the "life" of the project and the discount rate is shown as follows:

		r = 6%		r = 10%	
		(Pula million)			
		Fin	Ec	Fin	Ec
Life =	10 years 1.3	3.5	0.7	2.5	
	30 years na	7.6	na	4.6	

Notes:

1. Stock units are weighted numbers of wild species.

2. The internal rate of return is the rate of interest that makes the present value of costs just equal to the present value of revenues. The IRR may then be compared to the prevailing rate of interest, see text.

3. The net present value is the present value of benefits (revenues) minus costs. To be potentially attractive a project should have a NPV ﹥ 0.

4. The economic rate of return is the IRR but with all values shadow priced (see text).

Source: authors' calculations

to such problems. Of the limited selection of studies that do exist on the value of wildlife tourism, the valuation is usually confined to the direct costs and benefits of tourism, with little, if any, analysis of external impacts of wildlife tourism. For example, indirect use benefits from tourism may accrue to local communities from employment in the tourist trade and the creation of a market for handicrafts. However, these positive indirect use benefits need to be offset by any detrimental impacts the wildlife has on the local community, e.g. crop or other damage caused by animals. In addition, tourist pollution and congestion may have negative impacts. There may also be significant non-use/preservation benefits generated by wildlife tourism. The total economic value derived from the non-consumptive use of wildlife for tourism may have important implications for decisions as to whether or not to conserve or deplete wild resources.

The viewing value of elephants in Kenya

The exploitation of elephants for their ivory is perceived to threaten their survival in many African nations. However, the revenue accruing to Africa from ivory exports – approximately $35-45 million in the late 1980s – is a tiny fraction of the value of all African exports. Although the revenue derived from ivory exports is significant for a few individual countries, it is not anticipated that the loss of this revenue would seriously impair African development. What is more, other non-consumptive values of the African elephant, such as its importance for tourism in some countries, may be considerably more significant in terms of foreign exchange earnings.

In a recent study, Brown and Henry (1990) estimated the viewing value of elephants in Kenya. Kenya is visited by approximately 250,000 to 300,000 foreign adult tourists annually. Based on survey responses filled in by safari tourists and tour operators in Kenya, the non-transportation cost of safaris averaged $1,400. This represents potential expenditures of around $375 million, of which about $200 million is spent in Kenya. The authors then estimated the actual viewing value of elephants using two valuation techniques: the travel cost approach and contingent valuation method.

The *travel cost* procedure exploits the fact that individuals coming from different countries bear different costs for the same quality safari. Thus, individuals purchase different amounts of safaris. Using data obtained from survey responses the demand curve for safaris can be constructed. The consumers" surplus for safaris is the value of safari that is greater than the cost of safari. The part of this value that is attributable to elephants is based on information from survey respondents that identifies how tourists distribute the satisfaction they receive from a safari over a variety of activities and types of wildlife, including elephants. The *contingent valuation* method simply involves asking people on safari hypothetical questions about how much they are willing to pay or willing to accept in exchange for the maintenance or change in elephant numbers (Brown and Henry, 1990).

The results of the travel cost and contingent valuation techniques are reasonably comparable, and suggest that the value of viewing elephants in Kenya is US$25 million per year. Given that special interest tourism is estimated to be growing at 10-15 per cent each year, the future value of viewing elephants is also anticipated to increase. However, respondents to the survey reported that if the elephant population in Kenya was to decline by 50 per cent (25 per cent), at least one-half (31 per cent) would no longer find Kenya an attractive destination for themselves, their family or to recommend to friends. In contrast, tour operators believed that there would only be a decline of 10 per cent in safari activity if the elephant population decreases by 50 per cent in the next decade. Expectations of the impact of declines in the number of elephants on tourism differ between tourists and tour operators, but it is clear that the loss of elephants will directly lead to a significant reduction in tourist visits and the revenue derived from tourism.

Although the study reviewed above provides an estimate of the direct use value from viewing elephants, there is no attempt to estimate: a) the *option value* of individuals who wish to preserve the elephants in order to have the option of elephant viewing in the future; b) the *bequest value* of individuals who have no intention of viewing the elephants but value the opportunity of future generations viewing them; nor c) the *existence value* of individuals who just derive satisfaction from knowing that the elephants will be preserved. Given the widespread public concern over the plight of the African elephants, it is reasonable to suggest that the beneficial externalities of tourism – the non-use and preservation values – are highly significant.

The elephant also has an important *indirect use value*, which is derived from its natural ecological functions and role as a "keystone species" (Western, 1989). The elephant plays a major part in diversifying savannah and forest ecosystems, acting as seed disperser, reducing bushlands, expanding grasslands and so on. The ecological benefits of elephants are dependent on their population density being neither too low nor too high. For example, in the protected areas of Amboseli National Park in Kenya where elephants crowd in, or in the areas of non-protected lands that are abandoned, impoverishment results. The most equitable mix, and high relative abundance, of species occurs at the park boundaries where elephant densities are moderate. However, wildlife tourism may have an indirect adverse effect on the quality of the environment if level and type of wildlife tourism exceeds the carrying capacity of the wildlife park.

It is extremely difficult to place a monetary value on the additional costs and benefits of elephant viewing. To date, little progress has been made with such valuations. However, even without accounting for these additional costs and benefits, the above case study has shown that the direct use value of elephant tourism in Kenya may be as much as ten times the value that Kenya derives from exports of ivory – most of which has been illegally exploited in the past anyway. The relatively high economic value of non-consumptive use of elephants for wildlife tourism poses a powerful economic argument for sustainably managing the African elephant, at least in major savannah range states such as Kenya.

The value of ecotourism at a tropical rainforest site in Costa Rica

Tobias and Mendelsohn (1991) estimated the value of ecotourism at a tropical rainforest site in Costa Rica. Using the travel cost valuation technique, they examined the willingness to pay of local tourists to visit the Montverde Cloud Forest Biological Reserve (MCFR). Based on data from the reserve's headquarters on the frequency of ecotourist visits, distance from the site, population density and illiteracy from each of Costa Rica's eighty-one cantons, the authors derive a demand function for visits to the site. The travel cost demand function describes how many times people are willing to purchase a trip depending on the price of a trip. With high prices per trip people will tend to visit less often, and the travel cost demand function will be downward sloping. The demand function reveals the quantity a consumer would purchase at any given price and the price a consumer would pay for any specific quantity. The net benefits (or consumer surplus) from visiting the site is given by the area below the demand curve (D) but above the cost line (C) in Figure 6.1.

After calculating the consumer surplus for each canton, the results are summed across all cantons to derive a national recreational value of the entire site of approximately $100,000 per annum. The present value of the loss of the entire site is the discounted value of the future stream of net benefits from the site. Assuming that the real value of the site remains the same over time and a real interest rate of 4 per cent, Tobias and Mendelsohn 1991 estimate the present value of domestic recreation at MCFR to be between \$2.4 million and \$2.9 million. Given that there are approximately 3,000 domestic visitors annually, the site is valued at about \$35 per visit.

Figure 6.1: Visitation Demand and consumer surplus

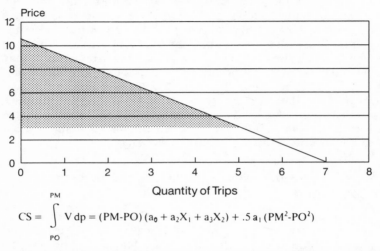

$$CS = \int_{PO}^{PM} V\,dp = (PM\text{-}PO)(a_0 + a_2X_1 + a_3X_2) + .5\,a_1\,(PM^2\text{-}PO^2)$$

Notes: Assuming that the price of the trip is \$3, the consumer surplus is given as the area above \$3, but below the demand function.

Source: D. Tobias and R. Mendelsohn 1991, 'Valuing Ecotourism in a Tropical Rain-Forest Reserve', *AMBIO*, Vol.20, No.2, pp.91-93.

The estimate of the value of ecotourism at MCFR is likely to be an under-estimate of the true value of the site for three reasons:

(i)   the real value of recreational visits to the site is assumed to be constant over time, whereas the visitation rate has been growing at 15 per cent a year for the past five years;

(ii)   the estimate only represents the value of the site by national visitors, although foreign visitors out number domestic visitors by around four to one. Assuming foreign visitors value visiting the site the same as domestic visitors at \$35 per trip, an additional \$400,000 to \$500,000 needs to be added to the recreational value of MCFR. However, given the higher incomes of, and lack of nearby substitutes of the site for, foreign tourists this value may be even higher;

(iii)   the recreational value of the site does not capture any potential preservation values of the site, such as the sustainable harvesting of non-timber forest products such as fruit and latex, protection of watersheds, protection of wildlife habitats and rare species. As discussed in Chapter 7, these values may be significant.

Given that the net present value of domestic and international recreation combined is about $12.5 million and that the reserve covers 10,000 ha, the recreational value per hectare is about $1,250. By comparing the going price for land surrounding the reserve, which ranges from $30 to $100 per ha, to the value of land for ecotourism, Tobias and Mendelsohn assert that expansion of the reserve is economically warranted. Although this assertion is appealing, there are several problems that may constrain this approach.

First, it is not clear that the recreational value of the site is captured by the site managers. Given that the site is privately managed, the decision to expand will be based on the financial returns, i.e. the gate receipts in the case of ecotourism, rather than the net value to society. It would only be possible to fund additional land purchases by raising the entrance fee or obtaining a subsidy from central government. Raising the entrance fee may effectively discourage local tourists from visiting the site. This could result in the reserve being viewed by the local community as a high priced leisure item for foreign tourists and alienate them from the benefits of the park. The failure to encourage the support and participation of the local community in the park may undermine conservation efforts.

In addition, the comparatively lower value of land outside the reserve may reflect its lower value as a potential ecotourism site. The land outside the reserve may have significantly lower biodiversity, natural beauty, or other "amenity" values that are sought by ecotourists. In addition, there may be an opportunity cost of converting the land from existing or previous non-tourist uses (World Bank, 1991).

The value of tourism in Khao Yai National Park

Khao Yai, the oldest national park in Thailand, contains most of the remaining forest in north-eastern Thailand and is of critical importance for wildlife and local hydrology. It is a premier tourist destination for both Thais and foreigners, located approximately three hours away from Bangkok. Tourism in Khao Yai has increased dramatically over the past decade – in 1977 over 115,000 individuals visited the park and by 1985 the number of visitors had increased to over 400,000. Information from survey responses shows that individuals visit the park for a number of reasons, including enjoying the scenery, viewing wildlife, seeing the waterfalls, relaxation, hiking and camping (Dixon and Sherman, 1990).

Tourism directly contributes 3.03 million baht (26 baht equals approximately $1.00) in the form of gate fees and accommodation charges to the National Parks Division (NPD). The Tourist Authority of Thailand (TAT) also operates lodging facilities, restaurants, a golf course, souvenir shops and wildlife lighting activities in the park. The combined revenue generated from these services amounted to approximately 10 million baht in 1987 while its expenditures during that year were approximately 3.3 million baht. However, the profits from TAT's operations accrue directly to TAT, and do not contribute to the park.

Information from the Beneficial Use Project on tourist expenditures gives some indication of the value of tourism in Khao Yai (Dixon and Sherman, 1990). Although the overwhelming majority of visitors are Thai (95 per cent of the total) foreign visitors tend to spend more per person on average than Thai visitors. For example, a foreign visitor may spend between 500 to 800 baht on average each day, mainly on transport (42 per cent), food and drink (33 per cent), accommodation (19 per cent), guide service (5 per cent) and park admission (1 per cent). A Thai visitor, in contrast, spends around 350 to 600 baht on average per day. The total expenditures generated by tourism in Khao Yai amounts to between 40 million and 200 million baht given that over 400,000 tourists visit the park each year. However, only a small percentage of tourist expenditures actually accrues to the park through gate fees and accommodation charges. Tourist expenditures are expected to increase, and the Khao Yai Management Plan estimates that tourism could grow as much as 17 per cent a year over next five years if visitor improvements are undertaken.

Although there have been no attempts to estimate the economic value of ecotourism at Khao Yai National Park, a travel cost study of Lumpinee Park, Bangkok, in 1980 estimated the total consumer surplus from 2 million visits to this park each year to be worth more than 13 million baht (approximately $0.5 million). Although this value was estimated for short visits to an urban park, it does have implications for the potential economic value of Khao Yai. The total consumer surplus of Khao Yai is expected to be larger than 13 million baht owing to price increases and the wider nature of visitor attractions at Khao Yai. Assuming the average consumer's surplus is ten times the amount estimated for Lumpinee Park visitors, the total consumer surplus amounts to 26 million baht, or $1 million. Although the willingness-to-pay for Khao Yai is high, only a relatively insignificant proportion of this economic rent is currently captured in the form of entrance fees.

Wildlife tourism and conservation

Many environmentalists are uneasy with the notion of developing the *utilization* of wildlife as a means to protecting it. But given population pressures and the development needs of relatively poor nations, the idea of outright *preservation* through non-use becomes non-viable in many cases. The preservationist, "no use" option frequently fails because of the lack of incentives for local people to conserve the resource in question. Protected areas are then seen as unreasonable constraints on alternative uses of the land and the end result is the familiar erosion of protected areas through gradual encroachment and poaching. The utilization option, however, does provide incentives to conserve the resource. An essential element should be the requirement that some of the rents from the utilization option, in this case the profits from ecotourism and game tourism, should be returned to the local communities. One problem that does arise, as demonstrated in the Khao Yai National Park case study, is that the potential economic rent accruing to the wild area is not adequately captured due to low user charges, such as entrance fees.

However, even if rent diversion of this kind is not practised, the utilization option frequently creates employment where outright protection does not. In this way local communities can again benefit. The higher the rents the more potential there is for redistributing part of them to local communities, so that there are good reasons for focusing on high unit profit ventures, such as game viewing.

The second criticism of the utilization approach is that it tends to encourage over-expansion of demand for the resource with consequent loss of wildlife and natural habitat through stress and disturbance. There is evidence that Kenya's wildlife has suffered in this way in some very popular areas. This raises the issue of how to "market" wildlife tourism. Kenya has opted for high turnover, relatively cheap package tourism, often linked to time spent on the coastal resorts. South Africa has similarly encouraged low price domestic tourism through subsidisation of protected areas, e.g. the Kruger National Park. Botswana and, to a lesser extent, Zimbabwe have opted for a different approach of attracting fewer tourists but at higher prices. Measurement of carrying capacity is hazy in the context of wildlife tourism but early signs of breaches of carrying capacity can be detected from observation of wildlife populations for signs of stress and behaviourial change. While Kenya certainly exhibits these signs in some areas, Western (1986) has argued that even there the carrying capacity is four to five times the existing tourist use rate. Barnes (1990b) suggests that Southern Africa's better quality protected areas might support 133-980 hectares per lodge bed, with an average of 700 hectares. A lodge of 50 bed capacity, then, would require a minimum area of some 35,000 hectares and smaller lodges of 20 beds would require 14,000 hectares. These calculations offer further support for the high-price, low quantity approach.

While the high-price approach has the very substantial advantage of ensuring that the carrying capacity of wildlife areas is not exceeded, it has a distinct disadvantage in that it limits the "wildlife experience" to the relatively well off. This may confine the conservation message to the rich and foreign, whilst alienating the local community from the sustainable management of the wild plants and animals in the park. It may be preferable to maintain the high-price, low quantity approach but combine this with some sort of limited allocation of low-cost trips to enable the participation of the local community (for further discussion of community based wildlife development, see Chapter 5).

In Botswana, the main factor competing with wildlife is the increasing development of livestock herds, which are favoured by subsidies in a society where cattle have both market and non-market (cultural) significance. The aim of district land use plans in Botswana is to minimize this conflict. Cattle numbers have grown rapidly in parallel with human population growth.

"Smallstock" – mainly goats – have also increased rapidly since the mid 1960s. The main cattle holdings belong to the relatively wealthy: some 8 per cent of farmers held 45 per cent of cattle in 1984 (Arntzen and Veenendaal, 1986). Not only are ranches in competition for wildlife areas, but also ranching itself is widely held to be responsible for land degradation in several areas (Pearce, Barbier and Markandya, 1990). The "trade off" between cattle ranching and wildlife utilization favours cattle ranching because of price and input subsidisation. Without subsidies, cattle ranching would appear to be a financially non-viable proposition in many areas (see Box 2.2 in Chapter 2). Additionally, the land degradation associated with over-grazing means that the social rate of return to cattle ranching is even lower than the private non-subsidized rate of return. Adequate protection for wildlife thus requires some outright protection for critical wildlife areas (the "no use" option), but also a level playing field between ranching and wildlife utilization options. It is through the proper design of economic incentives, and the removal of economic distortions, that wildlife protection can best be advanced.

References

Arntzen, J. and Veenendaal, A Profile of Environment and Development in Botswana, [Amsterdam: Institute of Environmental Studies, Free University of Amsterdam, 19866].

Barbier, E., J. Burgess, T.Swanson and D.W.Pearce, Elephants, Economics and Ivory, [London: Earthscan, 1990].

Barnes, J., "Development of Botswana's Wildlife resources as a Tourist Attraction", Proceedings Botswana Society Symposium on Tourism in Botswana, Gaborone, 346-369 [1990].

Barnes, J., "Economic Aspects of Tourism in National Parks and Game Reserves", Paper presented to SADCC Workshop on Wildlife Based Tourism, Musungwa Lodge, Kafue National Park, Zambia [1990].

Borge, L., W. Nelson, J. Leitch and F. Leistritz, "Economic Impact of Wildlife-Based Tourism in Northern Botswana", Department of Agricultural Economics, North Dakota State University, Discussion Paper No.262, mimeo [1990].

Brown, G. and W. Henry, "The Economic Value of Elephants" LEEC Discussion Paper 89-12 [London: London Environmental Economics Centre, 1989].

Dixon, J. and P. Sherman, Economics of Protected Areas: a New Look at Benefits and Costs [London: Earthscan, 1990].

FGU-Kronberg, The Contribution of Wildlife to the Economy of Botswana, Botswana Ministry of Commerce and Industry, Gaborone [1988].

Pearce, D.W., E. Barbier and A. Markandya, Sustainable Development: Economics and Environment in the Third World [London: Earthscan, 1990].

Robinson, J.G., and K.H. Redford (eds), Neotropical Wildlife Use and Conservation [Chicago and London: University of Chicago Press, 1991].

Swanson, T., Wildlife Utilization as an Instrument of Natural Habitat Conservation: a Survey of the Literature and of the Issues [London: London Environmental Economics Centre, Paper DP 91- 03, 1991].

Tobias, D. and R. Mendelsohn, "Valuing Ecotourism in a Tropical Rain-Forest Reserve", AMBIO, Vol.20, No.2, pp.91-93 [1991].

United Nations Environment Programme, Environmental Data Report, third edition, 1991/1992 [Oxford: Blackwell, 1991].

Western, D., "Tourist capacity in East African Parks", United Nations Environment Programme, Industry and Environment, 9 (1), 14-16 [1986].

Western, D., "The Ecological Value of Elephants: A Keystone Role in African Ecosystems" in the ITRG Report, The Ivory Trade and the Future of the African Elephant, prepared for the Second Meeting of the CITES African Elephant Working Group, Gaborone, Botswana [1989].

World Bank, Malawi – Economic Report on Environmental Policy, Southern African Division Washington, D.C., World Bank, [1991].

7

SUSTAINABLE RAINFOREST UTILIZATION

Edward B. Barbier

Tropical moist forest (TMF) – the "rainforest" as it is more popularly known – includes wet evergreen, moist semi-deciduous, moist deciduous, and freshwater swamp forest. It is the rate at which the world's remaining TMF areas is being deforested that is causing so much global concern, particularly as only 5 per cent of rainforest currently receives legal protection (Swanson, 1991).

Approximately 8.4 million ha of tropical moist forest area were being cleared annually by the end of the 1980s, with over 4 million ha deforested in Latin America alone (Schmidt, 1990). Perhaps most worrying is that deforestation is occurring with little regard to long-term management of the forests. Much of the loss of forest is the result of clearing for agriculture – both planned and unplanned – with little regard to the social opportunity costs of the disappearing forests. Even management of forests for timber production is precarious. For example, a study by Poore et al. (1989) concluded that, on a world scale, operational management of tropical forests for sustainable production of timber is negligible.

Yet the cost of forest conversion and degradation to developing countries can be high. For example, in Indonesia, the forgone cost in terms of timber rentals from converting primary and secondary forest land is in the order of US$625-750 million per annum. With logging damage and fire accounting for additional costs of US$70 million, this would represent losses of around US $800 million annually. The inclusion of forgone non-timber forest products would raise this cost to US$1 billion per year. In addition, the loss of timber on sites used for development projects could be another US$40-100 million (Pearce, Barbier and Markandya, 1990 ch. 5). The total cost of the depreciation of the forest stock would include not only the cost of conversion but also the cost of timber extraction and forest degradation. One study estimated this total cost for Indonesia to be around US $3.1 billion in 1982, or approximately

4 per cent of GDP (Repetto, et al., 1987). However, this estimate must be considered a lower bound, as it does not include the value of the loss of forest protection functions (e.g., watershed protection, micro-climatic maintenance) and of biodiversity. The latter may particularly be important in terms of *option* and *existence values*, i.e., values reflecting a willingness to pay to see species conserved for future use or for their intrinsic worth, which could translate into future payments that the rest of the world might make to Indonesia to conserve forest lands.

There is now sufficient economic evidence linking the tropical deforestation problem to economic policies. The core of the policy problem concerning tropical deforestation is, first, proper economic valuation of the forest losses incurred, second, rigorous analysis of the economic and social causes driving deforestation, and third, design of appropriate incentive structures to correct for the problem.

This chapter discusses the role of economic policy in contributing to tropical deforestation. If we are to slow down the pace of TMF destruction, then modifying incentive structures through the design of better policies is required.

Economic valuation of tropical deforestation

Tropical deforestation is an economic problem because important values are lost, some perhaps irreversibly, when closed forests are "opened up", degraded or cleared. Each choice or *land use option* for the forest – to leave it standing in its natural state, or to exploit it selectively, e.g. for timber or "minor" (i.e. non-timber) products, or to clearcut it entirely so the land can be converted to another use, such as agriculture – has implications in terms of values gained and lost. The decision as to what land use option to pursue for a given tropical forest area, and ultimately whether current rates of deforestation are "excessive", can only be made if these gains and losses are properly analysed and evaluated. This requires that *all the values* that are gained and lost with each land use option are carefully considered.

For example, if the forest is to be cleared for agriculture, not only should the direct costs of conversion (e.g. clearing and burning the forest, establishing crops) be included as part of the costs of this land use option but so must the *forgone* values of the forest that has been converted. These may include both the loss of important environmental functions (e.g., watershed protection, micro-climate maintenance) and resources (e.g. commercial hardwoods, non-timber products, wildlife).

In other words, we must determine the *total economic value* (TEV), both marketed and non-marketed, that is being surrendered through modifications of the prevailing forest land use that any development option entails. These values comprise direct and indirect use values, option values and existence values (see Box 7.1). Direct use values include timber and non-timber products and ecotourism. Indirect use values are essentially the ecological functions of tropical forests: their watershed protection, microclimatic and material cycling functions. All these values may have an "option value" component if we are interested in preserving them for future use. Finally, existence values are the values that people place on the forest "in itself" and are unrelated to any use.

Calculation of the above components of total economic value is important for assessing the costs and benefits of different forest land use options. However, care should be taken in adding up the various components of TEV, as there are inevitable trade-offs among them. Furthermore, a measure of TEV in itself does not tell us anything about the opportunity cost – the next best land use option foregone – of a given development option. Only by carefully comparing the full costs and benefits of different options is it possible to determine which development option should take place.[1]

In addition, many of the component values in total economic value have no market – especially subsistence or underdeveloped non-timber products and the indirect use, option and existence values of forests. Actual choice of land use is therefore often biased in favour of land uses that do have marketed outputs, e.g. development options such as ranching, timber exploitation, agriculture, mining, hydroelectricity. The result is too much conversion and over-exploitation of forest and too little natural management of forest land.

The basic reason for the imbalance is that the non-market values of the natural/managed systems are not automatically reflected in the price of forested land. For example, the market value of land converted to agriculture fails to reflect the lost environmental benefits, such as watershed protection. If "owners" (i.e. those with legal title and those who have acquired the land on a first-come basis) had to pay the full social cost of developing forested land, less land would be converted or over-exploited. Forested land is clearly *underpriced*. An important consequence is that once the land occupied has become sufficiently degraded and thus significantly less productive, the "owners" have a strong incentive to abandon the land for new, virgin forested land that is "cheap" to acquire and develop. The process repeats itself until it becomes difficult to get access to new forest lands, for example due to the lack of roads or waterways into a region.

Box 7.1: Total economic value of tropical forests and development options

The table indicates the many *use* and *non-use* values of a tropical forest that may comprise its *total economic value* (TEV):

Classification of total economic value for tropical forests

Use values			Non-use values
(1)	(2)	(3)	
Direct value	Indirect value	Option value	Existence value
Sustainable timber products	Nutrient cycling	Future uses as per (1), (2)	Biodiversity
			Culture, heritage
Non-timber products	Watershed protection		
Recreation	Air pollution reduction		
Medicine			
Plant genetics	Microclimatic functions		
Education	Carbon store		
Human habitat			

Source: D.W.Pearce, *An Economic Approach to Saving the Tropical Forests*, LEEC Paper 90-05, London Environmental Economics Centre, London, 1990.

Direct use values are the resources and "services" provided directly by the forest. *Indirect use values* are essentially the environmental functions of the forest, which indirectly support economic activity and human welfare. *Option value* relates to the amount that individuals would be willing to pay to conserve a tropical forest, or at least some of its uses, for future use. Individuals are essentially valuing the guaranteed "option" of future supply of these uses, the availability of which might otherwise be uncertain. *Existence value* relates to valuation of the resource as a unique asset in itself, with no connection to its use values. This would include forests as objects of intrinsic and "stewardship" value, as a bequest to future generations and as a unique cultural and heritage asset.

Thus the failure to account more fully for the economic costs of deforestation is a major factor behind the design of inappropriate forest policies. For example, a common assumption by policy makers is that the values of tropical forests that are so difficult to quantify must be less significant. This may not be the case. Pearce (1990) has shown how the existence value of the Amazonian tropical forests may easily dominate its direct and indirect use values. On the assumption that the Amazon forest is valued at an average of US$8 per adult in the advanced economies of the world (only), existence value would total US$3.2 billion, or a quarter of the entire GDP contribution of Amazonia to the Brazilian economy, inclusive of mineral extraction, timber and agriculture. If this money was collected from individuals in the advanced economies and placed in an "Amazon Conservation Fund", it could be used to compensate those people in the Amazon contributing to more than 25 per cent of its economic output for "ceasing" their activities.

Additionally, tropical forests could be given "carbon credits" for their role in averting global warming. In this case, the benefit of conserving existing forests would relate to the avoided damage of *not* releasing the stored greenhouse gases (mainly carbon) through deforestation. Pearce (1990) estimates that the value of this function may amount to around US$1300 per ha for a single year, with perhaps similar benefits for about five years. For newly forested areas values might be of the order of US$130 per ha per annum. Again, provided adequate collection and transfer mechanisms could be found, such "carbon credits" would be a powerful incentive for promoting conservation over development and deforestation.

Potential economic losses in terms of non-timber products, such as essential oils, honey, wildlife products, resins, bamboos, fruits and nuts, from deforestation may also be significant. For example, in Indonesia, exports of non-timber products rose from US$17 million in 1973 to US$154 million in 1985, comprising 12 per cent of export earnings. Exports of rattan alone were US$80 million in 1985 (Pearce, Barbier and Markandya, 1990 ch. 5). However, the commercial potential of many non-timber products may be currently under-exploited. The forgone future value of these products may therefore be much higher than their value at present. Moreover, many of the important economic uses of non-timber products, e.g. the use of "wild" forest foods to supplement food security and meet subsistence needs, are non-market and thus are not often properly accounted for. Consequently, both the forgone commercial and non-market benefits of non-timber products must be incorporated into any assessment of the costs of deforestation.

Table 7.1: Financial returns to non-timber products and other forest uses, in one ha of forest at Mishana, Rio Nanay, Peru

(Net Present Value, US$/ha 1989, 5 per cent discount rate)

1. Non-timber harvesting fruit and latex	6330
2. Sustainable timber harvesting periodic selective cutting	490
Total natural forest value (1. + 2.)	**6820**
3. Clear-cutting timber harvesting	1001
4. Plantation harvesting timber and pulpwood [1]	3184
5. Cattle ranching [2]	2960

Notes: [1] 1.0 ha plantation of *Gmelina aborea* in Brazilian Amazon.

[2] gross revenues/ha of fully stocked cattle pastures in Brazilian Amazon, costs of weeding and fencing and animal care not deducted.

Source: C. Peters, A. Gentry, R. Mendelsohn, 'Valuation of an Amazonian Rainforest', *Nature*, Vol. 339, 29 June 1989, pp. 655-656.

Table 7.1 shows the results of one study in Peru that calculated the comparative financial returns from non-timber products and other commercial uses of the same forest. The results indicate that the discounted returns to fruits and latex compare highly favourably with the alternative options of clear-cutting timber and forest conversion.[2]

Box 7.2 illustrates the type of comprehensive cost-benefit analysis required for tropical forest land use options, with the example of the Korup Project, Cameroon. Although this example is of a *conservation* rather than a *development* option, the approach is essentially the same. Thus the net benefits of the Korup protected area and project in terms of sustained forest and subsistence use, tourism, genetic value, watershed protection, control of flooding and soil maintenance, all compare favourably with the opportunity costs of forestry and other development options, thus generating a substantial overall net benefit to Cameroon.

Box 7.2: Cost-benefit analysis of land use: Korup Project, Cameroon

The Korup Project is an on-going programme to promote conservation of the rainforest in Korup National Park in Southwest Province, Cameroon. A social cost-benefits analysis (CBA) of the project undertaken on behalf of the government of Cameroon and World-Wide Fund for Nature, UK, yielded the following results:

Base case result
(NPV 000, 8 per cent Discount Rate)

Direct costs of conservation	**−11,913**
Opportunity costs	−3,326
lost stumpage value	−706
lost forest use	−2,620
Direct benefits	**11,995**
sustained forest use	3,291
replaced subsistence production	97
tourism	1,360
genetic value	481
watershed protection of fisheries	3,776
control of flood risk	1,578
soil fertility maintenance	532
Induced benefits	**4,328**
agricultural productivity gain	905
induced forestry	207
induced cash crops	3,216
NET BENEFIT PROJECT	**1,084**
Adjustments	6,462
external trade credit	7,246
uncaptured genetic value	−433
uncaptured watershed benefits	−351
NET BENEFIT CAMEROON	**7,545**

Source: H.J. Ruitenbeek, *Social Cost-Benefit Analysis of the Korup Project, Cameroon*, Prepared for the World-Wide Fund for Nature and the Republic of Cameroon, London, 1989.

The CBA includes not only the *direct* operating and capital costs of the project, but also the *opportunity costs* of lost timber earnings (lost stumpage value) and lost production from the six resettled villages (lost forest use). Against this must be weighed the *direct benefits* of the project in the form of sustained forest use beyond the year 2010 when the forest would otherwise have disappeared, replacement subsistence production of the resettled villagers, tourism, minimum expected genetic value of the forest resources in terms of pharmaceuticals, chemicals, agricultural crop improvements, etc., and environmental functions – watershed protection of fisheries, control of flooding and soil fertility maintenance. Also included are *induced benefits*, agricultural and forestry benefits of the project's development initiatives in the buffer zone. The external trade credit shows a positive benefit to Cameroon of direct external funding of the project. "Uncaptured genetic value" is a negative adjustment reflecting the fact that Cameroon will be able to capture only 10 per cent of the genetic value through the licensing structures and institutions that it has in place, and "uncaptured watershed benefits" indicates that some of the watershed protection benefits will flow to Nigeria and not Cameroon.

Thus the analysis indicates that the Korup Project offers substantial net economic benefits as a land-use option at the project level and to Cameroon as a whole.

Economic policies and the incentives for deforestation

If the costs of excessive tropical deforestation are not properly evaluated and the direct and indirect impacts of deforestation are ignored, then policies to improve forest management have less chance of succeeding. Corruption and the political clout of powerful interest groups that profit from immediate returns from tropical deforestation also weaken "political will". Whatever the underlying reason, too often the pricing and economic policies of countries with tropical forests distort incentive structures to favour excessive deforestation. This occurs in two ways:

- First, the "prices" determined for tropical timber products or the products derived from converted forest land do not incorporate the lost economic values in terms of forgone timber rentals, forgone minor forest products and other direct uses (e.g., tourism), disrupted forest protection and other ecological functions, and the loss of biological diversity, including any option or existence values.
- Second, even the direct costs of harvesting and converting tropical forests are often subsidized and/or distorted, thus encouraging needless destruction.

For example, in the Brazilian Amazon subsidies and other policy distortions are estimated to have accounted for at least 35 per cent of all forest area altered by 1980 through tax incentives for capital investment (e.g., industrial wood production and livestock ranching); rural credits for agricultural production (mechanized agriculture, cattle ranching and silviculture); subsidized small farmer settlement; and export subsidies (Browder, 1985).

Similarly in Malaysia and Indonesia, government policies to encourage the switching from the export of raw logs to processed timber products have led to substantial economic losses, the establishment of inefficient processing operations and accelerated deforestation (Repetto and Gillis, 1988). Throughout Southeast Asia the allocation of timber concession rights and leasing agreements on a short time scale, coupled with the lack of incentives for reforestation, have contributed to excessive and rapid depletion of timber forests. In the Philippines, the social gain from logging old-growth forest was found to be negative (around -US$130 to -US$1175 per hectare), once the social costs of timber stand replanting, the costs of depletion and the costs of off-site damages were included (Paris and Ruzicka, 1991).

In addition, government-financed investment programmes – for road-building, colonial settlement and large-scale agricultural and mining activities – may *indirectly* be contributing to deforestation by "opening up" frontier areas that were previously inaccessible to smallholders and migrants. Past estimates for Brazil allege that road-building may have accounted for as much as one quarter of deforestation. More recent analysis confirms that, at the state and municipal levels, changes in deforestation appear to be generally related to increasing road density, which also appears linked to changes in the other indicators of agricultural frontier expansion (Ruis and Margulis, 1990). In Indonesia, both official and spontaneous migration may have accounted for as much as 2 million ha of deforestation, with roads and existing frontier settlement areas serving as the main "launch pads" into the forest areas (Pearce, Barbier and Markandya, 1990, Chapter 5).

There is also evidence of *non-economic* policy distortions contributing to extensive deforestation.[3] Formal property law and titling regulations often ensure that clearing of land is a prerequisite for guaranteeing claims to frontier forest landholdings. Given the insecurity of many frontier tenure regimes, private individuals and firms often excessively clear forest lands in order to safeguard their tenuous claims to holdings and to "capture" agricultural rents. For example, a statistical analysis of deforestation in Ecuador indicated that the extent of land clearing for agriculture was a function not only of rural population pressure but also of tenure insecurity (Southgate, Sierra and Brown, 1989).

As the capacity of many governments to "manage" vast tracts of publicly owned tropical forests is often minimal, encroachment into forest reserves and protected lands are not controlled. At the same time, proper consideration of customary land tenure arrangements and access claims by indigenous forest dwellers and users is often lacking in government decisions to allocate forest land or determine titling. The failure to recognize explicitly the *adat* (customary law) rights of traditional cultivators within forest boundaries in the Outer Islands of Indonesia and the resulting absence of secure tenure give rise to an increase in shifting cultivation and thus deforestation. Attempts to resettle shifting cultivators into sedentary agriculture have generally not been successful; for example, over the period 1972–82 only 10 000 families were resettled (Pearce, Barbier and Markandya, 1990 Chapter 5).

In sum, there are a host of government policy failures that directly and indirectly distort the costs of deforestation. Such policy failures usually have several effects:

- it means that developing countries are being insufficiently compensated for the depletion of their forest resources, as individuals over-exploit forest resources for immediate gain;
- it encourages "rent-seeking" behaviour, i.e., an acceleration in the rate of deforestation as those responsible for forest clearing and over-exploitation seek to secure even larger and larger rents;[4]
- it leads to a policy emphasis on maximizing production from forest development activities (timber extraction, agricultural production, mining) as a means for governments to increase their revenues and for the economy to "develop".

Table 7.2: Tropical timber rent capture
(US$ million)

	Potential rent from log harvest (1)	Actual rent from log harvest (2)	Official gov't rent capture (3)	3/2 (%)	3/1 (%)
Indonesia (1979-82)	4,954	4,409	1,644	37.3	33.2
Sabah (Malaysia, 1979-82)	2,198	2,094	1,703	81.3	77.5
Philippines (1979-82)	1,505	1,033	171	16.5	11.4
Phillipines (1987)	256	68	39	57.1	15.3
Ivory Coast	204	188	59	31.5	28.9
Ghana	- -	80	30	38.0	- -

Source: R. Repetto, "Macroeconomic Policies and Deforestation", Prepared for UNU/WIDER Project *The Environment and Emerging Development Issues*, 1990 and R. Repetto and M.Gillis (eds), *Public Policies and the Misuse of Forest Resources*, Cambridge University Press, Cambridge, 1988.

Short-term concessions and poor regulatory frameworks coupled with inappropriate pricing policies often contribute to excessive rent-seeking behaviour in tropical timber production. Table 7.2 indicates government rent capture from tropical timber in five countries. By not charging sufficient stumpage fees and taxes or by selling harvesting rights too cheaply, by and large most governments have allowed the resource rents to flow to timber concessionaires and speculators as excess profits.

For example, in the Philippines, if the government had been able to collect its full share of actual rents, its timber revenues would have exceeded US$250 million – nearly six times the US$39 million actually collected. Instead, profits of at least US$4500 per ha went to timber concessionaires, mill owners and timber traders (Repetto, 1990). Although the total area of production forest in the Philippines is 4.4 million ha, the total area under timber concession exceeds this at nearly 5.7 million ha – almost 90 per cent of the entire forest area. Concessions are awarded for 25 years but some for as little as five, even though the minimum realistic felling cycle is 30 years and the rotation 60 years. Almost all the large logging companies have senior politicians on their boards, and it is generally the politicians, not forestry officials, that ultimately determine concession policy and allocation (Poore et al., 1989, Chapter 5).

Deforestation and frontier agriculture expansion

Clearing forest land for agriculture is thought to be the major cause of tropical deforestation. As indicated in the previous section, economic policies and government-financed investment programmes both directly and indirectly encourage frontier agricultural expansion at the expense of tropical forests. However, there can be direct implications in terms of lost economic benefits. Table 7.3 indicates that more than half the forest logged in the African ITTO producer countries would subsequently be deforested in 1981-85.[5] The annual loss of almost half a million hectares of productive forest – much of which could have been reharvested in 30 to 40 years time - will have a severe negative impact on future timber supplies in the African continent.

A number of economic studies have been launched, particularly in Latin America, to analyse the main factors inducing people to settle in and to clear 'frontier" forest lands for agriculture.

For example, Binswanger (1989) and Mahar (1989) make the case for the role of subsidies and tax breaks, particularly for cattle ranching, in encouraging land clearing in the Brazilian Amazon. However, more recent analyses by Schneider et al. (1990) and Reis and Margulis (1991) emphasize the role of agricultural rents, population pressures and road building in encouraging small-scale frontier settlement. In the Northern Brazilian Amazon, the total road network (paved and unpaved) increased from 6,357 to 28,431 km from 1975 to 1988. A simple correlation between road density and the rate of deforestation shows that as road density increases, the rate of deforestation increases in larger proportions (Reis and Margulis 1991). Schneider et al. (1990) argue that these factors encouraging frontier agriculture – "nutrient mining" - far outweigh the more publicized impacts of fiscal incentives for cattle ranching. A statistical analysis by Southgate, Sierra and Brown (1989) of the causes of tropical deforestation in Ecuador indicates that colonists' clear forest land not only in response to demographic pressure but also to "capture" agricultural rents and to safeguard their tenuous legal hold on the land.

Table 7.3: The relation between timber harvesting and deforestation in African ITTO Producer Countries, 1981-5

Country	Area logged [1] (thousand ha)	Area logged deforested [2] (thousand ha)	Unlogged area deforested [3] (thousand ha)
Cameroon	272	75	3
Congo	57	20.5	1.5
Côte d'Ivoire	330	290	E
Gabon	150	15	E
Ghana	n.a.	22	n.a.
Liberia	104	44	E
Total	>913	466.5	>4.5

Notes: ITTO = International Tropical Timber Organization
E   = unknown but small
n.a. = no data

[1] total average area selectively logged per annum
[2] estimated area of [1] subsequently deforested
[3] unlogged area deforested per annum

Source: Barbier, E., Rietbergen, S. and Pearce, D., "Economics of Tropical Forest Policy" in J.B. Thomas (Ed.), Deforestation: Environmental and Social Impacts (London: Chapman and Hall, 1992). FAO, Tropical Forest Resource Assessment. Part 1: Africa, FAO, Rome, 1981.

Although there are an increasing number of case studies examining the factors behind tropical deforestation and agricultural frontier expansion, there have been few attempts to explore these linkages through statistical analysis. One such analysis by Palo, Mery and Salmi (1987) for 72 tropical forest countries identified a strong link between tropical deforestation and population density, population growth and increased food production.

A study by Capistrano (1990) and Capistrano and Kiker (1990) examined the influence of international and domestic macro-economic factors on tropical deforestation. The authors use changes in timber production forest area as a proxy for total deforestation. Although they argue that there is a close correlation between average area of closed broadleaved forest and timber production forest area, there are many tropical forest countries where industrial logging is not a significant source of over-all deforestation. Thus their analytical results are more rele-vant to the deforestation of tropical timber production forests than to overall tropical deforestation. Nevertheless, the econo-metric analysis indicates the role of high agricultural export prices in inducing agricultural expansion and forest clearing, as well as the influence of domestic structural adjustment policies, such as exchange rate devaluation and increased debt servicing ratios.

A comparative analysis of 24 Latin American countries also highlights the strong but indirect relationship between population pressure and frontier expansion – increasing numbers of urban consumers raise the demand for domestic production and hence for agricultural land – and the countervailing role of increased agricultural productivity and yield growth in slowing agricultural expansion (Southgate 1991). A statistical analysis by Burgess (1991), covering all tropical forest countries, confirms the relative importance of frontier agricultural expansion (represented by an index of food crop and livestock production) and debt-servicing on tropical deforestation. Increases in domestic roundwood produc-tion (representing both industrial use and fuelwood) and GNP per capita also had significant but much smaller positive impacts. Sur-prisingly, population had a slightly negative effect on deforestation. The latter results conflict with the earlier findings by Palo, Mery and Salmi (1987) and suggests that further empirical work needs to be undertaken to examine the explicit relationship between popu-lation growth, population density and deforestation.   A recent study in Thailand highlights the complex linkages between agri-cultural crop prices, the relative returns from different crops and the demand for land (Phantumvanit and Panayotou, 1990). In Thailand, approximately 40 per cent of the increase in cultivated land in recent years has been met by converted forest land. The most important factors affecting the demand for cropland, and thus forest conversion, appear to be population growth followed by non-agricultural returns, although agricultural pricing also has a significant influence (see Table 7.4). Higher aggregate real prices may have a slightly positive influence on the demand for cropland, and thus increased forest clearing; however, this direct effect may be counteracted by the indirect impact of higher agricultural prices on raising the productivity of existing land and increasing the cultivation of previously idle land, thus reducing the demand for new land from forest clearing. Changes in relative prices also influence the demand for new cropland by affecting the relative profitability of land-saving as opposed to land-extensive cropping systems.[6]

Table 7.4: Thailand – the demand for agricultural land (cultivated), 1962-89

Explanatory variables	Coefficients and T-statistics
Real price of agricultural crops (lagged one year)	0.081 (2.00)
Agricultural population	1.337 (12.82)
Agricultural productivity (lagged one year)	−0.280 (−2.43)
Relative return to land from landsaving crops to land using crops	−0.155 (−3.95)
Relative return to labour from non-agriculture	−0.308 (−3.37)
Time dummy	−0.352 (−4.12)
AR(2)	0.437 (−2.27)

R squared adjusted = 0.987
DurbinWatson = 2.00
F-statistic = 330.00
Degrees of Freedom = 19.00

Notes: **1.** Coefficients indicate the responsiveness of the dependent variable to changes in the explanatory variables; e.g., a 10% increase in aggregate real crop prices leads to a 0.8% increase in the demand for land.

2. Statistics indicated in parentheses.

Source: D. Phantumvanit and T. Panayotou (1990).

Conclusion and further policy issues

Excessive tropical deforestation is a matter of concern for both tropical forest countries and the international community. In this chapter we have stressed the importance of proper valuation of forest resources, proper analysis of land use options and the causes behind tropical deforestation and correcting market and policy distortions that provide incentives for excessive depletion and conversion of forest lands.

However, tropical forests may have some important economic values that are internationally significant. In particular, their functions as "stores" of carbon and biological diversity may have a global value. As argued in this chapter, as other nations benefit from these global values, they should be willing to pay tropical forest countries for conserving the forests. Not only is it important to begin estimating these values in monetary terms, but also it is essential to begin discussing appropriate international transfer mechanisms and agreements through which these values can be translated into financial resource flows that can benefit tropical forest countries directly. In this respect, the emergence of the International Tropical Timber Organization (ITTO), which is essentially a commodity organization bringing together the major tropical timber consumers, traders and producers as a basis for formulating a policy consensus on the trade, is an important step in encouraging more effective efforts globally to bring tropical forests under sustained management. At the same time, the ITTO may be effective in discouraging well-meaning but unhelpful policy developments concerning the trade, such as a ban on tropical timber imports proposed by some consumer nations.[7]

Ultimately, however, the management of the world's tropical forests will remain in the hands of those countries that contain these great ecosystems. In many TMF countries, most of the forested land is in the public domain, or at least nominally under government control. Good forest management depends, therefore, on the effective implementation of appropriate government policies. This chapter has particularly emphasized the role of economic policies in forestry management. However, effective economic policies have to be complemented by appropriate institutional and regulatory frameworks for forest land use management, such as land use planning and zoning, land titling and registration, monitoring and enforcement of protected areas, co-operating with local inhabitants in community-based development initiatives (see Chapter 5) and developing technical and administrative suport for the line agencies responsible for forest resource management.

References

Barbier, E.B., *The Economic Value of Ecosystems: 2 - Tropical Forests*, LEEC *Gatekeeper* 91-01, London Environmental Economics Centre [1991a].

Barbier, E.B., *Tropical Deforestation*, Ch. 9 in D.W. Pearce et al., *Blueprint 2: The Greening of the World Economy*, [London: Earthscan, 1991b].

Barbier, E.B., J.L. Burgess, T.S. Swanson, and D. W. Pearce, *Elephants, Economics and Ivory* [London: Earthscan, 1990].

Binswanger, H. *Brazilian Policies that Encourage Deforestation in the Amazon*, Environment Department Working Paper No. 16, [Washington, DC: World Bank, 1989].

Browder, J.O., Subsidies, Deforestation, and the Forest Sector in the Brazilian Amazon [Washington, DC: World Resources Institute, 1985].

Burgess, J.C., "Economic Analysis of Frontier Agricultural Expansion and Tropical Deforestation", M.Sc. Thesis, Economics Dept., University College, London [1991].

Capistrano, A.D., "Macroeconomic Influences on Tropical Forest Depletion: A Cross-Country Analysis", PhD Dissertation, Food and Resource Economics Dept., University of Florida, Miami [1990].

Capistrano, A.D. and C.F. Kiker, "Global Economic Influences on Tropical Closed Broadleaved Forest Depletion, 1967- 85", Food and Resource Economics Dept., University of Florida, Miami, mimeo. [1990].

Mahar, D. Government Policies and Deforestation in Brazil's Amazon Region, [Washington, DC: World Bank, 1989].

Palo, M., G. Mery, and J. Salmi, "Deforestation in the Tropics: Pilot Scenarios Based on Quantitative Analysis", in M. Palo and J. Salmi (eds.), Deforestation or Development in the Third World, Division of Social Economics of Forestry, Finnish Forestry Research, Helsinki [1987].

Paris, R. and I. Ruzicka, Barking Up the Wrong Tree: The Role of Rent Appropriation in Tropical Forest Management, Environment Office Discussion Paper, Asian Development Bank, Manila [1991].

Pearce, D.W. An Economic Approach to Saving the Tropical Forests, LEEC Discussion Paper 90-05, London Environmental Economics Centre, London [1990].

Pearce, D.W., E.B. Barbier, and A. Markandya, Sustainable Development: Economics and Environment in the Third World [London: Edward Elgar, 1990].

Phantumvanit, D. and T. Panayotou, Natural Resources for a Sustainable Future: Spreading the Benefits, report prepared for the 1990 TDRI Year-End Conference on Industrializing Thailand and its Impact on the Environment, December 8-9, Chon Buri, Thailand [1990].

Poore, D., F. Burgess, J. Palmer, S. Reitbergen, and T. Synott, T. No Timber Without Trees: Sustainability in the Tropical Forest, [London: Earthscan, 1989].

Reis, E. and S. Margulis, "Economic Perspectives on Deforestation in the Brazilian Amazon", Paper presented at the EAERE Conference on Economics of International Environmental Problems and Policies, Stockholm, June 10-14 [1990].

Repetto, R. "Macroeconomic Policies and Deforestation", paper prepared for UNU/WIDER Project, The Environment and Emerging Development Issues, Helsinki [1990].

Repetto, R. and M. Gillis, Public Policies and the Misuse of Forest Resources [Cambridge: Cambridge University Press, 1988].

Repetto, R., M. Wells, C. Beer, and F. Rossini, Natural Resource Accounting for Indonesia, [Washington, DC: World Resources Institute, 1987].

Schmidt, R.C. *Current Tropical Moist Forest Management Activities in Brazil*, Report prepared for the Government of Brazil, FAO, Rome [1989].

Southgate, D., *Tropical Deforestation and Agriculture Development in Latin America*, LEEC Discussion Paper 91-01, London Environmental Economics Centre, London [1991].

Southgate, D., R. Sierra, and L. Brown, *The Causes of Tropical Deforestation in Ecuador: A Statistical Analysis*, LEEC Paper 89-09, London Environmental Economics Centre, London [1989].

Swanson, T. "Conserving Biological Diversity", in D.W. Pearce, et al., *Blueprint 2: Greening the World Economy*, [London: Earthscan, 1991].

Notes

1. For further discussion of the methodology for economic appraisal of different tropical forest land use options see Barbier (1991a).
2. The results of the study presented in Table 1 have to be interpreted with caution (Barbier, 1991b). First, the financial returns to fruit and latex are the *potential returns*. Whether actual returns will reach this magnitude is uncertain, as the marketing, post-harvesting processing and exporting prospects necessary for establishing new non-timber products is generally underdeveloped. Second, the particular hectare of forest studied is in an advantageous position near town markets, whereas most tropical rainforest areas are less favourably located for the marketing of non-timber products. Finally, fruit harvesting in the Amazon can be destructive, especially to palms, and certain techniques of rubber-tapping, such as "slaughter tapping", have also been known to cause severe tree damage. In general, the record for harvesting non-timber forest products for commercial exploitation is not good, especially where harvesting is potentially desstructive, such as in the case of tree barks and gum.
3. For a review, see Binswanger (1989); Majar (1989) and Peaarce, Barbier and Markandya (1990), ch. 5 and 9.
4. The *resource rent* is the full resource value except for the cost and labour and capital employed in managing and harvesting. The existence of a rent from resource exploitation suggests the presence of "excess" profits – i.e. profits exceeding the returns necessary to keep labour and capital employed in that activity. The combination of policy distortions, ill-defined property rights and uncontrolled access to new tracts of forest land all contribute to excessive deforestation through rent-seeking behaviour.
5. ITTO is the International Timber Trade Organization.
6. The authors also examined the effects of relative price changes on land productivity and the cultivation of previously idle land but found this relationship more difficult to estimate in such an aggregate analysis.

7. The use of bans on highly valued resource commodities that also have very widely dispersed, and fluid, trading routes has not been very successful. In general, a controlled and regulated trade linked to sustainable management practices may be more effective. In this regard, the lessons from the economic analysis of the trade in elephant ivory might be instructive for the timber trade (see Barbier et al, 1990).

8

WILDLIFE AND WILDLAND UTILIZATION AND CONSERVATION

Richard Luxmoore and Timothy M. Swanson

Many of the chapters in this book have made much of the capacity of wildlife utilization to render benefits for the conservation of wildlands. This is certainly true, in theory. However, it is not true that use, irrespective of the form that it takes, will necessarily confer benefits upon the wildlands from which the wildlife derives. The form that the utilization takes is crucial for conservation purposes.

All domesticated species were wild once, and the form of use chosen for these species does absolutely nothing to benefit the wilds. Similarly, current attempts to render wild species, such as the cane rat, into domesticated species generally do nothing for the conservation of wildlands and wildlife. The introduction of specialized uses of wildlife into wildlands merely converts them to domesticated habitat.

The *sustainable* harvesting of wild plants and animals for subsistence use by local communities is probably the least specialized use of wildlands. These forms of use are nearly always of conservation benefit, supporting both the biological and the cultural diversity of the wilds.

This chapter assesses the range of forms of wildlife utilization that lie between these two endpoints of domestication and sustainable harvesting. While it is clear that specialized use/domestication is not a force for conservation, it is equally apparent that its polar opposite is a positive force for diversity conservation. But what of the various forms of utilization that lie inbetween? Is it possible for other forms of human intervention in the wilds to confer any conservation benefits, or are these merely more gradual forms of wildlands erosion? That is, what are the characteristics of human intervention that render it a force for conservation, rather than a force for conversion? This is the critical analytical question that must be answered with regard to wildlife utilization.

Equally important are the practical questions. Even if in theory utilization can confer benefits for conservation, does it do so in practice? For example, although local peoples' wild harvests are theoretically forces for conservation, in practice they are often unsustainable and thus non-constructive. In the course of our analysis in this chapter, we attempt to sort out the differences between theory and practice. Although theory may dictate that utilization be made a part of the strategy for diversity conservation, it is equally clear that many problems for its implementation remain. Our analysis here is intended to spotlight these problems for their future resolution, not to indicate that their existence negates the importance of the theory.

Finally, the last question that we pursue is whether there is any profitability to be had from the forms of wildlife utilization that should convey conservation benefits. If not, then there is little reason to be supporting a strategy based upon utilization, because then the only forms of utilization that would occur would be the non-beneficial ones (conservation-wise). Hence the demonstrated profitability of constructive utilization must be clear; otherwise, more harm than benefit could result from embracing this policy.

Non-specialized production versus specialized production

With the possible exception of Antarctica, almost all terrestrial habitat has, to a greater or lesser extent, evolved with a human component within it. Therefore, the basic objective of diversity conservation should not be to remove people from the wilds; people-less parks are not "natural". The distinction is not between habitat devoid of humans or that populated by them; rather, it is a distinction between different methods of production.

Table 8.1: Distinctions between non-specialized and specialized production

Non-specialized production	
diverse species	one or few species
minimal capital goods	substantial capital goods
little human intervention	substantial intervention
nonsegregated resource	segregated resource base

The three key facets distinguishing specialized production from non-specialized production are homogeneity, intervention and segregation. *Specialization* arises when the methods of mass production are applied to natural resources. The mass production of a single commodity allows for the use of specialized capital goods (machinery, chemicals, bio-engineered seed varieties) that have comparatively high rates of productivity when introduced. This means that specialization results in substantial cost differentials between those resources processed by thes methods and those for which such capital goods are not available or not used.[1]

Such capital goods require substantial minimum efficient scales in order to be cost-effective, both in their own production and in their application. This minimum efficient scale requirement means that only a few species are capable of production on a world wide basis by use of these capital intensive methods. The logical consequence is that only a small number of species provide the bulk of the world's food. For example, of the thousands of species of plants that are deemed edible only 20 species actually produce the vast majority of the world's food. (Vietmeyer (1986)]. In fact, the four main carbohydrate crops (wheat, rice, maize and potatoes) feed more people than the next 26 crops combined (Witt, 1985).

Another consequences of the mass production of a small number of species is the necessity for continuous human intervention. The introduction of these species into habitats to which they are not naturally adapted, and especially when intensive agriculture is being practised, means that continuous human involvement is required in order to monitor the production process. Of course, nature is capable of producing biomass of its own accord through natural photosynthetic processes, but once substantial components of the existing ecosystem are removed and new ones are introduced, continuous human intervention is usually necessary. In essence, the displacement of the ecosystem production system from its equilibrium is a commitment to on-going (ie not a one-off) intervention.

The dynamics of this process are well illustrated by the case of the introduction of cattle throughout the range of the tsetse fly in AFrica. Because the fly carries a disease dangerous for both cattle and people, there have been numerous campaigns to eradicate it in order to make room the cattle introductions. The first attempts were direct: wildlife eradication programmes were initiated at the beginning of the century. Then, it was found that re-invasion of the tsetse was virtually certain, even after the removal of the wildlife, unless the brush was also cleared; this led to massive land conversion programmes in the post-war period. More recently, massive insecticide and fencing programmes have been initiated as possible control programmes. The problem remains unresolved; the impacts on the region have been enormous (matthiessen and Douthwaite, 1985).

In this fashion, substantial human intervention becomes translated from a one-off into an on-going process, as the consequences of earlier activities require future interventions. Often the causal link between past intervention and necessary future intervention is not so obvious; however, it is generally true that the conversion to less diverse methods of production renders the resource base more vulnerable, and hence more continuous methods of monitoring and intervention become necessary as well.[2]

The second distinguishing facet of specialized production is the segregation of the resource base. Segregation by the clear designation of individual property rights, usually accomplished through fencing, is often necessary for optimal individual investments. This is because the incentives for optimal individual investments are most cost-effectively conferred by this method; it provides the means by which the expected returns to investment are internalized *ex ante*. The notion of asset ownership is especially important when the investment process is an on-going one. Therefore, segregation and specialization go hand-in-hand when specialized production techniques are introduced into natural habitat.

However, biologists have demonstrated a causal connection between the segregation of natural habitat and the extinction of species. Empirical studies have estimated that a reduction of 90 per cent in the size of a particular piece of natural habitat will result in a halving of the number of species (Wilson, 1988). Although it would seem to require dramatic changes to the habitat in order to achieve this magnitude of reduction, this sort of impact could in fact be obtained by merely erecting two fences across the area. Therefore, the conversion of land from natural habitat to specialized production is driven by the economic *law of specialization*, and the productivity gains that it promises. However, a clear trade-off exists between productivity and variety under this law. This is because the necessary components of specialized production (homogenization, intervention and segregation) foster the former while diminishing the latter.

The theory of wildlife utilization attempts to break this cycle, by encouraging only *non-specialized* forms of production in the wilds. This raises the prospect of breaking this link between development and diversity destruction, by allowing intervention to take some form other than the most intensive and specialized, while still capturing the full range of the value of the wilds.

The question that must now be addressed is: which of the various forms of wildlife utilization are positive forces for conservation? That is, which are non-specialized, non-intensive interventions that act by capturing the value of the wilds, rather than converting them?

The range of methods available for wildlife utilization

The different wildlife exploitation systems, are known by a confusing variety of terms, often based on details of practical husbandry. One set of terminology to consider is that laid down by CITES, the international convention on trade in endangered species.

Under CITES, "captive-breeding" is the breeding of species in a "controlled environment" from a parental breeding stock which is "maintained without augmentation from the wild". A "controlled environment" is "one which is intensively manipulated by man for the purpose of producing the species in question, and that has boundaries designed to prevent the species in question . . . from entering or leaving". Thus, there is little to distinguish captive breeding of wildlife from the processes that are applied to domesticated species.

"Ranching", on the other hand, involves the rearing of animals in a controlled environment of specimens taken from the wild, and therefore differs from captive-breeding in that there is a continuous interchange with wild populations. The ranching of wildlife therefore has implications for wildlands, and must be more carefully analysed. There is a variety of different ranching methods available, ranging from fairly active intervention to virtually none, and thus this concept covers quite a broad range of possible activities in the wilds.

Table 8.2: The spectrum of methods available for wildlife utilization

Domestication/captive breeding		ranching	wild harvest
	Intensive	Extensive	

The fundamental distinction between the concepts of domestication and captive breeding versus ranching and wild harvest is that of interaction of the utilized animal with the wild population. It is this interaction that keeps the ecosystem intact, and provides the incentives to conserve the entire system rather than just the animal. The fundamental distinction between the various forms of ranching is the degree of specialization involved.

Captive-breeding – a survey of methods

The term captive-breeding implies separation from the wild population of the species, which is ually achieved either by removing the animals to an artificial enclosure (as with mink farms), fencing in an extensive area (as with deer farms) or close control of a free-ranging herd (as with reindeer husbandry). The essential feature is that the gene pool of the captive population is separate from that of the wild population.

All domestic livestock derives from early attempts to bring wild animals into captivity, but this process took place so long ago, mostly in the Neolithic period, that surviving stock are clearly differentiated, in law and genotype, from their wild ancestors. However, attempts at wildlife domestication continue and have been increasing in frequency during the last hundred years. Some of the more interesting examples are listed in Table 8.3. Those that have been most successful have been the species farmed for fur, the deer, the crocodilians and the ostriches. Several of the other species, such as the musk deer, moose, musk ox and cane rat, have yet to pass from the experimental phase to commercial production.

What is commonly termed "game ranching" is often the keeping of captive herds under extensive conditions. These methods of ranching are common in South Africa where a variety of native ungulates are kept on fenced properties. The habitat is managed by the provision of watering points and often a system of burning, and the species composition is manipulated by selective culling and the introduction of livestock bought from other farms or caught in nature reserves. Some interchange with wild populations is achieved by imperfect fencing and the purchase of stock from outside. Nevertheless, these regimes are probably most accurately considered to be more extensive forms of captive breeding, rather than more intensive forms of ranching; there is too little interaction with the wilds.

A vast aquaculture industry has sprung up fairly recently, consisting of mostly freshwater fish, such as tilapia, salmon and trout, and prawns, mussels and oysters. These represent the first steps in the introduction of the forces of domestication/specialization into the watery environments on earth. It shall probably not be many too years before the vast variety that we are accustomed to seeing arise from the seas is also diminished by this process.

Table 8.3: Selected species of wild animal (excluding fish and invertebrates) bred in captivity for commercial purposes

Common name	Scientific name	Main products	Date	Main countries
Mink	Mustela vision	Fur	1900	Widespread
Musk rat	Ondatra zibethica	Fur	1910	N. America
Racoon dog	Nyctereutes procyonoides	Fur	1969	Europe, USSR
Coypu	Myocastor coypus	Fur	1920	N. America
Silver fox	Vulpes vulpes	Fur	1890	Widespread
Blue fox	Alopex lagopus	Fur	1900	Widespread
Sable	Martes zibellina	Fur	1929	USSR
Chinchilla	Chinchilla laniger	Fur	1923	Widespread
Red deer	Cervus elaphus	Meat, antler	1830	USSR, New Zealand, Europe, N. America
Fallow deer	Dama dama	Meat		New Zealand, Europe, N. America
Silka Deer	cervus nippon	Meat, antler	1000 BC	China, Eyrope, Korea
Rusa deer	Cervus timorensis	Meat, antler		Mauritius, SE Asia
Moose	Alces alces	Meat, milk, draught	1949	USSR
Musk deer	Moschus spp.	Musk (experimental)	1975	China, India
Plains bison	Bison bison	Meat	19??	USA, Canada
musk ox	Ovibos moschatus	Fibre (qiviut)	1965	USA (Alaska)
Cane rat	Thryonomys swinderianus	Meat		Benin, Cameroon
Ostrich	Struthio camelus	Leather, meat, feathers	1860	S.Africa, USA, Zimbabwe, Botswana
Emu	Dromaius novaehollandiae	Leather, meat, feathers	1976	Australia
Crocodiles	Crocodylus spp.	Leather, meat	1950	Australia, SE Asia, Africa
Alligator	Alligator mississippiensis	Leather meat		USA
American bullfrog	Rana catesbiana	Meat		USA
Green turtle	Chelonia mydas	Meat, oil, shell, leather	1970	Cayman Islands

Ranching – a survey of methods

Ranching is bringing the wild population into contact with a human-controlled environment for some portion of their lives (prior to harvest). This intervention may be fleeting, such as the provision of additional food supplies or nesting facilities, or it may be very substantial, such as the removal of eggs for hatching. Various types of intervention include: removing competition with the focal species ("pests") and competitors for the same ("predators"); improving the food supply, possibly by rotational burning, fertilization, irrigation, introduction of food species or the direct provision of food; providing additional water or mineral supplements; creation of additional sites for nesting or breeding; and the introduction of species to regions where they did not naturally occur.

Examples of ranching are more difficult to find but are possibly best exemplified by some crocodile farms. In several countries, notably Zimbabwe, Australia, and the USA, eggs are collected from nests laid in the wild and are brought into captivity to be hatched and grown until the animals are large enough to slaughter for their skins. In Papua New Guinea, the eggs are usually allowed to hatch naturally in the wild and it is the hatchlings that are brought into the farms. Green turtles are ranched under a similar regime on Réunion in the Indian Ocean, the hatchlings being collected after emerging from their nests on the uninhabited islands of Tromelin and Europa. Under natural circumstances, there is a high mortality of young crocodilians and turtles, very few surviving to reach adulthood. Thus, taking 100 eggs from the wild probably only prevents one or two reptiles from reaching maturity and it is therefore much less damaging than taking 100 adult animals. A slightly different form of reptile ranching is being developed with green iguanas in Costa Rica. Eggs are collected from nests laid in the wild and the resulting hatchlings are reared in captivity for a relatively short period before being released to feed in the wild. Once they have grown sufficiently, they are harvested for food.

Eels are also ranched. They breed in an unknown location (presumed to be deep in the western Atlantic) and the juvenile elvers return to feed in rivers in Europe whereupon they are collected and removed to farms for ongrowing. Salmon are usually bred in captivity but they can also be ranched because they return to breed in their natal river having spent a period of time feeding at sea. Thus, by releasing juvenile parr or smolt at a stage that is past that when the peak natural mortality occurs, they can be allowed to feed at sea at no expense to the rancher after which they return to their release site and can be caught once more. This is the exact converse of the type of ranching practised with crocodilians, because the breeding occurs under controlled conditions while most of the growing phase takes place in the wild.

Civets are kept in Ethiopia for the purpose of extracting musk, a valuable substance used in the perfume industry. They are not bred in captivity but are captured from the wild and kept in cages, the musk being extracted at intervals of about ten days. The use of elephants for draught power in India and particularly Myanmar must be regarded as a form of ranching because they are rarely bred in captivity, but are captured from wild herds and trained with other "domesticated" elephants.

It is difficult to find other examples of ranching amongst the large mammals. "Game ranching" as practised in Canada with the native species of moose, wapiti, bison and white-taked deer, is probably the best candidate for the title.

Wild harvests – a survey of methods

The different methods of exploiting free-ranging, wild animals grade imperceptibly into what can reasonably be called ranching, depending on the level of management practised. Selective culling is one of the least intensive methods of intervention. In Zimbabwe, the culling of wild elephants for ivory, meat and hides generated approximately US$4.7 per annum in the 1980s.

The type of "mixed use" regimes found in Zimbabwe are also a form of wild harvest and involve little habitat manipulation. The rarer species, particularly elephant, buffalo, leopard, sable antelope, are generally preserved for hunting by overseas trophy hunters, which yields a very high price per animal. More common species, such as impala, may be simply shot for meat. Some of the best developed enterprises are to be found on private cattle ranches where game are exploited in conjunction with the more conventional agricultural products. This type of mixed use results in greatly increased species diversity and considerably less habitat alteration than cattle farming on its own. Whereas previously, buffalo were actively eradicated because of their ability to transmit disease (notably foot-and-mouth disease and TB) to cattle, they are now one of the most favoured species because of their high trophy value.

The attempts to involve local communities in the commercial management of game for a wide variety of uses (tourism, sport hunting, meat) are also very non-intensive forms of utilization. These are described in Chapter 4.

Although most East African countries have now prohibited the traditional hunting of wildlife for subsistence purposes, the use of game meat in West Africa is widespread. In many of the rural parts of Latin America and AFrica, it may contribute as much as 70 per cent of the animal protein (Ajayi, 1979; Sale, 1981). However, the systems of exploitation practised are not generally well managed and any resemblance to a sustainable management programme is fortuitous, resulting from the biology of the exploited species, the low human population or the difficulty of hunting.

Table 8.4: Comparative returns of mixed use versus monoculture in Zimbabwe

	Cattle and wildlife	Cattle alone
	Z$/ha.	Z$/ha.
Wildlife	4.47	1.16
Cattle	1.23	2.93
Total	5.71	4.09

Source: Child (1988)

One of the oldest and best documented traditional hunting systems is that of the Inuit culture of northern Canada, Alaska and Greenland. This depends on a mixture of species, including ringed seal, caribou, muskox and a variety of other marine mammals, fish and birds. Further south in Canada, the Indian communities depend to a large extent on meat harvested from the wild, estimates ranging from 253 kg to 1493 kg per capita per year (Klein, 1989).

Elsewhere in the Northern TEmperate Zone, the huge herds of saiga anteloupe have been hunted for many years in the USSR, yielding an annual average of 2800 tonnes of meat in the 25 years up to 1981 (Sokolov and Lebedeva, 1989). However, the fur harvest of North America and the USSR returns a substantial economic off-take from wild lands.

There are many non-consumptive forms of wildlife utilization as well. The great seabird colonies of Peru are used as a source of guano, as are various cave-dwelling bats and swiftlets in Southeast Asia. Slightly more damaging is the practice of removing the cave swiftlets' nests to eat. Eider ducks have been used as a source of down in Iceland for centuries, the feathers being collected from the nests, which are often built in specially constructed shelters and protected from the depredations of Arctic foxes. Vicuña are periodically rounded up in Peru and sheared of their extremely fine hair. This practice has been revived only recently but was originally used by the Incas. The fibre from musk oxen is of a similar quality and value to that of vicuña and can be collected from the ground at the annual moult. Although the collection of birds' eggs for food is usually a form of predation, involving direct mortality and a reduction in breeding success, it can be practised in such a manner as to minimize this this. The eggs of species of colonial-nesting birds, especially gulls, can be harvested at the correct time so that the parents re-lay and, although this involves additional energy expenditure, the same number of chicks can be raised.

Also included in the category of non-consumptive non-intensive wildland utilization are the variety of forms of recreational uses of the wilds., These interventions involve an indirect costliness for the wilds due to habitat degradation, but they also return tremendous value. The recreational uses of the wilds include tourism, trekking and various wildlife "sports". For example, a somewhat bizarre form of trophy hunting has recently emerged in South Africa where rhinos are shot with a tranquillizer dart. A mould is then taken of the unconscious animal's head which is later used to make a cast to hang on the hunter's wall.

The impact of the form of use on conservation

The most non-intensive, non-specialized uses of the wilds render a straightforward conservation benefit when they are practised sustainably. Without damaging or converting the natural capital of the wilds, these uses create benefits in their current state. This helps to maintain their existing status, and to recruit local communities to their cause.

In this section, the relative conservation merits of the "intermediate" forms of wildlife utilization (captive breeding and ranching) are considered. These are more complicated questions because the degree of intervention and intensity is much greater than with mere wild harvesting. First, two "indirect" ways in which utilization aids to conservation are considered: a) their contribution to an increase in the total numbers of the exploited species, and b) the diversion of trade away from wild populations. Finally, the "direct" contribution of these intermediate forms of utilization is considered: c) the conservation of natural and diverse habitats. The validity of these arguments will be reviewed in the following sections.

Population increases and conservation

Although captive-breeding can undoubtedly give rise to a substantial captive population, it is by no means clear that this benefits the wilds. As an example of the long-term conservation potential of captive-breding, one need look no further than the wild relatives of the current domesticated species of large mammals. Table 8.5 lists the species that are close relatives of the major domestic species. Of these, at least 33 are listed in the CITES Appendices or considered by IUCN to be threatened (IUCN), 1988). Captive-breeding, by definition, involves genetic isolation from the wild stock which, under the demands of commercial production, almost inevitably leads to selective breeding. After a period of time, the captive stock are no longer suitable for re-introduction or inter-breeding with the wild stock, and history shows that there has been little practical incentive to conserve the wild stock. Furthermore, even if no genetic divergence has occurred, fear of introducing disease may make the captive stock unsuitable for re-introduction to depleted local populations.

The main domestic species diverged from their wild parents many generations ago, but this process can occur very rapidly, as can be seen from some more recent domesticates. Ostriches were bred initially for their feathers, and the farmed stock in South Africa are markedly smaller than the wild stock. The distinction with fur-bearers is often more obvious because the breeding tends to select distinct colour varieties. The silver fox, one of the most widely farmed furs, is a colour variety of the red fox that is extremely rare in the wild. Captive-breeding is designed to function independently from the wild population and, after a period of time, almost inevitably does so.

Ranching does not have this disadvantage because not only does it involve a continuous interchange with the wild population, and therefore prevents inbreeding, but also it actually depends on the continued existence of a wild population to function. Furthermore, in many cases, the ranched animals are kept in semi-natural habitats, and are therefore still under some selection pressure to retain a resemblance to the wild type.

It is important to note that the line between domestic/captive and wild is sometimes a fluid one. The rabbit was originally introduced to the UK as a food source and kept under close control in "warrens", usually under the ownership of monasteries – clearly a form of captive-breeding. After some time, the warrens were allowed to slip into disuse and the proprietary rights over the rabbits were less strictly enforced so that they became free-ranging, feral animals.

**Table 8.5: Wild relatives of major domesticated species,
showing IUCN categories (Endangered, Vulnerable or
Intermediate) or CITES Appendix. Brackets indicate that
only certain subspecies are listed**

Suidae

Babyrousa babyrussa	babyrousa	V
Hylochoerus meinertzhageni	Gian forest hog	
Phacochoerus aethiopicus	Warthog	
Potamochoerus porcus	Bush pig	
Sus barbatus	Bearded pig	(V)
Sus salvanius	Pugmy hog	E
Sus scrofa	Wild boar	(V)
Sus verrucosus	Javan warty hog	

Caprinae

Ovis ammon	Argali	I
Ovis aries	Moufflon	(V)
Ovis canadensis	American bighorn	App II
Ovis dalli	Dall sheep	
Ovis musimon	Moufflon	(V)
Ovis vignei	Urial	App I
Pseudois nayaur	Bharal	
Ammortragus lervia	Aoudad	(V)
Capra caucasica	W. Caucasian tur	
Capra cylindricornis	E. Causasian tur	
Capra falconeri	Markhor	V
Capra hircus	Bezoar	
Capra ibex	Ibex	(E)
Capra pyrenaica	Spanish ibex	E

Bovnae

Bos sauveli	Kouprey	E
Bos gaurus	Gaur	V
Bos javanicus	Bantng	V
Bos gruniens	Wild yak	E
Bubalus bubalis	Water buffalo	E
Bubalus mindorensis	Tamaraw	E
Bubalus depressicornis	Lowland anoa	E
Bison bonasus	European bison	V
Bison bison	American bison	(App I)
Syncerus caffer	African buffalo	

Equidae

Equus asinus	African wild ass	E
Equus burchelli	Burchell's zebra	
Equus caballus	Wild Horse	E
Equus grevyi	Grevy's zebra	E
Equus hemionus	Asiatic wild ass	(E)
Equus kiang	Kiang	
Equus onager	Onager	(App I)
Equus zebra	Mountain zebra	(E)

Camelidae

Camelus bactrianus	Bactrian camel	V
Vicugna vicugna	Vicuna	V
Llama guanicoe	Guanaco	App II

For a while, they were exploited by full-time professional trappers but now they are only hunted intermittently and opportunistically.

This points to another problem. It matters not only what the size of a population is, but also where it is. Outside of its own habitat, a species can be much more of a detriment than a benefit for conservation.

Ever since the time of the rabbit introductions, a problem resulting from wildlife utilization is the possibility of introducing exotic species outside their natural range. It is a particular problem of captive-breeding. Entrepreneurs in countries that do not have native species suitable for farming may attempt to introduce alien species that can then escape and establish feral populations. There are numerous examples among the fur-bearers where this has happened with deleterious effects on the local fauna. Mink and muskrat are now established throughout much of Europe and the feral population of nutria was only exterminated in the UK after many years of costly control programme. There are serious concerns in Scandinavia about the racoon-dog escaping from farms. Recently, Nile corcodiles have been introduced to Brazil for the purposes of establishing a farm, posing a potential threat to aquatic ecosystems throughout the continent of South America. Similarly, Cuban crocodiles have been introduced to farms in South east Asia.

The threat of exotic populations is not theoretical and there are numerous documented ecological catastrophes resulting from species introductions. At a recent workshop convened by IUCN to discuss the problem of species extinctions, it was concluded that the majority of documented extinctions of vertebrates were attributable to the problem of exotic species. The red deer and Himalayan that have been introduced to New Zealand for sport hunting and have caused major disruption of the plant communities. The effects and economic impact of the introduction of the rabbit to Australia are well known.

Introduced species cause problems not only by direct predation and ecological competition, but also by more subtle means. One of the most widely cultivated species of oyster is the Japanese oyster. This does not breed in European waters and has to be maintained by the supply of larvae from hatcheries. There is thus no danger of it establishing feral populations and yet it has been responsible for the introduction of a disease that has seriously affected local stocks of the native oyster. The signal crayfish has been introduced from North America to the freshwaters of Europe for farming and has brought with it a disease that has spread to the local species of crayfish with devastating effect.

Introduction of disease is not only a problem of exotic species, however, but also may be spread by indigenous species when used

in unfamiliar ways. TB has been brought to previously uninfected
areas of Canada by the movement of wapiti and bison for game
farms. High intensity farming also exacerbates the problems of
natural diseases because of the locally high population density.
Atlantic salmon are naturally infected at low levels with various copepod ectoparasites. When the salmon are confined to the
crowded cages of farms, these parasites build up to lethal levels
and must be controlled with chemicals. This is certainly a problem
of the farmed stock but it also spills over into the wild stock of
salmon because the high population of parasites ensures that a
larger number of larvae are released into the water column where
they can infect the local wild salmon or sea trout. In some areas
of Ireland this is reported to have depleted wild populations and
caused the collapse of a profitable sport fishing industry.

Diversion of trade

Where a wild population is being over-exploited for trade, it is
possible that an alternative supply from captive sources could divert
some of the trade and reduce the pressure on the wild population.
The mechanism by which this can work is by increasing the
supply so that the market becomes saturated and the price is
driven downwards, making exploitation of the wild population
unprofitable. A practical example is the case of the ATlantic Salmon
which was first farmed in Europe in the 1970s and of which annual
production has now reached some 160,000 tonnes, many times the
size of the wild harvest. The effect on price can be seen in Figure
8.1, where the annual production in the Uk is compared to the
average wholesale price (1989 values). Apart from a period of low
production in the late 1970s, when the price rose to £11/kg, the
previous price of wild salmon was in the region of £7/kg. The rapidly
escalating production has driven the price down to nearly £4/kg
in 1989, which has had some profound effects. It has obviously
reduced the profit margins for the farming industry itself, which
has forced some farms out of business and made it less attractive
to new investment, but it has also affected the wild harvest. Many
commercial net fisheries on British rivers have declined in value so
that they have been bought out by anglers' associations wishing
to establish exclusive rights to the fishing. Whether it has affected
the illegal poaching of salmon has not been determined, but it is
probably that the legal fisheries suffered most, as poaching has
fewer overhead costs (Stansfeld, 1986).

The implications of this experience for other wildlife harvesting
systems are serious. It has been argued that those exploitation

Figure 8.1: Production of Atlantic salmon (*Salmo salar*) in the United Kingdom (FAO, 1960–1988) including both wild harvest and output from farms

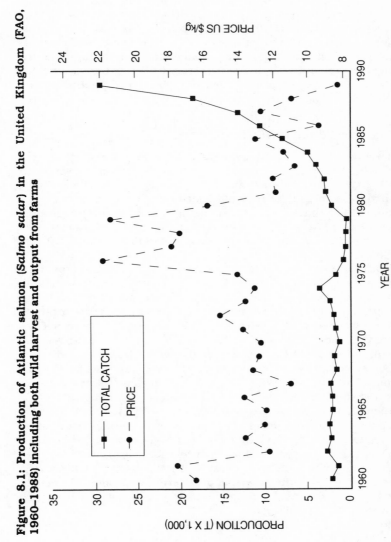

The 1989 production was estimated from a farm production of 28.5 T (Salmon Growers' Assoc., pers. commun.). The wholesale price of salmon in Scotland (Stansfield, 1986, pers. commun., 1990) was corrected for inflation to 1989 values.

systems that rely on wild populations, either direct harvest or ranching, have the greatest likelihood of giving value to, and therefore promoting, conservation of natural habitat. If a captive-breeding operation is set up in competition then there is a strong probability that it will depress the price of the wild commodity and result in reduced profitability for the legal wild harvests while allowing the illegal, unregulated trade to continue. In the longer terms, captive-breeding is therefore likely to have a seriously detrimental affect on any attempt to manage wild populations for commercial production.

Conservation of natural habitats

It is self evident that intensive captive-breeding makes little contribution to the conservation of natural habitats. It makes very little difference to the local environment if a farmer erects a chicken shed or a mink farm. Both are equally destructive to the pre-existing vegetation. Even the less intensive types of captive-breeding operation, such as deer farms, are comparable in their impact to domestic livestock agriculture: a monoculture of deer is similar to a monoculture of cattle.

The more extensive forms of wildlife use, ie the variety of ranching regimes, rely on the maintenance of extensive areas of natural habitat and are generally more beneficial for conservation. However, even the less intensive forms of ranching create forces contrary to diversity conservation. This is because, once a particular species from the wild becomes explicitly "valued", sthere is a danger that the other residents of the same habitat will be less tolerated.

For example, most game cropping exercises rely on a fairly small range of species. It is difficult to process an elephant and a duiker through the same facility or market their meat through the same outlets. As a result, game ranches based on meat harvesting tend to favour a restricted number of species, often at the expense of other indigenous wildlife. Sometimes the other species may be removed because they are viewed as competitors for scarce grazing. Other times they may suffer as a result of habitat manipulation (e.g. bush clearance or the provision of waterholes) designed to benefit the favoured species. Predators, in particular, are seldom tolerated and are usually destroyed.

In general, commercial game enterprises that rely on trophy hunting or game viewing rather than cropping for meat tend to encourage a wider variety of species and habitats. Even predators, such as lion and leopard, are some of the most valuable assets of hunting or tourist ranches in AFrica. However, this is not always the case. The historical conflict between gamekeepers and birds of prey in Europe shows that commercial sport hunting is also incompatible with some forms of wildlife. One of the strongest lobbies in western Canada for wolf control is the hunting lobby who fear that burgeoning wolf populations are a threat to the hunted populations of deer, mountain sheep and other quarry. Other species may be discouraged for less obvious reasons: aardvark and warthog are often unpopular because they make large burrows in which the farmer's truck may break an axle.

The comparative value of natural habitat production

This section discusses whether the constructive forms of wildlife utilization can ever be profitable. This is a fundamentally important question because the concept of wildlife utilization hinges upon the belief that utilization can unleash already existing forces for conservation. However, it is only the profitable forms of conservation that will be unleashed by a simple policy of wildlife utilization. If the profitable forms of utilization are not constructive, as discussed earlier, and if the constructive practices are unprofitable, then there is no practical conservation value to a simple policy of wildlife utilization.

Therefore, this section examines the issue of whether the less intensive methods of ranching and wild harvests identified as potentially constructive forms of utilization are also potentially profitable. There are three parts to this examination. First, there are the productivity trade-offs implicit in specialized/non-specialized forms of production. Second, there are the price trade-offs. Third, there are the observed aggregate comparative values demonstrated in various studies. It is apparent that this question has not yet been conclusively answered, but there are clear indications that less intensive utilization might be able to "pay its own way".

The productivity trade-off

It is undoubtedly true that there are tremendous productivity gains to be acquired through movements towards specialized production methods. This is because the law of specialization implies increasing returns to standardized production. This increased productivity of specialized production is the single most important reason why diversity has been reduced to the extent that it has.

Less obvious are the productivity advantages of diverse production methods. These arise precisely because of the diverse and indigenous nature of the resource base relied upon under these methods. First, natural habitat production allows for the tapping of a wider range of resources within the same habitat. For example, in Indonesia, it has been found that the value of the non-wood exports originating from that country's tropical rainforests equals over 10 per cent of the value of all rainforest exports (amounting to over $100 million annually since 1979) (Gillis, 1989).

This means that a wider range of the resource base is being utilized; in general, domesticated species are only able to tap a proportion of the resource value tapped by the wider range of species indigenous to an environment (the replacement value). It also means that there is a wider portfolio to rely upon, in the event of an unforeseen fall in production or value from the resource base.

The second general reason that natural habitat production methods can be expected to have productivity advantages is due to the better adaptation of indigenous species to prevailing environmental conditions. Two of the most important reasons are the indigenous species compatibility with pest and climate variations, resulting in better disease and stress tolerance (Eltringham, 1986).

Third, a recent study in Zimbabwe indicates that there are land degradation costs implicit in the introduction of non-indigenous species. This study found that the introduction of cattle within buffalo range produced favourable returns over a short time horizon; however, over a 30 year period the resultant land degradation caused the cattle to become an inferior asset (Child, B. 1990).

Therefore, non-intensive and diverse methods of production also have their own productivity advantages. These largely stem from the compatibility of the species utilized with the environment they evolved within.

Specialized methods of production have their own productivity advantages. These result from the compatibility of the selected species, not so much with the natural environment as with the human one. Specialization hinges upon a small group of species that are conducive to human management systems such as herding, selective breeding, and mass production.

The important question is the extent to which the existing specialized production systems can be extended beyond the environments within which they evolved. It should be anticipated that there will be decreasing returns to the application of the same methods in very different environments, although this might be evident only in the medium term with consequent environmental degradation. In any event, there is reason to suspect that the force of the law of specialization cannot by itself spread the same methods of production across the entire face of the earth.

The price trade-off

Even if productivity gains continue to favour specialized methods of production as they are applied across the globe, this alone does necessarily imply that diverse methods of production are doomed. The relative profitability of a use of habitat is, however, the product of two factors: the relative productivity of that use *and* the relative price of the goods and services flowing from that use. Therefore, it is equally important to consider the relative prices, as it is the relative productivities of these uses.

There already exists evidence indicating that a "premium" is frequently paid for the products of natural habitats, both on account of their "diverse" nature and also in recognition of their source. Customers will pay a premium for a "wild" salmon over a farmed one. Rhino horn products are now approximately the same price as gold.

This development is in part due to the increasing scarcity and hence increasing value of natural habitat, and its related production. It is also attributable in part to the prevalence of surpluses in the world's traditional commodity markets, and hence the decline in the prices of those goods usually produced through specialized agricultural methods. Therefore, the "dynamic" nature of comparative advantage might be such that future development is better orientated towards these scarcer commodities than the more abundant varieties.

During the past three decades the developing countries have engaged in "mass conversions" of natural habitats, thereby substantially increasing the proportion of their lands that are dedicated to specialized agricultural production. During the same period, developed countries have ceased conversions altogether. In spite of this, the increase in the value of production of these agricultural commodities has been precisely equal in the two regions. That is, there has been no relative return to the increased rates of conversion.

A possible explanation for this trend is the absence of significant demand for the additional quantities of the same commodities. Recently installed agricultural specialization in developing countries has focused primarily on meeting the demand for a small number of basic commodities that are already in mass production throughout the developed world.

However, Western production already goes far towards completely satisfying this demand, and Western agricultural subsidization policies palce developing country exports at the "end of the queue".

This means that the relevant elasticity applicable to less developed countries' exports is that of the marginal consumer. Frequently, inelastic demand exists for the additional quantities placed on the market by expanding producers.[3] For example, in Sub-Saharan Africa it has been estimated that 60 per cent of export earnings come from commodities for which the price inelasticity is such that an increase in production of those commodities would actually reduce earnings (Godfrey, 1985).

Table 8.6: Rate of return to agricultural conversions

Region	Conversion to agriculture	Increase in value
LDCs	37% increase	24% increase
DCs	No change	21% increase

Source: Holdgate, M. et al. (1982).

One theory of comparative advantage indicates that it is the *uniqueness* of the supply of a good that determines its terms of trade. Under this theory, for greatest comparative advantage, countries must produce those products that are most uniquely within their exclusive capabilities, by reason of natural characteristics peculiar to those countries. Therefore, a good that is produced in obviously limited quantities will always produce the best exchange rate.[4]

This is the theoretical basis behind the expectation that the value of goods and services produced from more obviously limited resources, such as natural habitats, should be increasing as their supply becomes more limited. The empirical record developed during the recent period of mass conversions of natural habitat does not contradict this theoretical expectation. It is possible that the comparative advantage of countries that retain natural habitat resources might now lie (or will in the future lie) in the fuller appropriation of their value as such, rather than their conversion into different forms of more intensive production.

Case studies demonstrating favourable comparative valuation

There are a number of case studies that demonstrate the comparatively favourable valuation of natural habitat production over specialized agricultural production in various areas. These are presented here as possible examples of situations in which the non-intensive use of land compares favourably with the intensive.

However, the conservation impact of these non-intensive uses is not positive, unless they are also sustainable. In practice, much of the wildlife harvest currently being undertaken is not being sustainably managed. In these cases substantial short-term returns are realized as the resource is being depleted. Of course, this is equally as harmful for the wildlife resource. Nevertheless, these unconstructive practices of wildlife utilization do not obviate the conclusion that it is possible for utilization to render conservation benefits, if sustainably practised. The following studies lend credence to this theory, but only if they represent the sustainable management of wildlands. For example, it is now the case that the overall value of game production in Zimbabwe compares well with that of beef ($106 million against $260 million) (Martin, 1984). Similarly, a year's use of natural habitat for wildlife in that country was found to produce an aggregate return of $2.49/ha, rivalling the returns from the most intensive forms of cultivation there (Child, 1984).

Table 8.7: Comparative value of natural habitat and specialized production

Country	Natural habitat use and value	Alternative use and value
Kenya	Wildlife tourism	Cattle ranching
Zimbabwe	Wildlife product. Z$4.20/ha	Cattle ranching Z$3.58/ha
Malaysia	Forest production $2455/ha	Intensive agriculture $217/ha
Peru	Forest production $6820/ha	Clearcut $1000/ha

Sources: Zimbabwe, Child & Nduku (1986); Kenya, Western (1984); Malaysia, Watson (1988); Peru, Peters, et al. (1989).

Where natural habitat tourism is a significant factor, the comparison is even more favourable. Several studies of the value of national parks in Kenya indicate that natural habitat is by far the most profitable use (Thresher, 1981; Henry, 1978; Western, 1984). Again, as was indicated above, the recreational value of many resources will often outweigh their other production values; for example, throughout Arizona, sport hunting earns returns that are a factor of four times greater than the returns to beef grazing on the same lands (Robinson and Bolen, 1989).

The removal of rainforests in Brazil in favour of beef production has been economically analysed as well. It was found that, whereas the former economy was sustainable, the transition to intensive beef production actually reduces value throughout much of this environment. The revenues from beef ranching cover only about 45 per cent of recurring costs (Browder, 1988). Similarly, the conversion of tropical forests in Malaysia for intensive cultivation results in a substantial net loss in value ($2455/ha per year for forest production against $217/ha per year for agricultural production) (Watson, 1988). Pearce has provided a general review of these studies (Pearce, 1990).

Conclusion

The conservation effectiveness of wildlife utilization depends on the form of the use involved. The only difference between constructive use and destructive conversion is the degree of intervention involved. Therefore, it is fundamentally important that a critical analysis be applied to any proposed use before it is exercised in the cause of conservation.

The more intensive forms of utilization, captive breeding and intensive ranching, have little to distinguish them (in terms of conservation effectiveness) from domesticated methods of production. If anything, these forms of utilization may be more damaging to the environment, due to problems with exotics and through indirect market-driven effects. The current trend towards encouraging captive breeding in the name of conservation, as under CITES, is therefore discouraging.

The less intensive forms of utilization, extensive ranching and wild harvests, have the potential to contribute substantially to wildland and wildlife conservation. This is so because these uses can extract value without converting the habitat.

The fundamental problem here is whether such uses are financially or environmentally sustainable. Often times, the extensive use of wildland will commence a slow process of diversity degradation, as the forces of specialization lead to greater and greater interventions. There are theoretical reasons to expect that, at some point, the advantages of specialization (productivity and price) will be exhausted; however, it is uncertain whether that point has yet been reached.

Where wildlife utilization is the predominant practice, it is often practised unsustainably. This means that the financial returns can be comparable in some instances, but only while the diversity is being mined. Thus, there are many reasons to believe that the theoretical advantages of wildlife utilization remain largely theoretical at present. However, the challenge is to develop systems that will ensure that the theory can be put into practice in the future, rather than to abandon the principles on account of poor practices. This chapter has attempted to isolate a few of the important characteris-tics of wildlife utilization for conservation effectiveness, which can be summed up as low intensity and high diversity. This is the path down which the sustainable management of wildlife should be pursued.

References

Ajayi, S., *Utilization of Forest Wildlife in West Africa*, FAO, Rome [1990].

Browder, J., "Public Policy and Deforestation in the Brazilian Amazon", in R. Repetto, and M. Gillis, *Public Policies and the Misuse of Forest Resources* [Cambridge: Cambridge Univ. Press, 1988].

Child, B., "Assessment of Wildlife Utilization as a Land Use Option in the Semi-Arid Rangeland of Southern Africa", in Kiss, A. (ed.) *Living with Wildlife* [Washington, DC: World Bank Draft Report, 1988].

Child, G., "Managing Wildlife for People in Zimbabwe", in J. McNeely and K. Miller (eds) *National Parks, Conservation and Development [Washington, DC: Smithsonian Institute, 1984]*.

Eltringham, K., *Wildlife Resources and Economic Development*, [New York: John Wiley, 1984].

FAO, *Yearbooks of Fisheries Production Statistics*, Food and Agricul-ture Organization of the United Nations, Rome [1960].

Gillis, M., "Indonesia: Public Policies, Resource Management, and the Tropical Forest", in R. Repetto, and M. Gillis (eds), *Public Policies and the Misuse of Forest Resources* [Cambridge: Cambridge Univer-sity Press, 1988].

Goldstein, J.H. (in prep.) "The prospects for using market incentives for conservation of biological diversity".

Holdgate, M., M. Kassas, and G. White (eds), *The World Environment 1972–1982* [Nairobi: UNEP, 1982].

Honacki, J.H., K.E. Kinman, and J.W. Koeppl, *Mammal species of the world* [Lawrence, Kansas: Association of Systematics Collec-tions, 1982].

ITRG, *The Ivory Trade and the Future of the African Elephant, Volume 2, technical reports*. Report prepared by the Ivory Trade Review Group for the 7th meeting of the Conference of the Parties to CITES [1989].

IUCN, *The ICUN Red List of Threatened Animals* [Gland, Switzerland: IUCN, 1988].

Klein, D.R., "Northern subsistence hunting economies", R.J. Hudson, K.R. Drew, and L.M. Baskin, (eds), *Wildlife Production Systems: economic utilization of wild ungulates* [Cambridge: Cambridge University Press, pp. 96-112, 1989].

Lebedeva, N.L., "Commercial hunting in the Soviet Union", R.J. Hudson, K.R. Drew, and L.M. Baskin, (eds), *Wildlife Production Systems: economic utilization of wild ungulates* [Cambridge: Cambridge University Press, pp. 96-112, 1989].

Martin, R. "Wildlife Utilization", in R. Bell and E. McShane-Vicuzi (eds), *Conservation and Wildlife Management in Africa* [Washington, DC: US Peace Corps, 1984].

Matthiessen, P. and D. Douthwaite, "The Impact of Tsetse Fly Control Campaigns on African Wildlife", *Oryx* xix:202-209 [1985].

Pearce, D., "An Economic Approach to Saving the Tropical Forests", LEEC Discussion Paper 90-96 [London: IIED, 1990].

Robinson, W. and E. Bolen, *Wildlife Ecology and Management*, [New York: Macmillan, 1989].

Sale, J., *The Importance and Values of Wild Plants and Animals in Africa* [Gland, Switzerland: IUCN, 1981].

Stansfield, J.R.W., "The effect of the competition of farmed salmon in the market place on the present state of commercial salmon fisheries", D. Jenkins, and W.M. Shearer (eds) *The status of the Atlantic Salmon in Scotland*. Institute of Terrestrial Ecology, Monks Wood, UK [1986].

Vietmeyer, N., "Lesser Known Plants of Potential Use in Agriculture and Forestry", *Science* 232:369-382 [1986].

Watson, D. "The Evolution of Appropriate Resource Management Systems", in F. Berkes (ed.), *Common Property Resources* [London: Belhaven, 1988].

Western, D., "Amboseli National Park: Human Values and the Conservation fo a Savannah Ecosystem", in J. MeNeely, and K. Miller (eds), *op cit.*

Wislon, O. (ed.), *Biodiversity* [Washington, DC: National Academy Press, 1988].

Witt, S., "Biotechnology and Genetic Diversity", California Agricultural Lands Project, San Francisco [1985].

9

ILLEGAL EXPLOITATION OF WILDLIFE

E.J. Milner-Gulland and Nigel Leader-Williams

Utilization of wildlife

Wildlife utilization takes several forms. Legal forms, such as ranching, tourism and community-based development, have been dealt with in other chapters. Here we look at the illegal utilization of wildlife. "Illegality" in most circumstances implies both irregularity and immorality. With regard to the exploitation of wildlife, this may not be the case, for the traditional use of wildlife by subsistence hunters often breaks wildlife laws imposed by outsiders. In terms of the quantity of the resource used and the economic value of the industry, illegal hunting is probably the most important and widespread form of wildlife utilization throughout much of Africa. For example, in the wildlife-rich country of Tanzania it has been estimated that around 60 per cent of wildlife utilization is illegal (ITC/IUCN, 1988).

In broad terms, there are two distinct elements to illegal utilization. First, traditional subsistence hunting, where products are used mostly for local consumption. Second, larger-scale commercial hunting, where products are bartered or sold further afield, often in the international market-place. Both forms have been practised traditionally for centuries, as shown, for example, by remains of animal kills in archaeological sites or the long-standing trade in ivory between Africa and the Far East. The right to practise these forms of utilization went largely unquestioned until this century, when laws establishing protected areas and limiting the use of wildlife were passed.

Wildlife laws in Africa were usually first passed by alien colonial administrators (Graham, 1973; Marks, 1984). Laws often resulted in the enclosure of land in attempts to form pristine areas of wilderness. Local people were evicted to new areas, often without compensation for the loss of property, title and traditional hunting rights. In the eyes of local people, colonial wildlife officers favoured the protection of animals over the welfare of humans living around the newly created protected areas. This problem was particularly acute because, by then, most wildlife remained on marginal agricultural land whose occupants were poorly integrated into the mainstream economy. Such disenfranchisement occurred throughout much of Africa, on the assumption that conservation was equated with land use restrictions, although there were regional differences in the extent of the restrictions. For example, cattle-herding Masaai in East Africa were allowed to continue their traditional use of wildlife land for water and grazing, but local hunters living in tsetse-infested areas of Zambia, where cattle herding is impossible, had their traditional rights more severely curtailed.

This chapter examines both subsistence and commercial illegal hunting and their impact on the wildlife resource. The strategies that are needed to conserve the resource and bring the profits of utilization into the mainstream economy are discussed. We use the hunting of rhinos and elephants in the Luangwa Valley, Zambia, as our case study.

Background – the recent history of the Luangwa Valley

The Luangwa Valley has a fairly typical history among protected areas (PAs) in Africa. The four national parks (NPs), with an area totalling 16,660 sq. km, were originally established as game reserves in the colonial era. The local inhabitants, who had previously used the area's products both for subsistence (meat, firewood, honey) and trade (ivory, rhino horn), were evicted. People were allowed to remain in seven sparsely inhabited hunting areas, totalling around 46,300 sq. km, that border on the reserves, but were subjected to game and gun laws and to licence quotas set to protect wildlife. Both reserves and hunting areas were managed increasingly for the benefit of outsiders, chiefly tourists and safari hunters, and earnings from wildlife went largely to central government and the private sector. Apart from two far-sighted exceptions where revenue-sharing schemes were established, local residents, denied access to resources that were previously under their control, became increasingly impoverished and resentful (Marks, 1984; Abel and Blaikie, 1986).

After independence in 1972, Zambia established NPs over 9 per cent and game management areas (GMAs) over 22 per cent of its surface area. At that time, Luangwa Valley held large populations of elephant (100,000) and black rhino (between 4,000 and 12,000). However, Zambia's economy then began to decline because of falling copper prices and although central government spent quite heavily on conservation, the amount was low in relation to the vast areas under protection. Consequently, park infrastructure and law enforcement began to collapse. By the late 1970s, Zambia's internal socio-economic problems, coupled with dramatic price increases of ivory and rhino horn on the world market, had resulted in a serious outbreak of poaching in Luangwa Valley (Western and Vigne, 1985; Douglas-Hamilton, 1987).

By the mid-1980s elephant numbers were reduced by 75 per cent to around 25,000 and rhinos to probably a few hundred. Profits from this slaughter went not to the Zambian mainstream economy, but elsewhere – the smallest share to local poachers, a larger share to members of organized gangs who killed and extracted horn and ivory from animals within the parks, and the largest share, including foreign exchange, to middlemen who smuggled the trophies out of Zambia. The slaughter provided little direct benefit to Luangwa residents, because most of the organised poachers came from areas bordering onto, but outside, Luangwa Valley (Leader-Williams, Albon and Berry, 1990).

In late 1979 an anti-poaching operation was set up, funded in part by the Zambian government. The following year an external conservation agency donated a relatively large sum in conservation terms (half a million US dollars over three years) to the operation. The government bought vehicles and mobilized staff into units that undertook regular foot patrols in important areas with the aims of arresting poachers and protecting rhinos and elephants. In spite of this protection, the elephants and rhinos still declined rapidly in numbers. Clearly law enforcement was not adequately deterring poaching.

Illegal exploitation as an economic activity

The effects of law enforcement on poaching rates can be examined in detail for the Luangwa Valley because the anti-poaching patrols kept detailed records of all interactions with poachers, showing the number of hunters and carriers in the gang, the number and type of firearms and trophies with them, and the number arrested. There are also details of the subsequent sentencing of the gang members (Leader-Williams et al., 1990). These data allow the effects of law enforcement to be included accurately in the costs that a poaching gang incurs when hunting. A model of a poaching gang's incentives to hunt was produced using this information. It was used to explore the effects of changes in the probability of being caught and in the penalty received on a poacher's decision to hunt (Milner-Gulland and Leader-Williams, 1992).

In the Luangwa Valley, the elephant and rhino stocks are now so low that the government's main objective is to prevent further large-scale exploitation. Thus the poachers' incentives must be altered in order to make it uneconomic to poach. This could be done in several ways. First, on an international level, the demand for trophies could be reduced. There is still controversy over whether the best way to achieve this objective is to ban the ivory trade or to promote a more regulated legal trade (ITRG, 1989; Barbier et al., 1990). Second, the cost of poaching could be raised by increasing the wages that an employee could gain elsewhere, either in the economy as a whole or in the Luangwa Valley area. Third, penalties could be made more severe so that hunters must be paid more in order to persuade them to risk capture.

A wildlife authority with a budget to spend on law enforcement has the option to increase the probability that a gang will be caught. It can also press the courts for an increase in the penalty that a captured poacher faces. Both changes feed into the costs of the poaching operation in a rather different way to straightforward increases in the cost of mounting a poaching operation, and it is these two options that we examine in more detail.

The structure of the poaching industry

There is a very clear difference between the types of poacher encountered. On the one hand, there are local people, who use their area of Luangwa Valley for subsistence hunting. For them, meat hunting is a traditional and cultural necessity in an area where domestic stock cannot be herded because of the presence of tsetse fly (Marks, 1976, 1984). They hunt mostly in the GMAs, in small gangs, and stay close to home, usually only going out for one day at a time. They use primitive firearms such as muzzle loading guns, as well as spears, snares and dogs. Although they mainly hunt for meat, they will occasionally kill an elephant or rhino. On the other hand, there are organized poaching gangs that usually contain two professional elephant and rhino hunters with automatic weapons and about six carriers. The gangs penetrate deep into the NPs, and are out for several days. It is this type of gang that can reduce elephant and rhino populations most seriously. The members of the gang come not from within Luangwa Valley, but from above the escarpment to the north and west of the valley, next to the Great North Road, so that transport is excellent. Their trophies can quickly be removed by middlemen and exported (Leader-Williams et al., 1990).

Any action to reduce incentives to hunt will affect these two gang types very differently. The gang types vary both in the costs and prices they face and in the structure of the industry within which they work. The local gangs are exploiting a tribal resource over which no one now has control, apart from the limited capability of the wildlife authority, so that anyone is free to exploit it. The organized gangs are employed by middlemen, who organize poaching activity along with other similar activities. Ivory and rhino horn are often discovered with other contraband such as drugs, gems and electrical equipment. There are relatively few middlemen, who effectively control the exploitation of the wildlife resource. There is evidence that a single dealer controlled most of the hunting in Luangwa Valley. The organized part of the poaching industry is probably operated by this dealer much like any other business with exclusive rights in its territory.

The incentives to poach

In order to understand how changing rates of detection and penalties affect the poacher, the economic context of the poacher's decision must be taken into account. The two distinct groups of poacher, local and organized gangs, must both be deterred. The local hunters have relatively low hunting costs, since most are self-employed farmers who earn little from their work. However, the price that a trophy fetches is also relatively low, because rather than being employed by a dealer, the hunter must try to sell his trophies to the dealer. By the 1980s, the density of elephants in the GMAs was quite low, and of rhinos was very low indeed, and so the chances of a local hunter coming across either in a hunt specifically intended to kill elephants or rhinos were small. Even if a herd of elephants was encountered, a gang with a single muzzle loading gun could only shoot one and the gun is so unreliable that there would probably only be a 50 per cent chance of killing it (Marks, 1976). Even without the chance of being caught and incurring a penalty, the economics were such that in 1985 the small cost of mounting a special expedition to kill rhinos or elephants outweighed the probable returns. Thus it was not worth hunting elephants and rhinos simply for their trophies. Box 9.1 shows the economic decision faced by a local hunter.

The penalty if caught is significant compared to the low costs and prices obtained by local poachers and so further militates against hunting specifically for trophies. However, a local hunter is primarily concerned with meat, and if he happened to encounter an elephant or rhino while out hunting other game, it would be worth killing for its large carcass with the added bonus of ivory or horn. Thus the model confirms what is seen in the Luangwa Valley – local gangs are caught primarily with meat, but also with the occasional elephant and rhino trophy.

The story is very different for the organized gangs because the dealer has exclusive rights over the territory and so can control the speed at which the animals in it are harvested. He may want to harvest less today in order to invest in the resource for the future. This decision depends upon two main factors. The first is the growth rate of the asset. Elephant and rhino populations grow rather slowly. An elephant population will grow at up to 6 per cent per year, a rhino population at up to about 11-16 per cent per year. The growth rate is fastest at low population sizes. The second factor is the weight the investor gives to future earnings as compared to earnings today. In Africa, the future is discounted at a high rate due to factors such as political uncertainty and the high lending rate.

A local poacher makes a decision to hunt or not at a particular moment, ignoring the future because the resource may not still be there. Because the dealer has sole control over his assets, he will try to maximize their value over time. The best way to do this is to hunt as hard as possible until the asset, in this case the elephant or rhino population, reaches an optimal level. Then as the population grows, he will remove the increase in population size each year. The optimal level of the population depends on how much present income is preferred to future income. A dealer with no preference for the present over the future will reduce the population until it produces the maximum yield each year. In elephants and rhinos, this is at around 75 per cent of the maximum population size. If the dealer has high preference for the present, he will remove more individuals now, giving a lower sustained harvest later. This investment decision comes on top of the economic decision as to the level of hunting that maximizes short-run profits. Law enforcement affects the decision because the more a gang hunts, the more likely it is to be caught and a penalty imposed.

The dealer's costs and prices are much higher than those for the local hunter, and so law enforcement has less potential effect on his decision making. Elephants and rhinos are also more abundant in the national parks than in the GMAs, and the superior weapons used by the gang mean that most of any herd encountered can be killed. Thus the chances of finding and killing an elephant or rhino on an expedition are far higher for an organized than a local hunter. Longer expeditions and the presence of carriers also mean that a single expedition can produce a large output. These differences meant that it was profitable for organized gangs to hunt elephants in Luangwa Valley.

Box 9.1: The economic decision faced by a local hunter

All the economic variables are in Zambian Kwacha and are for the situation in 1985. In 1985, K5.7 equalled US$1. A local hunter could earn K270 from the ivory of one elephant. Killing a rhino would earn him K670 for its horn. The cost of going on a hunting expedition was K14. The fine if the gang was caught was K500/hunter, plus the confiscation of the gang's trophies. There were usually two hunters, with one trophy between them. Each time a gang went out, it had a 5 per cent chance of being caught. For a local gang to find and kill an elephant, it had to go hunting on average 20 times, while to find and kill a rhino the gang would need to go out 9,600 times.

From these data, the expected profit from one expedition can be worked out. If the gang were hunting elephants, the expected profit would have been:

K270/20 K14 0.05 x (2 x K500 + K270) = -K64
[Price/expeditions - cost - probability of detection x (fines + confiscation) = profit]

Thus a local gang would on average make a loss if it went elephant hunting. The loss if the gang was hunting rhinos would have been even larger. It was not worth a local hunter's while to go hunting specifically for elephants or rhinos. This is true even without the expected cost of law enforcement – the cost of mounting an expedition was K0.5 more that the expected revenue earned from it.

Source: E.J. Milner-Gulland and N. Leader-Williams (1992), "A model of the incentives for illegal exploitation of rhinos and elephants: poaching pays in Luangwa Valley, Zambia". *Journal of Applied Ecology 29.*

At the 1985 parameter values, the fate of Luangwa Valley rhinos was being determined by the incentives to hunt elephants. It was profitable for the organized gangs to go out specifically to hunt elephants, but not rhinos. However, as with the local hunters, if an organized gang happened to encounter a rhino, killing it would be very profitable, particularly since rhino horn is far easier to carry than ivory and so the number of elephants that could be killed would not decrease. The situation in the Luangwa Valley in 1985 was consistent with these findings: organized gangs were usually found with ivory, but occasionally with rhino horn as well. Thus the profitability of ivory actually contributed to the decline in the rhino population, despite rhinos being too scarce to be worth hunting alone.**Box 9.2

The effects of changing the incentive framework

This case study has shown that illegal exploitation of wildlife can be the result of the predictable reaction of individuals to a given framework of economic incentives. It is important to know by how much the factors affecting a poacher's decision to hunt need to change to produce a marked change in the poacher's behaviour. For the local poacher, elephants and rhinos were scarce enough that the cost of the hunt itself was enough to deter hunting. Even if the price of ivory or horn doubled, it would still not be worth the local hunter's while to mount hunts specifically for elephants and rhinos. The opposite situation held for the organized gangs hunting elephants. Only if both hunting costs doubled and the price per kill was reduced fivefold would it be unprofitable to hunt, and it was only near these levels that the hunters became at all sensitive to changes in costs and prices. The rhino population was so low that their hunting was only incidental to elephant hunting (Milner-Gulland and Leader-Williams, 1992).

Changes in law enforcement were essentially irrelevant to local hunters, since the simple economic calculation would imply a decision not to hunt, although as discussed later, law enforcement has some bearing on whether or not elephants or rhinos are killed in a casual encounter. For the organized elephant hunter, law enforcement could have more impact, but the prices and costs involved in hunting were large enough that changes in the penalty or the risk of incurring it would have to have been very large for any effect to occur at all.

Detection or penalty?

There are two components to law enforcement, but they are rather different in their effects and in their costs of implementation. In the literature on crime in the United States, from which some lessons can be drawn, opinion is divided as to whether the severity of a sentence has a deterrent effect at all. The studies do agree, however, that the penalty level is less of a deterrent than detection rate (Ehrlich, 1973; Avio and Clark, 1978). Taking a severe penalty such as prison, an offender's perception of the severity of the sentence before it is delivered depends on how much he

Box 9.2: The economic decision faced by an organized hunter

All the economic variables are in Zambian Kwacha and are for the situation in 1985. In 1985, K5.7 equalled US$1.

A dealer could earn K2570 from the ivory of one elephant. Killing a rhino would earn him K4390 for its horn. The cost of going on a hunting expedition was K500. The fine if the gang was caught was K500 per hunter, plus the confiscation of the gang's trophies. There were usually two hunters, with one trophy between them. Each time a gang went out, it had a 5 per cent chance of being caught. On average, an organised hunting expedition killed 3.5 elephants, while seven expeditions were needed to kill a rhino.

The optimal population sizes for an organized poacher.

	Population size	
	Optimal	**Actual in 1985**
Species		
Elephant	8	77
Rhino	42	16

The table shows the optimal population sizes of elephants and rhinos for an organized hunter, based on the information above. These are given as percentages of the maximum populations that the area can hold. The actual population sizes of elephants and rhinos in 1985 are also given as percentages. The gang will hunt as much as possible if the population is above the optimal size, not at all if the population is below optimal and at the population growth rate if the population is at the optimal size. Thus the table shows that the organized gangs would have wanted to hunt elephants as hard as possible in 1985, and not to hunt rhinos at all until the population was larger. The differences in the optimal population sizes for the two species are due to the different expected revenues from an expedition – the expected revenue from a rhino hunting expedition is lower than that from an elephant hunting expedition.

Source: E.J. Milner-Gulland and N. Leader-Williams (1992), "A model of the incentives for illegal exploitation of rhinos and elephants: poaching pays in Luangwa Valley, Zambia", *Journal of Applied Ecology 29.*

values the present over the future and how far into the future he looks.

In Africa, there is a lot of uncertainty about the future, so people tend to value the present more than the future and not look far ahead. Thus a sentence of two years might look much the same as a sentence of five years when the poacher is deciding whether or not to go hunting. The expected number of years spent in prison is the same if a poacher has a 20 per cent chance of one year in prison or a 10 per cent chance of two years in prison. However, if things are valued less the further into the future you look, a 20 per cent chance of one year in prison will appear to be a worse option than a 10 per cent chance of two years in prison (Cook, 1977). Thus increasing the probability of a poacher being caught will probably be a more effective deterrent than increasing the penalty.

There is a further reason why it is appropriate to concentrate on detection rates rather than penalties. The courts are completely separate from the wildlife authority that is attempting to protect the wildlife resource, and do not always set the same priority on elephant and rhino conservation. In Zambia, concern about the loss of elephants and rhinos and ivory and horn trafficking led to the government introducing mandatory 5 to 15 year prison sentences for elephant and rhino offenders in 1982. However, even though magistrates tended to deliver more prison sentences to elephant/rhino offenders, not all received prison sentences after 1982 and they were usually very short. The maximum length given up to 1985 was three years. Magistrates also did not distinguish clearly between elephant/rhino offences and other offences in terms of the severity of sentences. The legislation to increase penalties was slow and difficult to enact and has been incompletely carried out (Leader-Williams et al., 1990).

What kind of penalty is best?

The detection rate is probably the major determinant of poaching activity, but the type of penalty given once the poacher has been caught can also have a major effect on the incentives to poach. The two forms of penalty that are commonly used to deter illegal exploitation of wildlife in African conservation areas are fines and prison sentences (IUCN, 1986). It has been argued that fines are a better form of penalty than prison sentences, because they act as a "tax" on illegal activity and a direct transfer payment from the offender to the victim, in this case the state, which has lost a valuable animal (Becker, 1968). Fines are also easier to administer than prison. In contrast, prison sentences incur large costs both to the state and society and also to the prisoner, whose powers to earn legitimate wages may be seriously compromised by a spell in gaol. In the Luangwa Valley, the effectiveness of one or other type of penalty depends crucially on who suffers the penalty as opposed to who decides whether or not to hunt.

In the case of the local gangs, the hunters themselves are the decision-makers and also suffer the penalty. Because of this, and because they may have difficulty paying fines they are likely to be deterred by a fine. Local hunters are marginal offenders and so are likely to be easily turned from crime by the threat of a high penalty (cf. Thurow, 1980). If a differential were maintained between the penalty for entering a PA and killing game for meat and that for elephant and rhino hunting, this would deter local poachers from killing elephants and rhinos that they came across. A prison sentence might well be unnecessary, and would be a very severe penalty to a local hunter, having a serious effect on the welfare of his family since most are self-employed farmers.

Deterring organized gangs presents a far more serious problem. The decision-maker is the dealer employing the gang rather than the hunter in the gang, but the hunter is convicted. Confessions and evidence from the sentences delivered to poachers suggest that dealers often bought the acquittal of hunters with small fines while the more disposable and unskilled carriers were sentenced to prison. Therefore small fines for hunters were just part of the economic equation of ivory and horn trading, suggesting that much higher fines for hunters could act as a deterrent for the dealer. However, the size of fines delivered to hunters would require careful adjustment because they would only be effective as long as the dealer paid. If fines were set too high the dealer would allow the hunter to go to prison in default. Equally, delivering a prison sentence to an employed hunter probably would not deter the dealer from funding poaching until he ran out of skilled hunters. There might, however, be an increase in the risk premium needed to attract hunters into organized poaching if the sentences were perceived as severe, particularly if prison were involved. The ideal solution would, of course, be to deliver appropriate sentences to dealers in ivory and rhino horn, rather than to their employees.

There is one simple modification to the law enforcement structure that dramatically reduces the incentive to poach. At present, court records indicate that convicted poachers are penalized only for illegal hunting, not for the number of animals poached. However, if the fine paid were made proportional to the number of animals killed, then the optimal percentage of the population for the organized hunter to kill could have been reduced from

90 per cent to 2 per cent. This modification also penalizes the poachers who kill the most animals and so do most harm to the elephant and rhino populations. Making the fine larger for the more endangered rhino could also act to discourage opportunistic rhino killings.

A shoot-to-kill policy for poachers has been instituted by certain countries with prior political approval, initially Zimbabwe (Tatham, 1988; Tatham and Taylor, 1989) and latterly Kenya. The policy was never politically acceptable in Zambia because most poaching is carried out by Zambians (Leader-Williams et al., 1990). Elsewhere, however, illegal exploitation of rhinos and elephants has been carried out by nationals of other countries – Zambians in Zimbabwe and Somalis in Kenya. Crossing national boundaries with automatic weapons represents a threat to national security that, together with poaching, is deemed to merit such a punishment (Tatham, 1988). Wildlife managers have pushed for shoot-to-kill because it allows them to have sole control over law enforcement, circumventing lack of co-operation between ministries and particularly between neighbouring countries. However, it also sets an unacceptable precedent by imposing summary executions without trial. This undermines justice and human rights in the countries practising the shoot-to-kill policy.

Apart from the considerations of justice, there is evidence that the policy may not work. One disadvantage of a very high penalty is that although it may lower the overall level of crime, there is evidence that the level of serious crime may increase (Stigler, 1970). This suggests that a shoot-to-kill policy should not be applied to all poachers entering a PA, for then there is no incentive just to kill warthog as opposed to elephant or rhino, and no incentive to avoid killing approaching scouts. Thus local poachers may turn to serious crime if the punishment is applied unselectively. But are the serious poachers deterred by the death penalty? As yet no data are available to assess the situation in Kenya. In Zimbabwe, small gangs without carriers hunt for rhino horn, so the policy stands the maximum chance of success because a high proportion of hunters are killed. However nearly 300 rhinos were killed there between 1984 and 1987, despite 29 Zambian poachers being shot (Tatham, 1988; Tatham and Taylor, 1989).

How to achieve adequate detection

Given the importance of raising the probability of being caught as well as of deciding upon the most appropriate penalty, we now consider how the detection rate of offenders could be increased.

The key to effective deterrence remains simple in principle. It requires a wildlife authority that is well-manned and funded with motivated field staff. In Luangwa Valley the anti-poaching units were greatly understaffed, given the levels of illegal activity aimed at rhinos and elephants there in 1979-85. Field staff densities of at least around one per 10 to 20 sq. km of PA are needed to prevent the loss of valuable species in Africa (Leader-Williams et al., 1990). Indeed the highly successful mountain gorilla programme in Rwanda had staff densities of one per 2.5 sq. km (Harcourt 1986). Given that only 56 staff were available for the whole of Luangwa Valley during 1985, at densities of one per 300 sq. km of NP, it is scarcely surprising that very low detection rates were achieved and conservation measures for rhinos and elephants were unsuccessful.

The lesson here is that the infrastructure of PAs must be invested in if countries are to retain their natural resource base. As yet few countries earn enough from their PAs to be able to pay for their protection. In 1980 the total recurrent expenditure on conservation in the whole of Africa was around US$75 million per year, compared with US$167 million in 1979 for the United States alone (Morse, 1980; Bell & Clarke, 1986). Efforts in the USA to apprehend people hunting white-tailed deer in the closed season are sophisticated and have met with considerable success (Glover, 1982). Using an Africa-wide comparison of the success of different countries in conserving their rhinos and elephants, it was shown that a minimum of $200 per sq. km of recurrent expenditure was needed in the 1980s to prevent organized poaching (see Box 3) and with inflation and raised stakes, this has probably risen to $400 per sq. km today.

Such results illustrate a dilemma that will have to be faced increasingly in Africa. Poor countries that do not earn much from their wildlife resource often have large areas of PAs theoretically under protection, yet relatively few staff in national conservation agencies actually to undertake law enforcement duties. In different African countries in 1980, staff: area ratios varied from 1 per 580 sq. km to 1 per 7 sq. km (Cumming, Martin & Taylor, 1984; Bell & Clarke, 1986). In countries with low overall staff densities, such as Zambia, it is necessary for national conservation agencies and external funding bodies to make selective decisions about how much of their PAs and valuable species they can afford to patrol at effective staff densities. Although military tacticians and businessmen find no difficulty in concentrating effort and being selective when resources are short, this policy does not come easily to conservationists (Leader-Williams and Albon, 1988; Parker & Graham, 1989; von Clausewitz, 1976; Kraushar, 1985).

Box 9.3: The economics of investing in protected areas

Background: Rhinos and elephants have shown marked overall declines throughout Africa. However, their numbers have increased in several countries, especially in the richer countries of Southern Africa. It has been suggested that an important factor in the overall decline in rhino and elephant numbers across Africa was a shortage of manpower and ultimately of resources within national conservation departments.

Results: This suggestion was examined on a local scale in Luangwa Valley. It was shown that effort expended by anti-poaching patrols was directly related to success in conserving elephants and rhinos. On a continental scale, gross population trends of both species vary between countries. There are wide differences between the amounts of money spent by central governments on protected areas. There is a relationship between spending and the rate of rhino population decline in a country (see graph). The countries with high rates of rhino decline spent less than $50 per sq km on their protected areas, while the countries with stable or increasing rhino populations spent at least $200 per sq km. Similar results were found for elephants. The exception to this rule was Kenya, which although it spent nearly $200 per sq km, had a high rate of rhino population decline.

Conclusions: From this evidence, the rate of decline of a species in a particular country seems to be related to the resources available for conservation in that country, although the exception of Kenya suggests that other factors also play a part. It is important to invest adequate funds in law enforcement if species are to be conserved.

Other options to increase patrol coverage within PAs might include reducing patrol size, increasing time spent in the field, or using helicopters or aeroplanes. All these options require increased infrastructural input, the first needing well armed and trained patrols with effective logistical support, the second needing better servicing, provisioning and pay arrangements for staff, and the third needing good vehicular and mechanical support (Bell, 1986; Tatham, 1988). Unfortunately, all three options are less readily affordable or available in poor countries already in a state of infrastructural collapse. Perhaps the most effective option to raise detection rates in Africa is to make more arrests outside PAs (Bell, 1986b; Tatham, 1988). However, this still requires sufficient staff to achieve a balance between gathering intelligence information

Figure 9.1: The relationship between conservation spending and change in black rhino numbers between 1980 and 1984, for various African countries.

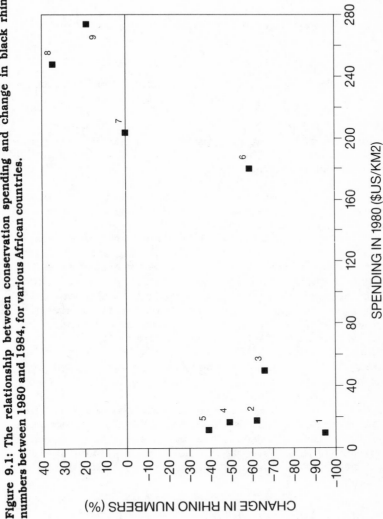

SPENDING IN 1980 ($US/KM2)

CHANGE IN RHINO NUMBERS (%)

Note: 1 = Central African Republic; 2 = Tanzania; 3 = Somalia; 4 = Mozambique; 5 = Zambia; 6 = Kenya; 7 = South Africa; 8 = Namibia; 9 = Zimbabwe.

Source: N. Leader-Williams and S. Albon 1988, "Allocation of resources for conservation". *Nature* 336, 533–5.

from captures made within PAs and mounting police-style operations, often in conjunction with other law enforcement bodies,
to achieve arrests of organized poachers, and possibly even the
all-important dealers, outside the PAs. This balance is made very
difficult if there is a high level of corruption and little political or
local support for conservation.

Local involvement in resource management

Increasing the opportunity cost of poaching through increasing
legitimate earning potential within PAs presents a politically appropriate solution that is within the power of an enlightened wildlife
management authority, and the most likely to gain popular support for conservation. Local hunters are marginal elephant/rhino
offenders, who are hunting meat illegally because meat hunting
is a traditional and cultural necessity. If hunting carries a penalty
whatever the species, then there is no barrier to elephant and rhino
hunting. If meat hunting by locals without a licence were better
managed or even legalized, the decision to poach elephants and
rhinos would become more clear cut.

Projects that give some responsibility for management decisions,
return some of the proceeds of safari hunting and tourism to
local people and secure jobs locally have been very successful. The
CAMPFIRE project in Zimbabwe is an excellent example (Martin,
1986). A similar project in the GMAs of Luangwa Valley has caused
a reported drop in illegal activity, because local people have received
revenues from the PA and have been employed to supplement law
enforcement efforts. Thus local poachers are no longer helped or
tolerated (Lewis, Kaweche and Mwenya, 1990).

Improvements in legitimate earning potential for organized gangs
living outside the PAs of Luangwa Valley are harder to achieve
because they cannot be included in community-based conservation
schemes as easily. Neither can the reduction of economic incentives
for hunters to enter a dealer's employment be achieved by increased
wages, given Zambia's declining economy. Thus the only chance
of increasing the effective wage rate of hunters is to increase the
perceived risk of poaching and so impose a large risk premium on
the dealer.

How best to reduce poaching?

We have concentrated on the Luangwa Valley but there is a serious
poaching problem in many African PAs. For example, buffalo
numbers in the Serengeti in Tanzania are now limited by poachers

supplying local meat markets (Dublin, et al., 1990). The themes discussed here are relevant to many areas where the main concern is not traditional subsistence hunting, although it may contribute to the decline of already endangered species, but large-scale commercial hunting.

Local hunters could easily be deterred by fairly small penalties. They are particularly suited to local involvement schemes and the return of some dividend from the resource that was once theirs. Hunting for meat is their main objective when entering PAs and better regulation of legal meat hunting could stop the hunters killing trophy species. Community involvement schemes have shown a reduced poaching rate by locals who feel that they now have some stake in the preservation of the resource.

Organized gangs present a less tractable problem, since the dealer who decides the level of poaching is sheltered from law enforcement, and treats the penalties imposed as simple costs to be borne. Our analysis showed that in Luangwa Valley the profits to be made out of ivory were such that neither the costs of labour nor fines were significant in reducing hunting mortality. This is likely to be true for other wildlife products and other areas. If law enforcement is to be effective, the dealers need to be convicted rather than the gang members. However, a high perceived risk of detection and a serious penalty could make the risk premium added to the hunters' wage high enough for the costs of poaching to rise significantly.

There are other ways of reducing poaching rates such as effective demand reduction by end-users, either nationally or in importing countries, or a well-regulated legal trade lowering the price for illegal trophies. However, until these kinds of system can be instituted, illegal exploitation will continue to be an important form of utilization in most of Africa's PAs, and law enforcement the only means of combatting it. Given that resources for conservation are limited and a high detection rate is the best way to deter commercial poaching under these circumstances, the wildlife manager's best short-term strategy seems to be two-pronged. Local involvement schemes give local people a share in the proceeds from the exploitation of their resource and create a political climate favourable to conservation. At the same time, high levels of law enforcement concentrated on the areas of key biological importance reduce commercial poaching in those areas. Thinly spread patrols have a detection rate low enough to make no difference to the commercial poacher, and are thus a waste of precious resources (Leader-Williams and Albon, 1988).

References

Abel N. and P. Blaikie, "Elephants, people, parks and development: The case of the Luangwa Valley, Zambia", *Environmental Management* 10, 735-51 [1986[.

Avio K.L. and C.S. Clark, "The supply of property offenses in Ontario: evidence on the deterrent effect of punishment", *Canadian Journal of Economics* 10, 1-19 [1978].

Becker, G.S., "Crime and punishment: An economic approach", *Journal of Political Economy* 76, 168-217 [1968].

Bell, R.H.V., "Conditions of service in a conservation agency" in R.H.V. Bell and E. McShane-Caluzi (eds), *Conservation and wildlife management in Africa*, pp. 529-42. [Washington, DC, US Peace Corps, 1986].

Bell R.H.V. and J.E. Clarke, "Funding and financial control" in R.H.V. Bell and E. McShane-Caluzi (eds), *Conservation and wildlife management in Africa*, pp. 543-6 [Washington, DC, US Peace Corps, 1986].

Cook P.J., "Punishment and crime", *Law and contemporary problems* 5, 164-204 [1977].

Douglas-Hamilton, I., "African Elephant Population Study", *Pachyderm* 8, 1-10 [1987].

Dublin H.T., A.R.E. Sinclair, S. Boutin, E. Anderson, M. Jago, and P. Arcese, "Does competition regulate ungulate populations? Further evidence from Serengeti, Tanzania", *Oecologia* 82, 283-8 [1990].

Ehrlich, I., "Participation in illegitimate activities – a theoretical and empirical investigation", *Journal of Political Economy* 81, 521-65 [1973].

Glover, R.L., "Effectiveness of patrol techniques for apprehending deer poachers", *Proceedings of annual conference: Southeastern Association of Fish and Wildlife agencies* 36, 705-16 [1982].

Graham, A.D., *Gardeners of Eden* [London: George Allen and Unwin, 1973].

Harcourt, A.H., "Gorilla conservation: anatomy of a campaign" in K. Bernishke (ed.), *Primates: the road to self-sustaining populations*, p 31-46 [New York: Springer-Verlag, 1986].

ITC/IUCN Reference to follow...

IUCN Environmental Law Centre, *African Wildlife Laws*, Gland: International Union for the Conservation of Nature and Natural Resources [1986].

Kraushar, P., *Practical business development: What works and what does not* [London: Holt, Rinehart & Winston, 1985].

Leader-Williams N. and S.D. Albon, "Allocation of resources for conservation", *Nature* 336:533-5 [1988].

Leader-Williams N., S.D. Albon and P.S.M. Berry, "Illegal exploitation of black rhinoceros and elephant populations: patterns of decline, law enforcement and patrol effort in Luangwa Valley, Zambia", *Journal of Applied Ecology* 27, 1055-87 [1990].

Lewis, D.M., G.B. Kaweche and A. Mwenya, "Wildlife conservation outside protected areas – lessons from an experiment in Zambia", *Conservation Biology* 4, 171-80 [1990].

Marks, S.A., *Large mammals and a brave people: Subsistence hunters in Zambia* [Seattle: University of Colorado Press, 1976].

Marks, S.A., *The Imperial Lion: Human Dimensions of Wildlife management in Africa* [Boulder, Colorado: Westview, 1976].

Martin, R.B., "Communal area management plan for indigenous resources (Project CAMPFIRE)", in R.H.V. Bell and E. McShane-Caluzi (eds), *Conservation and wildlife management in Africa*, [Washington, DC, US Peace Corps, 1986].

Milner-Gulland, E.J. and N. Leader-Williams, "A model of the incentives for illegal exploitation of rhinos and elephants: poaching pays in Luangwa Valley, Zambia", *Journal of Applied Ecology* 29; in press [1992].

Morse, W.B., "Wildlife law enforcement", *Proceedings of annual conference, Western Association of Game and Fish Commissions* 60, 162-80 [1980].

Parker, I.S.C. and A.D. Graham, "Men, elephants and competition", *Symposium of Zoological Society of London* 61, 241-52 [1989].

Stigler, G.J., "The optimum enforcement of laws", *Journal of Political Economy* 78, 526-36 [1970].

Tatham, G.H., "The rhino conservation strategy in the Zambezi Valley codenamed Operation Stronghold", *Zimbabwe Science News* 22, 21-3 [1988].

Tatham, G.H. and R.D. Taylor, "The conservation and protection of the black rhinoceros Diceros bicornis in Zimbabwe", *Koedoe* 32, 31-42 [1989].

Thurow, L.C., "Equity versus efficiency in law enforcement", in R.L. Andreano and J.J. Siegfried (eds), *The economics of crime* [New York: Halstead, 1980].

von Clausewitz, C., *On war* (originally published 1832), M. Howard & P. Paret (trans., eds), [Princeton, New Jersey: Princeton University Press 1976].

Western, D. and L. Vigne, "The deteriorating status of African rhinos", *Oryx* 19, 215-20 [1985].

10

THE END OF WILDLANDS AND WILDLIFE?

Timothy M. Swanson and Edward B. Barbier

The world's wildlands and wildlife are severely depleted, and the pressures that the remainder will face over the next century are set to be of phenomenal proportions. There is little that can be done at this time to avoid vast increases in the populations of those countries that still harbour substantial amounts of diversity. These peoples want, and deserve, a better lifestyle than that which their current stage of development affords. To the extent that population growth and development threaten diversity, the next century's threat is unprecedented in terms of the proportion of wildlands and wildlife that are affected.

Currently, only about 4 per cent of wildlands have any "protected" status, and even these will be in jeopardy as buffer stocks erode. Although it might be possible to provide for more preservation areas in these developing countries, it is not really fair to ask for them. These are "special" resources to the developed world, largely because of the small amounts of natural habitat remaining in the North. To the local communities, however, these resources are their lands – their lifestyles, opportunities, and hopes for the future are tied in with these places that we, as Northerners wish to "preserve", sometimes as museum pieces.

The role of a wildlife utilization strategy

It is possible to make the North's desire for diversity compatible with the South's need for development. This is the role for a carefully defined strategy of wildlife utilization. In point of fact, there is no "natural habitat", in the sense of a terrestrial ecosystem that has evolved without the presence of a human element. There is only the choice between different methods and forms of human involvement in the habitat.

Until a few decades ago, almost the entirety of the developing world's habitat had been used by the indigenous communities for subsistence and trade. It was only with the coming of colonial regimes that communities were removed from habitats, and people-less parks were born. This was not the "natural" state of these habitats; it was manufactured to satisfy the desires of millions of absentee landlords. Because the wilds became disengaged from their neighbouring peoples, these resources became increasingly less valued by the local communities. Moreover, the new "owners" of these resources – the public authorities – were unable, or even unwilling, to control access and use of the wilds. For these reasons, the wildlife of these areas has been mismanaged and overexploited as never before, and the wildlands are being converted to seemingly more "profitable" uses at accelerating rates.

Wildlife utilization affords the possibility of making development consistent with diversity. At the heart of a new conservation policy is enabling local communities to make use of the diversity that exists all around them. This is a fundamental element of a biodiversity conservation strategy because it addresses the root of the problem, namely the undervaluation of diverse resources by local peoples and their consequent conversion. It is not a policy that by itself can solve all of the problems of wildlife and wildland conservation, but it is a necessary component of such a policy. And, most importantly, it does not sacrifice the needs of the developing countries for the satisfaction of the desires of the developed. Wildland utilization is a strategy that does not aim to continue the disenfranchisement of peoples from their rightful property. The development of their lands is possible, without the need to convert the land to non-diverse products.

The problems of wildlife utilization

Of course, there is a very substantial gap between theory and prac-tice in the case of wildlife utilization. To date there has been little conservation benefit from much wildlife exploitation, and many attempts at wildland utilization have gone astray. However, it is possible to identify and isolate the problems raised by production in "the commons". These are the problems that we must address if continued existence of substantial amounts of natural habitats is to be assured in the future. We do not wish to imply that these problems do not exist; we simply wish to stress that they must be solved, not forsaken.

The facets of a wildlife utilization strategy

In this volume we have attempted to identify what the elements of a potentially successful policy might be. First and foremost, it is important to return the resources (or, at least, the revenues earned from the resources) to the communities. Any time there is a divergence between the objectives of local communities and absentee landlords, the result is likely to be waste and inefficiency. Local communities are the best managers of these assets, for themselves and for the global community. There are clear roles for "outsiders", but ownership (i.e. the disenfranchisement of the local community) is not one of them.

The second point that we have tried to emphasise is the importance of low intensity utilization strategies. The "natural habitat" that we now observe evolved in the context of low intensity human utilization – hunting and gathering, etc. – so it is clearly not incompatible with such activities. However, other forms of utilization, deforestation and/or conversion to cattle ranching, are at the other end of the spectrum of intensity. The positive impact of utilization dwindle as the form it takes moves from low to high intensity.

In particular, this means that overly specialized or capital-intensive methods of production generally should not be encouraged in wildlands, as there is very little positive conservation impact from schemes that substantially alter the environment. Minimal well-slotted interventions can have very substantial productivity impacts. The collection of reptile eggs and subsequent return to the wild of juveniles can increase their rates of survival by 5000 per cent, for example. In addition, the value of diverse production can often far exceed the value of specialized; oft-cited studies indicate that the aggregate value of rainforest production (from nuts, wood products, subsistence etc.) can far exceed its value in specialised production. Therefore, it is not always necessary to move to capital intensity or specialization in order to generate reasonable returns from the land. Where specialization is not necessary, diversity is a possibility.

The role of the developed world in diversity conservation

Finally, there is a very significant and wholly necessary role for the conservation-minded community in the developed world. The wildlands of the South cannot be maintained in their present volumes unless substantial and continuing sums of money are transferred there on an ongoing basis. This is the ultimate role of the concerned Northerner: to pay the bill.

However, the manner in which the bill is paid is as important as the payment itself. A simple transfer of funds does nothing to alter the decision-making framework of those who must decide whether to keep or to convert. What is required is a method of payment that compensates the developing countries at the end of each day that the wildlands are maintained. Wildlife utilization, by the developed world, in a controlled fashion that generates maximum revenues and returns them to the source habitat is one means of creating such a dynamic system of incentives. However, this is not intended to belittle the wide range of other values that these resources represent; it is equally as important to provide recognition and compensation to the less easily appropriated values. This policy is not sufficient to guarantee the continuing existence of adequate diversity; it is merely the necessary starting point.

The end of wildlife and wildlands?

Therefore, wildlife utilization is important because it is an important value to harness for the sustenance of wildlands. In essence, all that "wildlife utilization" means as a concept is the recognition of the North's obligation to pay for the maintenance of diversity in the South. It makes little difference whether these payments arise out of wildlife trade, tourism, safari hunting or even television royalties – so long as there is an irrevocable and ongoing obligation to make them.

And, perhaps more importantly, concentration on a policy of wildlife utilization is important because the problems of managing wildlands must be resolved *now* if diversity is to be made compatible with development. Development is certainly going to happen in the areas of most diversity in the coming century; the only question is whether we will simultaneously create a clear link between development and diversity. If we do not, we face the prospect of completing the long-commenced process of mining this clearly undervalued resource.

It is only by way of a policy that develops the investment potential of these lands *as wildlands* that a significant proportion of them will remain in 100 years' time. There really is no other option for the vast majority of existing wildlands. It is to be hoped that there will be a sea change in the developed world's perspective, as the importance of wildlife utilization for wildland conservation sinks in. Otherwise, it may be the "ark" that sinks.

INDEX

*(Numerals marked in **bold type** indicate a chapter / section devoted to the subject entry. For names of authors of books and studies, see references at end of each chapter.)*